Also by Joni B. Cole and B. K. Rakhra:

This Day in the Life: Diaries from Women Across America

•

This Day: Diaries from American Women

Also by Joni B. Cole:

Toxic Feedback: Helping Writers Survive and Thrive

Water Cooler Diaries

Women Across America Share Their Day at Work

Selected and edited by

JONI B. COLE and **B. K. RAKHRA**

Da Capo
LIFE
LONG

DA CAPO LIFELONG
A MEMBER OF THE PERSEUS BOOKS GROUP

Designed by Pauline Neuwirth, Neuwirth & Associates, Inc.
Set in 11.5 point Mrs. Eaves by the Perseus Books Group

Cataloging-in-Publication data for this book is available from the Library of Congress.

First Da Capo Press edition 2008
ISBN-13 978-1-60094-009-5
Published by Da Capo Press
A Member of the Perseus Books Group
www.dacapopress.com

Note: The views expressed by each day diarist are her own. Each day diarist's statements do not necessarily reflect the views of any other contributor or any of the organizations of which the day diarist may be a part, nor do they necessarily reflect the views of the book's creators,
Joni B. Cole and B. K. Rakhra, or the publisher.

Da Capo Press books are available at special discounts for bulk purchases in the United States by corporations, institutions, and other organizations. For more information, please contact the Special Markets Department at the Perseus Books Group, 2300 Chestnut Street, Suite 200, Philadelphia, PA 19103, or call (800) 255-1514, or e-mail special.markets@perseusbooks.com.

1 2 3 4 5 6 7 8 9

For my dad, who took care of all of us; and for my mom, who took care of my dad
JONI B. COLE

For my parents, who daily show me the value and joy of a working life
B. K. RAKHRA

We would like to express our deep gratitude to Nancy Fontaine. *Water Cooler Diaries* is as much a project as a book, which means someone needs to provide expertise in databases, Web sites, and how to communicate efficiently with hundreds of project participants and supporters. That someone is Nancy, our webmistress and technologist. Her skills, creative insights, and enduring friendship have made this book possible and kept us sane and centered from the beginning.

Contents

Introduction

WORKING WOMEN are creating quite the buzz. We see it in all the ink that has been spilled over the dubious "Mommy Wars," pitting moms with jobs against moms who stay at home. We hear about trends among young professionals who are "off-ramping" their careers to work part-time, and about "Alpha Moms" who thrive on multitasking to the max. We read about the persistence of the wage gap and the glass ceiling, and the rise of women in industry and self-owned businesses. We are told over and over, *Yes! Women can have it all!*—or not—depending on what you read.

But who are some of the real women reflected in these statistics and sound bites? And what is it really like to own the company . . . work from home . . . have a "glamorous" gig . . . occupy cubicle-land?

Water Cooler Diaries touches on the important issues that affect our working lives, in the most intimate of ways. How, for example, does an award-winning fashion designer keep her growing business afloat, when she can't even afford rent for a decent studio? What happens when a university librarian has four scheduled meetings, and her child wakes up with a 103.4-degree temperature? How does a boxing manager deal with hot flashes, a complicated love life, and signing a new heavyweight all on the same day?

On Tuesday, March 27, 2007, hundreds of women across America created an on-the-job "day diary" for this book project, chronicling their activities, thoughts, and feelings throughout this single day. Featuring thirty-five full-day diaries and dozens more diary excerpts and highlights, this collection reveals a wealth of workplace details, water-cooler drama, and laugh-out-loud moments. While publishing parameters made it impossible to include every contribution in the book, all the diarists informed these pages and strengthened the project with their collective enthusiasm.

I am proud to note that *Water Cooler Diaries* is the third volume in the "This Day" book series. The idea for the book project came from a day in my own life six years ago—a very bad day when I was dealing with a family illness, a lull in my freelance writing business, and a four-year-old daughter who refused to wear socks, despite freezing temperatures. Sitting at my desk feeling blue and still in my pajamas past noon, I wondered what other women were doing at that very moment. In my mind, I envisioned their lives as perfect. Their workdays were productive. Their kids were properly dressed. These women were "normal," while I . . . Well, I felt anything but. And so a book—and then a series—was born, out of self-pity, curiosity, and, in retrospect, a real need to connect.

In interviews, I am often asked if any themes emerged in the day diaries that speak to gender or American culture. Certainly, one refrain of many diaries is, "Rush, rush, rush." Women are masters at multitasking, but that doesn't mean we always like it (except for all those Alpha Moms who just can't get enough). The diaries also suggest that a woman's perceived success and happiness are determined as much by her attitude as by her job title or the size of her paycheck. We received entries from ranchers, truck drivers, bloggers, race car drivers, doctors, CEOs, mechanics, and relief workers. These diverse roles speak to the fact that, clearly, there is nothing a woman can't do—except be in two places at once.

These diaries affirm something else as well, as compelling as our many points of connection. Every woman is interesting; every woman's voice matters, including those who doubted their own contribution to this book project. ("Why would anyone want to read about *my* day?") After having the privilege of sharing a day in the life of so many women from all walks of life, I believe this now more than ever. Young, old, rich, poor, working with or without a paycheck, every woman has something unique, surprising, and inspiring to offer—her own perspective.

Bindi Rakhra, my partner in the book project, and I would like to express our gratitude to the 515 women who volunteered their day diaries to help create *Water Cooler Diaries*. You shared with us your work life, your home life, and your inner life, with remarkable honesty and generosity. You also reminded us, time and time again, of all the meaningful moments in this day—and any given day—if we just take the time to notice and appreciate them.

—*Joni B. Cole*

Water Cooler Diaries

Orthopedic Trauma Surgeon

ERIKA J. MITCHELL, 33, NASHVILLE, TENNESSEE

What she likes most—and least—about the job? The unpredictability. "A call night can bring anything and everything. Few orthopedic residents choose a career in trauma because of its impact on lifestyle." Her soapbox: "The media has turned surgeons into money-hungry, calloused beasts and the public has bought into this. No one realizes that we go to sleep and wake up thinking about our patients, questioning if we did enough or the right thing, and cry behind closed doors when there is nothing more we can do."

5:30 a.m. So many injuries, so little time. Eight phone calls through the night and a full list of operative cases to do today. Everyone and their brother were out on a motorcycle, or on their roof, or out driving like an idiot. Reviewing the X-rays of the patients that came in overnight has become my morning ritual whether or not I'm on call. Coffee in hand, I stare at the black and white of people's bony innards. A couple of good injuries: pelvic bones no longer attached to the spine; hip fracture; tibial plateau fracture; and a bunch of routine stuff—ankle, femur, forearm. How much of it can I get done today? And why is it eight hundred degrees in my office?!

6:15 a.m. Rounds with the residents. I hate this part of the day—reviewing the overnight events of each patient and creating the care plan with residents. The residents just don't seem to be interested in the day-to-day care of patients. Learning to operate is certainly the "fun" part for us surgeons, but the mundane aftercare is just as important. Perhaps if I were more patient or a better teacher I could make better use of this time. I'm still working on that. . . .

7:00 a.m. Met my first patient of the morning. Simple ankle fracture. A poster child for why you don't wear six-inch heels and get drunk at a post–St. Patrick's Day party. She's pleasant enough but already asking about pain meds. I tell her she will get the routine medications, she'll need crutches for six weeks, and, yes, I will fill out her work excuse until she's back on her feet.

9:00 a.m.-ish One down, one bigger one to follow. The ankle fracture was boring, but a short simple case is nice every now and then. This next fellow is less fortunate.

9:58 a.m. Long talk with the family of the next patient, a teenager who reminds me of another kid I had operated on who died last week. This patient didn't wear a seatbelt and has a bad head injury, with multiple facial fractures and a pelvic fracture such that half of his pelvis is a free piece of bone. These are injuries that could have been prevented with a simple piece of strapping standard on every vehicle. It makes me angry.

I had to convince the family that I was the surgeon, yes, the one who does the surgery. Typical. *Believe it or not, ma'am, they now let girls into medical school.* It's just like my patients who come into my clinic after their hospitalization—where I operated on them and rounded on them every day—and complain that they never met their surgeon. Argh! But this family was thankful and hung on to every word I said. They started crying. I gave them a hug. We'll take care of him.

10:07 a.m. In the OR, patient getting intubated by anesthesiologist. They always seem to take too long, but I realize this is part of my impatience problem. I rehearse the case in my head, just like my athlete days when I used to run or row entire races in my head before reaching the starting line. Finally . . .

1:36 p.m. The surgery took less time than I planned. He was thin and muscular, which helps oh-so-much. Big incision, a half

. . . . water cooler diaries

smile from the pubis to the ilium (hip), a big beefy iliopsoas muscle (unfortunately, I can't help but think of filet mignon, which is made of the iliopsoas muscle from cows). He also has a well-defined femoral artery (*don't cut the artery, don't cut the artery, don't cut the artery*—a simple mantra for the safety of a vessel that sits in the way). Young bone is nice to work with. Doesn't crush under my clamps, and each screw has satisfying purchase. It all came together nicely. I hope I didn't retract on his nerve and vessel too hard.

These types of cases exhaust me physically and mentally but are far more fun to fix than the ankle. I once told my boss that I get a high from fixing femoral neck fractures. I couldn't tell if he thought I was crazy or agreed with me. Maybe we're all nuts.

1:50 p.m. Can't find the patient's family post-op. Now I'm aggravated. I'm sure I'll get a phone call later from his nurse, saying the family is upset that no one talked to them after surgery. But I tried in the three different places a family is asked to wait—the surgical waiting room, trauma waiting room, and lobby outside the ORs. I'm hungry and have other things to do.

3:11 p.m. Did I call it or what? Nurse paged me while I was in the OR nailing a femur, saying the teenager's family is all pissed off. Now I'm pissed off. And now I've got a patient who just showed up at the clinic unannounced, assuming this way there'd be no wait. He missed his appointment last week and is out of pain meds. I tell the clinic he'll have to wait because I need to get back to the OR, but maybe the physician's assistant can help him. Sorry, the drive-through is closed.

Is it too much to ask to be left alone while operating? The pager keeps going off, secretaries are calling into the room, and the OR managers keep asking me when I'll be done! For God's sake, I have this guy's leg in my hands, trying to hold the fracture in place while the resident taps a metal rod into his thigh bone. I'm sweating like a pig and there's an OR nurse relaying messages between me and whoever is on the phone.

The rod finally went down, the bone looked well aligned and appropriately rotated, so I let the resident put in the screws. One more down and how many more to go? I still haven't eaten and now the next patient is in the OR ready to go, damn it.

5:00 p.m.-ish I seem to have lost my watch, and I've left my pager in the OR. Third watch I've lost this year. Ridiculous.

It turns out the family of the teenager with the pelvic fracture isn't even in the hospital. They took off, according to the nurses, and somehow I'm supposed to seek them out on the streets? Call me jaded, bitter, asshole, whatever, but at some point people need to realize there are other people in the world with things to do beside themselves. I'm getting tired and grumpy. Better shut up and just get the work done.

5:43 p.m. Ah, I am finally fed. Where would the world be without Cheez-Its? In the dictation room, I had a nice chat with a transplant surgeon who thinks I should eat more real food. I asked him if he would rather operate on me or the average-size American? He conceded. I hate lunch because it makes me sleepy, although also less grouchy, I suppose.

One more case to go. I decided to move my other big case that came in last night to tomorrow. It's another pelvic fracture but much worse. I'm too tired to take on a potentially six- to eight-hour case right now, with those scary blood vessels and nerves in the way. The patient has other injuries to his spleen and liver, but is stable for now. No need to hurry this one. Does this make me wimpy? I wonder what my colleagues think.

Talked to the missing family of the teenager. They finally showed up in the waiting room. Put on my happy face. Said it went as well as it could. Not too much blood loss. The breathing tube is still in right now. He needs it until he recovers more from his other injuries. I went over the pre- and post-op X-rays. Always hard to explain the three-dimensional pelvis on a two dimensional X-ray, but everyone likes to see the pictures of plates and screws. They're nice folks. I feel bad about getting angry earlier. More hugs.

9:56 p.m. Nice to be humbled by a "simpler" case every now and then. This was a twofer deal on a woman patient. Open kneecap fracture and distal femur. I didn't let the resident do much. He's probably miffed. Again, my problems with teaching. I know I'm very particular about how things are done, and this resident tends not to listen very well to what I say.

"Aim the drill toward me more . . . Control . . . Don't plunge . . . Toward me, toward me, more toward me!" Maybe if I were a stodgy old white guy, the resident would listen better. Or maybe that doesn't matter, but when it's *my* patient, the case is done *my* way. I thought the kneecap would be the easier part of the case but it was in so many friggin' pieces. She's going to get arthritis between that and the cartilage injury from the other fracture. Frustrating.

10:20 p.m. Done dictating my notes so that anyone (be it another surgeon or a lawyer) could look at them and understand what I saw and did. I could be more efficient and dictate notes after every case, instead of all at the end of the day, but I guess I like reviewing the day's work this way. I'm tired. Not so interested in going to see how my patients are doing post-op. But I've already wasted enough time dreading rounds. Now I should just pick my butt up and go do it. Happy face time again.

10:45 p.m.-ish The teenager that I operated on with the pelvic fracture is doing well. More alert. He follows commands, moves his feet up and down, and his bandages are still nice and dry. Hopefully, he'll get the nasty breathing tube out tomorrow. One of my other patients is not so lucky. He is fully sedated and unarousable on a ventilator. No changes since he arrived, except now he has pneumonia and his kidneys have shut down. His family is withdrawing care tomorrow. His wife and children have gone home for the night. He's fought for three weeks but is just getting sicker.

I lost a patient last week in this same manner—a seventeen-year-old kid who was catapulted from his car. He tried to die on day one, but we got him to the OR and stopped the bleeding from his pelvic fracture. He fought and almost made a comeback—the trauma team and I patted ourselves on the back. Then four

orthopedic trauma surgeon

weeks later, despite being able to demonstrate his physical therapy exercises and look me in the eye when I talked to him, he succumbed to the stepwise failure of each major organ system, the consequence of a massive resuscitation effort in his early hospital course.

I cried with the family that day, and apologized that we couldn't do more. Would it have been easier for them if he had died that first day? Did I torture him for a month in the ICU? Did I torture his family? They said they were thankful for the extra time we had given them, but I'm still unsure. What is the right answer? It still makes me cry to think about it.

1:08 a.m. Home sweet home. My first house. Have yet to get any furniture, but I kind of like the big open space. But what a mess. I've started some pasta to silence my belly. I need to review films for tomorrow, but I really just want to feed and sleep. When did my life get so pathetic?! At least I have the weekend off. Maybe I can get my scull out on the water if the weather holds.

1:32 a.m. Gave up on reviewing films for cases tomorrow. No longer so happy that I moved that case. Need to sleep. Besides the pelvic fracture from last night, I have a patient on tomorrow's schedule from clinic last week. Oh why did that damn fracture shift? This case is a teenager struck by a drunk driver. Young, healthy, plays hockey and basketball. Now with a bad hip fracture that I fixed two weeks ago, and a pelvic fracture I tried to treat without an operation. Everything behaved for the past two weeks, but now the pelvic fracture moved. Nature failed me this time. His family is terrified. I don't blame them. He faces a long operation, big scar, three months off his feet. He's scared, too, but trying to be strong. I told him he'd be okay. I hate saying that. I'm very superstitious. And very tired. Enough now.

Dr. Mom

3:15 a.m. Woke up, not to my pager, but to the sound of my nine-year-old son coughing. Poor kid, it's tough to be the child of a pediatrician. I still feel a little bad about loading him up with Motrin and sending him to school yesterday. I knew he wasn't contagious—he's been coughing for days at this point—and that he'd feel fine once he got to school, but my husband looked at me like I was Attila the Hun.

—*Leslie Fall, 43, Hanover, New Hampshire; hospital pediatrician*

●

Rancher

DIANE TRIBITT, 48, HILLMAN, MINNESOTA

She owns and operates the Rolling Thunder Ranch—520 acres of grass (and rocks), plus an additional 1,500 leased acres to accommodate her custom grazing operation. Summers, she tends up to seven hundred head of beef cattle. She also runs her deceased husband's bin-building business. When he died in a rodeo accident three years ago, she was pressured to sell. "I had to find peace with God and with my decision to stay." Now she's refound herself . . . and she's found love. "I'm engaged to another wonderful man, and, yes, he's also a cowboy."

7:30 a.m. I can smell the coffee as I rise to stumble out to the kitchen. Tom (a neighbor-rancher), TJ (Tom's son), Lloyd (a neighbor-friend), and Sam (my fiancé) are already sitting at the breakfast counter, probably on their second pot of coffee. It's the ritual here every weekday morning. I call them the Koffee Klutch. They converge in our kitchen to gather, gossip, and solve the world's problems. This has been an ongoing tradition since 1987, long before I moved here six years ago.

This morning the guys are talking about when they'd all be free to help Tom load out his fall calves that were ready to ship to market. Jason (another neighbor) isn't here this morning. Sam says he is on his way to pick up an "all natural" pig to take to Kimball for butcher. Jason raises "natural" cattle.

9:00 a.m. The Klutch left a half hour ago. I wash last night's dishes (oops!), and start sorting laundry. Sam has gone out to grind hay, but he stops back in to tell me there is a newborn calf I need to check on in the east pasture. The temperatures were in the high seventies last week, but we're back down to the low thirties again today, so I grab my winter Carhartt jacket.

My four-wheeler is cold-blooded so I have to keep the choke on awhile. Damn, it's cold on the wheeler! The wind is bringing tears to my eyes and they are freezing on my face. I pull my sweatshirt hood up over my head, but the wind is coming straight at me so the hood just puffs up like a balloon around my head. If it still had its drawstrings, I would tighten it up.

The pasture I need to drive to is a mile east of the house. The snow has all melted, but the sky looks overcast. I drive down the minimum-maintenance road, past the barn and corrals. As I pass the creek, I can look out across the pasture and see the cattle— three hundred head lined up in a row where Sam had ground hay for them. I love the smell of the high-moisture hay, kind of sweet and musky, like silage. I must have been a cow in my prior life if I think silage smells good!

9:20 a.m. I find the little red heifer calf on the bare ground about one hundred yards from where the cows were eating. The calf looks dead, but when I park the four-wheeler next to it I can tell it is still breathing. Its momma stands close by with her head down low. She is pawing at the ground, not looking happy to see me messing with her baby.

Sam drives up on the tractor and motions for me to wait for him to help. No problem there. I really am not wanting to piss that cow off all by myself, anyway! I use the four-wheeler to keep the cow at bay, while Sam picks up her calf and loads her onto the vehicle. She is a good 105 to 110 pounds, which is big. Given her size, it's possible that she came out backward and got some of her mother's fluids in her lungs.

Sam drives the tractor and I haul Penny (the calf was the color of a new penny, hence the name) back to the barn on the wheeler. She basically lies across my lap with her head resting on my right arm, making it hard for me to press the throttle and steer. In the barn, I put down some straw bedding. Then I go into the kitchen and mix up some colostrum (like baby formula), which is important for the calf to get within twenty-four hours after birth.

Otherwise, bacteria enters its bloodstream. This calf can't stand up, so it is obvious she hadn't sucked. Her eyes are rolled back and her breathing sounds raspy.

10:30 a.m. As I enter the barn, two horses are whinnying in the stalls to my left, demanding to be fed. The rooster is crowing in the chicken coop to my right. But I walk straight to the calf pen, bottle in hand, and sit on the floor next to Penny. She is still alive, but her legs are like rubber and she can't hold up her head.

I try to bottle-feed her but she won't suck, so I end up pouring the colostrum into a tube feeder. The feeder resembles an IV bag, with several feet of clear plastic tubing. The end of the tube gets threaded down the throat of the calf, so the liquid in the bag flows into the animal's stomach. I don't like tube-feeding, but it is the only option.

I grab an old towel from the saddle rack and give Penny a vigorous twenty-minute body massage. I do this to stimulate blood flow and loosen the muscles, and I like to think that the physical contact is beneficial. I try to make her get up by lifting her front end. Nothing. She's like a hundred-pound sack of potatoes. Sam brings a warming light over, so at least she'll be warm and dry.

11:30 a.m. Our neighbor Jason stops in. He told us he bought his "organic" pig and hauled it home in a crate in the back of his truck. Then he filled a pail with water to give it a drink, but when he opened the crate, the pig lay there dead. Evidently it had died of a heart attack. He says he had to call one of his buddies to come over to help him butcher it right there in the box of his pickup. We have to laugh at his hard-luck story.

12:00 p.m. I am working on listing all of my equipment and machinery for the insurance company. Tractors, four-wheelers, pickups, cars, and trailers . . . So far, the count is at twenty-eight, all needing documentation for VINs (vehicle identification numbers), mileage, costs, and dates of purchase. This compilation should have been done years ago. Over half of my vehicles are still in my late husband's name. I'm the world's worst (or best!) procrastinator when it comes to stuff like this. It seems like such a waste of time when I could be outside working. There are corrals to fix, miles of fencing to be done, cattle to be moved to different pastures, and I would love to go riding.

Sam comes in for a quick nap. The house is quiet . . . for five minutes. At 12:05 p.m., the phone rings, then UPS stops to deliver a package of vet supplies, then my dad shows up to visit. Dad's a retired mason, and I think the days tend to get long for him. My youngest sister lives a half mile down the road from me, so he spends most of his days floating back and forth between our places. Mom usually stays home.

No nap today for Sam. He heads to the corral to feed the horses. It's like a zoo around here most days, and even a catnap can be almost impossible.

1:30 p.m. My eyes are starting to cross, but there is a light at the end of this motor-vehicle tunnel. Every piece of equipment (that I know of) is listed with its year, date of purchase, cost, license plate number, VIN, color, and registration papers. And damn near every one of them needs a title transfer, tags, or both. It's going to be an expensive trip to the DMV.

Sam brings seven fresh eggs in from the coop. The hens had quit laying over the winter, but just when we started to consider getting rid of them, they started laying again. Ha! I think they are smarter than we think they are!

2:00 p.m. Time to check on Penny. I bundle up and head back to the barn. Why the hell do we live in this godforsaken state during the winter? When I grow up, I want to be a snowbird. We could summer here and winter in Arizona!

Penny's eyes are no longer rolled back, but she still sounds lung-y and has no sucking reflexes. And her legs still don't work. Maybe she had a nerve pinched in her back during birth? After another twenty-minute massage, I head back to the house. Penny did bellow a few times while I massaged her, which got my hopes up. Our death loss of calves is typically 1 or 2 percent, but this year we've lost a few more due to a late snowstorm. I love it when we can save a calf.

My daughter JoJo (one of four children) calls for the third time today. She is doing really well in her second year of college in Rapid City, but she still gets homesick. During the college rodeo season she stays busy roping and practicing, but in her spare time she is constantly calling and wondering if I miss her. I tell her, "No, you call ten times a day! It's like you've never even left!"

3:30 p.m. We are supposed to go to the local ag dealer for a free steak dinner tonight. I don't want to eat now and ruin an opportunity to enjoy a good steak, so I grab an orange to hold me over. Sam's oldest son, Travis, calls and wants to know if we are interested in playing on a coed softball team this summer. I have twenty-eight years of softball experience and Sam has twenty or so, but hey, it's been over ten years since we've picked up our gloves. Of course, we tell him, we will play. Just keep the oxygen close by.

I go back to work on my insurance stuff. This *has* to get done today and I *have* to go to the DMV tomorrow. Our bin-building crew will be leaving in a few days for a job in Ohio. After my husband Randy's death, I had to deal with how to keep his construction business going, which I knew nothing about. I made crew changes, equipment changes, and job location changes. I asked Sam if he would be willing to learn, too, and now we're going into our third season, consistently increasing our gross sales each year. But it's been a struggle.

Two of the workers pull in the driveway to clean the trailers and grease the jacks. We just brought our bin equipment out of storage and hired them to make sure everything was in working order. I'm sure they're broke and they'll want to get paid right away.

5:00 p.m. I was right. Not only did they want to get paid for today's work, they also wanted an advance on their first paycheck! Construction is seasonal, and it happens every year. They come back to work with no money.

Sam and I go out on the four-wheelers to check for newborn calves again. Penny's momma doesn't seem to mind that her calf is missing. There were three more new babies this afternoon and they all look great. Each one is up and sucking! We end up tube-feeding Penny again. She'll lift her head now a little. I do a bit more massaging and Sam moves her leg joints around some, but she makes no effort herself. Even though her eyes look better, her raspy breathing still bothers me. I think she's trying to die on us.

6:00 p.m. Brianna, my youngest, just got home from softball practice at five forty and decided to go with us to the steak feed, so we're running a little behind (like, that's a surprise!). I don't know of any sixteen-year-old that can get ready in a hurry. On the way out, I grab one of my books that I agreed to donate to the raffle. (I write cowboy poetry and just published my first book!)

It's still cold outside, but when we arrive at the ag dealer there are three chefs standing post at their grills. The steaks smell wonderful! Inside, thirty-some people are already seated and eating. There is a table set up for door prizes, mostly ag-related products and tools, and I deposit my book. Then we head to the food table—steak, baked beans, potato salad, finger buns.

Oh, man, it is delicious. This steak is so tender we are able to cut it with our plastic knives! The Hubbard Feed rep comes and sits with us awhile and schedules to come out next week to get our mineral order. He says they are going to do a video presentation on cattle minerals and supplements [after the dinner], so we sneak out as soon as we are done eating, stopping to praise the chefs on our way to the truck. I want to be home to check on Penny (which is as good an excuse as any to leave).

7:00 p.m. She's still alive! Maybe, just maybe, she'll make it. My eighteen-year-old son Cody called. He's on his way home from baseball practice and hungry. It is *so* hard to cook when your belly is full! But I get lucky. All he wants is ramen noodles. Hey, I offered to make him a hamburger or spaghetti! Ramen noodles are kind of gross, if you ask me, especially after eating steak.

rancher

7:30 p.m. I call my oldest son, Scott, to bullshit a little. He lives two hours away and I miss him. His wife, Michelle, answers and says Scott is still at fire training. He teaches a class for the Department of Natural Resources at the vocational school. Scott and Michelle have given me the three cutest granddaughters in the world, so I talk to each of them. They all love their grandma. They tell me so . . . because I asked.

8:00 p.m. I start working on some song lyrics. I usually just write cowboy poetry, but when I performed in Kamloops, British Columbia, I met Joni Harms, a country singer, who asked if I'd be interested in writing lyrics. I told her I'd like to try! Last week I went online and ordered a couple of books to study up on it. Now, if I only had the time to read them!

9:00 p.m. One last peek in the barn. Penny is curled up on the straw bed and looks comfortable under the heat lamp. Brianna is in her bedroom and Cody is in the living room, both on their laptops and probably chatting with friends. Unreal! They see them all day in school, then talk all night to them on MySpace or Facebook, or whatever cyberspot is out there where kids chat with each other. Sam is already snoring. I start to run a nice, deep hot bath and dump in some scented bath oil.

10:00 p.m. I made my bath too hot, so I have to go stand outside on the balcony off my bedroom to cool off. It's so liberating to stand out in the wide open and look at a sky full of stars when you're buck-ass naked. Good thing I live in the middle of nowhere at the end of a dead-end road.

11:00 p.m. My mind is still going a hundred miles an hour. There's so much to do. If the weather is nice I'd like to work outside tomorrow, but the housework is so far behind. And I need to pay bills, but it seems like we're always broke. Where does the money go? It's raining outside, so I listen to the sound and worry about the new calves lying out in the pastures in the cold rain. Damn it! Then I say my prayers and thank God for everything and everyone in my life.

Can You Hear Me Now?

6:00 a.m. Babe calls me. Not on the telephone, but tele-pathically. Babe is a horse. The call comes through in strong, vivid thoughts of her sweet and goofy nature. She tosses her mane from side to side, her head up and down, whinnying. "What's going on, my dear one?" I ask, send-ing the thought question over 1,076 geographic miles. "The sheep's wool is very thick and plans for spring shear-ing are being made," Babe says. "They're feeling pretty itchy." My skin crawls.

—*Suzan Vaughn, 51, Sequim, Washington;*
pet and people psychic counselor

•

All in a Day's Work

10:03 a.m. Rumors are flying all around the office. We are in the middle of a reduction in our sales force, so everyone is uptight. It is unfortunate, but what can you do? People keep coming up to me thinking that just because I am the VP's assistant, I know everything . . . and then will tell them what I know. I want to scream. This is what being the assistant is all about, keeping confidential information, well, confidential.

—*Jennifer Milligan, 31, Rochester Hills, Minnesota; executive assistant*

11:15 a.m. Meet with my law clerk and give assignment to prepare a response to a motion in a child support case. Another deadbeat dad that we're trying to get to do the right thing. This one is affluent and had sex with a fifteen-year-old girl, who ended up pregnant. He hasn't paid a cent since the child was born last year, but has hired two different sets of lawyers to fight Maryland jurisdiction. It really pisses me off how misguided some people's priorities can get. The amount spent on lawyer fees alone would have covered two years of child support by now.

—*Adele Abrams, 53, Takoma Park, Maryland; attorney*

Noon A former resident comes in, asking to buy two rolls of toilet paper. We don't normally sell toilet paper to those who don't live here but she has only forty-eight cents to her name, so I pay for her two rolls and send her on her way.

—*Lana Janssen, 64, Billings, Montana; assistant program manager, Montana Rescue Mission*

4:00 p.m. I head to the nursing-care wing of the facility. We play a musical alphabet game. Residents name one song that starts with each letter of the alphabet, and we sing them.

... water cooler diaries ...

Valerie offers suggestions of words for every letter but can't think of any songs. Beth is perpetually one letter behind the rest of the group. James dozes off in the middle of every song, and I wake him up again after we finish singing. But Gloria beams as we sing. Gloria, who is almost always angry and resentful, who usually demands to be taken home and stalks from the room, is having a good day. She suggests song titles on her own and comments to a peer sitting nearby, "I remember my father singing these songs. They give me such a good feeling inside."

—*Patricia Little, 23, Villa Park, Illinois; music therapist*

5:22 p.m. The financial director (who sits in an office across the walkway from my cube) and one of his senior analysts are bickering over what chairs they will or won't sit in, in the financial director's office. It is getting louder and louder. I shout out, "Boys! Boys! Can you please solve this more quietly?" The scary and funny part? I use my "mom" voice. Both guys look up, stop bickering, and slink away deeper into the financial director's office, closing the door. My two executive assistant colleagues who sit right by me and I all fall out laughing.

—*Constance Boyer, 44, Lynnwood, Washington; executive assistant, Amazon.com*

6:45 p.m. Time to head home to the family. I walk in the door and it stinks like a sewer. My nanny has left for the day and my husband, Gary, is home with the kids. I ask Gary what is that horrendous smell and he thinks that maybe the cat farted!!! Of course, it doesn't register with him to check Charlie's diaper. Holy hell, he has crap all up his back. Time to pour a bath for the little guy and a glass of wine for me.

—*Caralyn Goeldner, 33, Redondo Beach, California; interior designer*

Assistant to a Literary Agent

TINA WEXLER, 30, BROOKLYN, NEW YORK

She works for a senior agent in the literary department of ICM, one of the world's top talent agencies. She also represents about two dozen of her own authors. Job perks: "I get to work with some of the most talented writers in publishing today." Job quirks: Dealing with difficult authors, having people think she sits around and reads all day, and handling query callers who don't understand that publishing is a business. "I'm always surprised by how many people call and expect to talk with me about their manuscript. Or they'll e-mail a query—'Dear Tina, What's up?'"

12:00 a.m. Before we go to sleep, my husband, Doug, reads to me. This is how we end most nights. Tonight it's Robert B. Parker's novel *Hundred-Dollar Baby.* Today's reading starts with a scene between Spenser and Susan, his longtime girlfriend. Spenser is recounting the day's events while Susan nibbles a doughnut. "Wait," I interrupt. "Who's Farnsworth again?" Doug gives me a look.

The truth is that I'm listening and I'm not listening. Part of what's so wonderful about Doug reading to me is that, unlike when I'm reading a manuscript for my job, I don't have to be focused on whether I want to consider representing the work, what might need fixing, or which editors I'd send it to were I to take it on. I just have to sit back and enjoy. And if I'm not fully paying attention, ah, well, that's part of the fun.

12:35 a.m. Doug's asleep. I'm awake. Every night I wonder how it is that my husband can just drop off to sleep, when I'm left running through the things I want to get done tomorrow (finish reading the new draft of a client's manuscript, follow up on submissions), the things I need to get done tomorrow (run a report on monies due in April; remind Lisa, my boss, to do her expenses), and the things I can afford to put off but not much longer (respond to query letters).

9:05 a.m. I click-clack a block and a half to the subway station—the A train—and pull a manuscript out of my shoulder bag. There are two in there. One is the latter half of a client's manuscript that I've been wanting to finish for some time. The other is a referral from a client. I don't get a seat right away so I have to balance the manuscript, my bag, and my purse while the train rattles through the tunnel to Manhattan.

At the first stop, Broadway-Nassau, nearly everyone piles out. I grab a seat and continue reading. I'm happy to see the revision is strong. By the time the train reaches the 42nd Street stop, I've finished the first batch of pages. If all goes smoothly, I could have the manuscript out to editors by the end of the week.

Transferring across the platform to the C train, I pull the second manuscript from my bag. It isn't bad, from what I'm able to read during the span of one stop. The writing is solid, the characters are engaging. But, unfortunately, it seems to be missing that special something. I'll read another couple of chapters on my way home to see if it improves. Sometimes the opening chapters are just throat-clearing and the real goods come around page thirty when the author hits her stride.

9:36 a.m. ICM occupies the twenty-sixth floor of Worldwide Plaza, with windowed offices lining the perimeter and a grid of high-walled cubicles, two to four deep. My desk is fourth in a clutch of cubicles. I unload the two manuscripts from my bag. The revision goes in my to-do pile. The other goes back in the box under my desk where I keep all of the manuscripts waiting to be read. I pull out another five chapters to take home with me tonight. No need to lug pages I've already read to and from Brooklyn. While I'm futzing with the manuscripts, I find an article about the publishing industry from the *New York Times* that Doug slipped into my bag. What a sweetie.

9:42 a.m. Time to check voice mail. A hang-up and a film rights inquiry for one of Lisa's client's books. I leave a message that the book is already under option.

9:45 a.m. Forty-two new e-mails. Not bad. Six are industry related (*Publishers Weekly*, *Daily*, *Deal Lunch*), seven are spam, and twelve are query letters (a way for authors to solicit agents for representation). I file the twelve queries, each about a page long, in a folder with the others waiting for a response (ninety-three at last count).

9:54 a.m. Lisa arrives with her fifteen-year-old daughter who is on spring break. "Can you make this go away?" She holds up her BlackBerry with a frozen screen. I call my go-to guy for all things BlackBerry and leave a voice mail: "Help."

10:00 a.m. In the break room, I add milk to my Lipton as two women chat by the refrigerator. I catch the words "sex" and "Shakespeare." Who says publishing is boring?

10:15 a.m. With the help of Lisa's daughter, I open the morning mail: three interoffice mailers containing checks for Lisa's clients and one for mine, six query letters for Lisa, one for me, one magazine subscription renewal, one piece of author mail to forward on, and copies of *Publishers Weekly* and *New York* magazine.

10:22 a.m. Tech calls regarding Lisa's BlackBerry: "Can you come by my desk?" Certainly. I always welcome a jaunt through the office. When I'm there, I'm shown how to pop out the battery, wait a second, and then reinstall it. That old trick. I bring the BlackBerry back to Lisa and show her what I've learned. For a moment, it sounds like I know a thing or two about fixing a BlackBerry.

10:32 a.m. Time to send out checks. Who doesn't like getting paid? One of the checks is for a new client; it's the first payment I've sent her. There's something special about this, like it makes the whole arrangement seem more official. The contract has been signed by the author and the publisher. Money has been exchanged. A book is being made.

10:52 a.m. The ICM office in London is gearing up for the big book fair in April and requests are coming in daily for cover art, catalog copy, galleys, and finished books. We've run low on galleys (mock-ups of an upcoming book to generate early interest or blurbs for the book jacket). Time to call the editors to see if 'there are any more floating around.

11:02 a.m. Final cover art for one of Lisa's clients comes in. I print a color copy and thumbtack it to my corkboard with all of our other upcoming titles. Right now there are a lot of blue covers on the wall. Coincidence, I suppose. I'm happy to be tacking this particular cover to the wall; there's been a lot of back and forth on it. At last, author and publisher (and agent) are really happy with the design.

11:05 a.m. Lisa's daughter leaves for the day, but not before asking if she can take a galley of one of the titles I've inherited following the departure of one of our agents. I'm happy to give her one. She's got excellent taste in young adult fiction—and lots of friends to help spread the word.

11:25 a.m. More mail is dropped on my desk. One piece for Lisa includes a headshot and résumé. The girl is pretty and she's got a few credits. I'm sure it's costing her a small fortune to mail these out. I've heard time and time again how difficult it is just to get the name of someone "on the inside." Too bad she's got the wrong name. Lisa is a book agent, not a talent agent. No headshots here. Just books.

12:00 p.m. Confirm publication dates, forward cover art, chase payments due, figure out who controls anthology rights to one of Lisa's client's books, mail contracts . . . I quickly scroll through my contract log to see if anything is outstanding—which publishers owe us contracts, which contracts are currently under review by our in-house attorneys, which authors were recently sent contracts to sign, which publishers have contracts to send back to us fully executed and with the first payment due. Everything looks to be on schedule. It's a good feeling.

12:20 p.m. Lisa's at my desk with a book proposal in hand. She has specific thoughts on how to improve it but wants my feedback, as well. She's hoping to speak with the client in a few hours and asks if I can read it now. I take the pages, pen in hand. I rarely get to sit and read manuscripts at my desk. That part of my job gets done on the subway, on my living room couch, or sitting up in bed at night. This proposal is nonfiction, forty-seven pages long, divided into five sections (overview, chapter breakdown, author bio, competitive works, and market). I start reading . . .

12:41 p.m. My friend Jessica calls. She's an editor at Technicolor (the postproduction company that first brought color to the big screen. How cool is that?!). We make plans to meet at my apartment at 7:15 p.m. It feels like ages since I've seen her.

1:04 p.m. Time to hit the gym. For someone who obsesses about things even when nothing can be done to take care of them (who was it who couldn't sleep last night?), sweating on the treadmill is a bit of heaven. Or hell. Isn't it time to get off this thing yet?

2:05 p.m. Back at my desk, eating the salad I picked up at the deli downstairs. More mail. It never stops. Two boxes of hardcovers just arrived. Inside are copies of *The Dream of the Stone* by Christina Askounis. This is one of the first books Lisa sold at ICM. When I started representing my own clients, fantasy was having a resurgence, thanks in large part to *Harry Potter*. Lisa suggested I try to sell reprint rights. And now, here are the fruits of that labor.

The book looks great. I e-mail the editor and author to ooh and ahh. This is one of my favorite things. A cardboard box arrives at my desk. Random House or Simon & Schuster or Bloomsbury or Scholastic is stamped on the side. Inside, packed in Bubble Wrap, are twenty books fresh from the warehouse. A year or so has passed since the manuscript was sold to its editor. Perhaps months of revisions followed. Cover art came in. Pages went into copy editing. Galleys were made. A publicity and marketing plan was put into motion. And then—finished books. It's not the end of a journey—there's so much more to be done once the book is published—but it's certainly a moment to enjoy.

2:45 p.m. Finish reading the book proposal and go into Lisa's office to discuss. We're both smitten by the idea—it's smart and timely—but the writing is too academic in sections and redundant in others. I offer suggestions on how to simplify and/or clarify specific sections and cross out those parts that unnecessarily revisit ideas.

3:30 p.m. The phone is for Lisa, a query caller who wants to pitch her novel. Lisa's already on the phone with a client, and in general prefers a written query, unless the caller has been referred to her or is a recognizable name. Frustrated about having to actually write a query letter (Um, are you *sure* you're a writer?), the caller asks for Lisa's voice mail.

"I am the voice mail," I say.

"I'll call back later," she says.

3:50 p.m. After grabbing an Evian from the break room, I take a quick look at the oldest query letters in my Outlook subfolder. Time to respond to at least ten. That will keep me out of striking range of hitting one hundred, which I've deemed critical mass and cause for intervention, or at least time out of my weekend until I get the number down.

Nix, nix, nix . . . Oh! This looks interesting. Request the complete manuscript on the exclusive. Nix, nix, nix . . . Hmm. This one could be good if the writing is fantastic. Or it could be awful. I'll ask for fifty pages. Nix, nix, nix . . .

I'm primarily looking to acquire literary fiction, memoir, young adult, and middle-grade fiction aimed at readers nine to fourteen. The reason I pass on most material has nothing to do with whether the story sounds saleable, or how strong the writing is, or whether the author has previous publishing credits. It's just that the manuscript is aimed at a market I'm not familiar with or not interested in pursuing. Sometimes I want to write something comforting like, "If I was ever going to represent a novel about a private investigator living on a remote island off the coast of Oregon, this would be it." But I know that would be inviting trouble.

By the time I've read and responded to seventeen queries, I've heard back from two. One, who received a rejection, thanks me for my time. The other is from one of the writers I asked to see work from. Another agent is also considering her manuscript. Is that a problem? No, I write back, as long as the other agent isn't with ICM and she'll give me time to respond in kind should she receive an offer of representation.

4:15 p.m. I do my best to read *Publishers Weekly* between answering e-mails. Lisa's left for the day but she's already e-mailed me three times on her BlackBerry, asking that I respond to a film rights inquiry, remind her to call such-and-such editor tomorrow, and check the payout in a client's most recent contract. One of these days I'll have to get a BlackBerry myself. I'm not in a rush, though. I think I was one of the last New York City residents to get a cell phone.

The latter half of *PW* is filled with book reviews. I flag Lisa's and my upcoming titles that have been mentioned. Lisa's got a lot this week. I'll have to scan them into the computer and share them with the agents in the London office and in Los Angeles.

4:35 p.m. We've got a new copier, a snazzy Sharp MX-5500N. I have skipped the tutorials on how to use it. After all, before I came to ICM, I worked at two "boutique" agencies, and one of my less glamorous responsibilities was taking care of the photocopier. So I'm damn near cocky when I approach the new copier nestled into a bank of cubicles. Of course, after stabbing at its LCD display a few times, I realize I have no idea how to get it to scan my documents. Once again, I'm not above asking for help.

4:45 p.m. I've got to make some follow-up calls regarding a manuscript I have on submission. I've found that many children's editors get in early so they can leave early (as opposed to yours truly who would happily sleep until noon, even if it meant working until ten at night). So, as expected, I get a lot of voice mails. Two editors are on vacation. Stab of envy? You bet. Mini-fantasy time—on the beach, warm in the sun, my husband and I frolic in the surf, a great book waiting for me back on my beach towel . . .

5:52 p.m. Jessica calls to confirm that she will be getting out of work at a regular hour. Woo-hoo!

5:54 p.m. Click and drag a few new query letters into the folder. Happily, I'm still not at one hundred. Another one of my job responsibilities is to place excerpts from our upcoming titles in magazines before the books come out. These are called first serial sales. Before I leave, I follow up on a first serial submission to *Harper's Magazine*.

6:26 p.m. Doug calls. He's going to his friend Nick's apartment to help move a TV. Trying not to sound too joyous about Jessica and me having the apartment to ourselves, I tell him to have fun, bend with the knees, and say hi to Nick for me.

6:30 p.m. Time to figure out what I'm going to read on my commute. I open my submission log. The list starts with two partial manuscripts and is followed by eight full manuscripts. Since I'm pretty strict about reading the material I request in the order it arrives, I put the two partials in my bag. I'm banking on being able to determine pretty quickly if these are something I want to represent. If not, I'll have lugged a lot of paper home only to lug it back and forth a few more times until I get to it.

6:43 p.m. Crap. I'm going to be late. Luckily, Jessica has keys to my apartment and the doormen know her. Stabbing the elevator button repeatedly is not going to make the doors open any quicker, but it's what I really want to be doing. Tick, tick, tick.

assistant to a literary agent

The doors open. Of course the elevator stops on nearly every floor. I think of the elevator joke that drives my husband crazy—"Looks like we got a local"—and smile.

7:15 p.m. On the sixteenth floor I find Jessica waiting outside my apartment. "I thought you had keys." She closes the book she's reading—*Marley and Me*.

"I left them at home."

I pour us both a pint of stout and ask about her day, even though I know I'll have to interrupt at least once or twice for clarification regarding some of the film terminology. It's amazing how much jargon comes with each industry. My day might consist of P&Ls and ARCs and D&A payments—all of which have stopped sounding foreign. Ultimately, our conversation turns from work to family to Jessica's upcoming wedding. And then, of course, to food. It's time to order in some sushi.

9:59 p.m. Jessica heads home. She lives exactly one mile from my apartment. It's such a blessing having a close friend who lives nearby. My family is in Maine, my friends are scattered throughout the country. Sometimes I wish the heart of publishing didn't so very clearly beat in New York City. I pull one of the partial manuscripts from my bag. Might as well get ahead on my reading.

11:08 p.m. Doug walks into the apartment. I can tell by his posture that he's tired. He gives me a kiss hello and heads to the shower. I decide I've read enough for the night and start puttering around the kitchen. By the time I'm finished, Doug's out of the shower. "Am I reading to you tonight?" he asks.

"Definitely."

Dear Author . . .

2:45 p.m. I check e-mail. An agent I queried responds, "I really loved the premise of the story, especially enjoyed the careless character of the punk mother, but I just did not fall in love with the writing." Ah, the joys of writing. Does the agent really need to fall in love with the writing to accept the project? If so, I'm doomed.

—*Diane Payne, 48, Monticello, Arkansas;*
writer, assistant professor of English

•

assistant to a literary agent

Aircraft Mechanic, Timco Aerosystems

JANICE DE LA GARZA, 52, STOKESDALE, NORTH CAROLINA

She's an FAA-licensed airframe and power plant mechanic with over twenty-five years' experience in the aviation industry. She's performed major repairs, modifications, and general maintenance on a wide variety of commercial jetliners but now supervises Timco's carpet shop. A "skirt" in a male profession, the line that really gets to her is, "You know how she got that position." She's a role model, not only for women but for her oldest son, also an aircraft mechanic. "I'm so proud of him. It's not often that the son's goal is to grow up to be like Mama."

7:15 a.m. Why didn't you take the suitcase out of the car, Janice? Oh well, too late now. Can't be late the first day back from vacation. Stuck in traffic, no music on the radio, just talk, talk, talk about nothing. Oh, yay! I have my iPod in the suitcase. Cool, there is some lotion, too. I love my Estée Lauder. Just because I work like a man, I don't have to smell like one.

8:00 a.m. Entering the parking lot, hundreds of cars, hope I can find a spot. I'll park in the visitor's space. I work in Hangar 4 but have to run into the shipping department in Hangar 1 (where I used to work) to pick up some tickets. There's a new guard at the security gate, checking everyone's photo badge. Glad I remembered mine. Since 9/11, it is next to impossible to get a temporary badge because of the airport runway access.

There are four United planes in Hangar 1—two Boeing 767s and two Boeing 757s. The way they have staged these planes in here a gerbil would have a hard time navigating this hangar. There are air hoses running all over the place, tool boxes, and parts racks.

Radios are playing, rivet guns are blasting, fork lifts are zooming all around. The buzz of aviation maintenance at its best.

"Hey, Sheila, long time no see." Cool, there is Vicki. Heard she had a heart attack, glad to see her back. "Hey Vivat, my hero, how are you?" I love my old crew down here, we really made it happen. I feel almost exiled since I have been working in Hangar 4. It's a lot quieter down there, not much foot traffic, and I am working with a much smaller crew now, only eight mechanics.

Oh well, better get those shipping tickets. They have the FedEx tracking numbers for all the shipments we've sent to United Airlines. With the three-hour time difference, I can get the information forwarded to United in San Francisco so they'll have it at the start of business. It's important, especially for their planes on the ground that are unable to fly.

8:15 a.m. Hangar 4 parking lot. Oh no, they tagged my son Joseph's car. The Barney Truck, that's what his kids call it, because it's big and purple. Joe hates that truck. He left it here after he got laid off a few weeks ago and took a temporary mechanic job in Dothan, Alabama. He didn't think the truck would make the trip. Now I need to get someone to help me move it. Glad I still have those jumper cables in the car; bet the battery is dead. I'll be glad when I get my taxes done. I will just pay the car off for him. With all those kids, he needs something even bigger.

8:25 a.m. My office is a white, cinder-block structure inside the loading dock area. Nothing fancy, but I love it. I even have windows. There is my co-worker Bojan, waiting at his desk for the shipping tickets. Nice, he rearranged the office. I like it this way, more efficient. Bojan is a war refugee from Bosnia. He is six foot four and, when he first started here, his accent reminded me of Arnold Schwarzenegger, especially when he would go to get supplies and say, "I'll be back." Bojan's come a long way. I am so glad to have him to help me. I could never take off time without him.

8:30 a.m. I check in on the carpet shop where I am the business planner. This is where we have the carpet-cutting machine, which is about 35 feet long. The carpet comes on either 6-foot or 4-foot-wide rolls. We load a roll (about 100 feet long) on the machine with a forklift, and feed it through on to a vacuum table, with a cutting head that runs the width and length of the table. No matter how complex the pattern, a push of the button and the cutting head cuts the carpet to any size or specs.

Jon is running the cutting machine. He and I go back to my first day at Timco almost twelve years ago. Jon rides a Harley. Some people only see his roughness, but he'll do anything for almost anyone, if he likes you. We've always had a special bond, and now that I have a Harley, too, maybe we'll go for a ride together. It's always nice to have an experienced motorcycle mechanic along on a ride. I fix airplanes, not motorcycles; Jon fixes both. (Ha-ha.)

Today Tu is in the sewing area, serging each cut piece of carpet to provide a finished edge to prevent unraveling. Little Tu is from Vietnam, and one of the hardest workers I've ever seen. She practically runs everywhere. Frank is hand-marking the part number on the cut parts. When the parts are finished, they'll be marked again with ink and stencil and put into kits and inventoried. Then they're boxed and sent off to shipping!

Things are running smoothly, so I pick up the finished paperwork—complete with certificates and conformances and inspection information—and head back to my office to enter the information into the computer.

8:45 a.m. Great, only eighteen e-mails. Oops, still loading. Wow, 238 unread e-mails. I forgot to turn on my out-of-the-office button. I finally have a response from Replin, a vendor in Scotland, and the only place that makes the type of material United requires for its sidewalls. I've been trying to get a quote from them for over six months now.

Great, a response from Willie about the thread we have on back order. Oh no, it has been pushed back another three weeks. We only have three rolls stashed, and that won't even cover the kits ordered today. Need to e-mail United to see if they have any in stock we can buy.

Another e-mail asking me if we can manufacture some engine inlet covers. I remember Tu has done this before. Need to check with her to see if she still has a pattern, or do we need to go measure the engine diameter.

United e-mails, too. Can we manufacture six kits to send to Beijing, China, by tomorrow? I know this is going to make Bojan mad. He has already scheduled the work for the day, and changes just blow him up. But he always gets the job done.

9:00 a.m. Yes Bo, I will go and smoke with you, and catch up on all the gossip. Bojan tells me "Rumor Control"—that would be Mark and Bobby—has it we are all going to get a bonus. We'll see. Those guys start rumors on everything from how the company is being sold, to who bought a new car, to who is being transferred, promoted, fired, or dating.

10:00 a.m. One of the leads from the 767 United lines calls to say the carpet they're installing doesn't fit right. I tell him everything we cut comes from a digitalized pattern, either by CAD-like files, or we plot the patterns, and then transfer the info into the cutting machine's computer. It doesn't change. I'll go down and check it out.

I had to look for the aircraft, which they'd pulled out to the blast fence to do engine runs. Good, they haven't started the runs yet. Inside, they've already put down double-back carpet tape, and are working on installing the pieces. One piece is too short, creating a gap. We review the installation drawing. All is well. They had the pieces in the wrong place.

Break time. Guess I will catch a smoke. Wow, what a nice day. A couple of mechanics ask about Joe. How he is doing in Alabama? When is he coming back? This will make him feel good, that people are missing him. Everyone is in a good mood. It must be the weather. Everyone has been so bitchy about the rain and cold. It's hard on them when the aircraft is outside, but that's why they call it work.

10:45 a.m. Cool, an e-mail from my director, Mark. He is back from Russia. I hope everything went well with the adoption. I can't imagine adopting a child from another country. I had a hard time raising my own two boys, and I gave birth to them.

11:10 a.m. United Airlines e-mail from Mark Davis, requesting a quote for producing the new color scheme carpet for their Boeing 767 fleet on twenty-one airplanes. Starting in August, they'll also be changing the color scheme on their Boeing 747s and 777s. Great! I love new projects. They keep things refreshing.

Oh, snap! Engineering picked up all the preliminary drawings before I left. I need them to scale out the yardage for the project, in order to work up a bid. I hope they are done revising them. I want to respond to Mr. Davis real fast. Can't let him down, especially after he wrote such a nice letter to the president of the company, telling him what a great job I was doing—"Janice has been instrumental in updating and maintaining the carpet process at Timco. . . ." I received employee-of-the-month out of that one. A dozen roses from the CEO. The president gave me beautiful plaque. And then the envelope! In it was a sizeable check. I also got my own parking place for December, close to the main entrance. To realize how valuable this is, just try to find a parking space at change of shift in the morning with over 1,500 employees trying to get to work on time.

It is great recognition when the customer takes the time to actually write a letter. Times like that, I really miss my mom. She would be so proud of me. Oh well, I guess she knows anyway. (She passed in 2002.)

Noon I am so hungry. I weigh myself on the new shipping scale on the loading dock just outside my office. Hope no one is around. It's digital, and those numbers are so big anyone could see them from across the room. Damn, another five pounds. I did want a steak and cheese, but guess I will go to a Weight Watchers meeting instead. I should take Joe's truck, which would charge the battery a little. Oh, snap! The tags are expired. Maybe no one will notice.

12:10 p.m. Oh, snap! I've never seen smoke coming from a car radio before. Can't pull over here, there is so much traffic. I don't smell anything burning. I better park far away from everything.

Weight Watchers meeting is boring. "Blab, blab, blab . . ." "You are fat . . . " "Don't eat anything that tastes good . . ." Sometimes I wonder why I bother. Seems I've always had to watch everything I eat.

The meeting is over. The truck is not on fire so I guess I will drive it back to work. Damn, the battery is dead and my cell phone is on my desk. And the extra one, yes a second cell phone, is in the console of my car back at work. Okay, think, Janice. Do you really want to jump it and catch it on fire? Great, there is a Starbucks. I can use the phone there and get a nice cup of coffee. And maybe a sweet roll. After all, this is a crisis, right?

1:00 p.m. Man, this maple bar tastes good. Bob, a co-worker, picks me up. The truck will be okay in this parking lot. It is out of the way.

1:45 p.m. Cool. Chuck, the new shipping supervisor, told me we are going to start shipping the carpet orders out of here tomorrow. Now I won't have to mess with transportation taking all the crates and boxes down to Hangar 1. Ever since they had to move out of this office so I could move in, they've been short with me. It wasn't my fault. My manager made the arrangements for me to relocate here. I hope they don't stay mad at me long. I like those guys.

2:00 p.m. I have so much catching up to do. I need to close out last month's service order and check the completed operations to make sure all materials were charged. It's going to be a short week, I don't have much time to get it all done, and I never know what orders I will receive tomorrow.

2:10 p.m. Just received an angry phone call from Ron at United in China. He has a carpet shipment stuck in customs. They're claiming that there are no international shipping documents with the shipment. I do not understand how this happens. We put a copy of all documents on the box, in the box, and I scan and e-mail them a copy. That is three copies. I will send them another one.

2:50 p.m. Guess I will go smoke a cigarette with Bo before he leaves for the day. I really like that young man. He is so much more relaxed now that he got his raise. He has wanted to buy a house and now he can. I can still remember that excited feeling of buying my first home.

3:00 p.m. I need to check my bank account to make sure my son has enough money. (He has my name on his account so I can transfer money to him if he is short.) What the he@%! My balance is negative $389! I didn't realize the twenty-third came before my next payday. I guess I need Joe to transfer some money into my account instead. Oh well, at least the bank paid my house payment.

I should sell that house. It's way too big for me. Now that my youngest son, Michael, is grown and gone, I'm by myself. I usually stay in my room most of the time. I have my TV and stereo in there. Those other three bedrooms are just being wasted. And I know I can find better things to do with my day off besides mowing the lawn and cleaning the pool.

4:00 p.m. I only have one hour to finish the invoicing. No way is this going to happen. Glad I told them Wednesday.

5:00 p.m. Off to play pool. Yes, T-Buddy, I will pick you up. I met T-Buddy playing pool about eight months ago. He was putting together a team and asked me if I would like to play on his league. I told him I had never played on a league, but he said no problem, he would teach me the rules. When I showed up the next week, I was told I was team captain!

7:00 p.m. I'm shooting pretty well. Oh, snap, here comes trouble. That guy is really drunk and loudmouthed. A lot of these guys take their games seriously. If he keeps running his mouth and bumping into people while they're lining up to shoot, he's going to get hit. He found out his wife is having an affair and is asking everyone if they've seen her. No wonder she left him, he's an idiot!!! Nobody wants to hear that mouth.

9:00 p.m. I just got a call from Joe, telling me that his fiancée was taken down to the police station and questioned for robbing a

Laundromat. Good God, he makes twenty-seven dollars an hour and will not even let her go to a Laundromat. I am so glad he bought those rims for his car. The police showed her a video of the car involved in the robbery. It looked just like her Honda, except it had stock rims. And the couple did look sort of like them. My poor baby boy. It seems like there is always something stressful happening with him.

10:00 p.m. I hope this game doesn't last much longer. I need to leave now! This has been a long day. "Blab, blab, blab . . ." When people get drunk, that is about all I hear. Come on T-Buddy, ready? Okay, one more game, more blab, blab, blab . . . and a bag of chips.

11:45 p.m. Finally, we are leaving. T-Buddy wants to have midnight breakfast at the Waffle House on the way home. Yes, that would be okay, if I didn't have to get up at five thirty in the morning. I have to be at work a half hour before everyone else to process the new orders that came in overnight. The crew can't get to work without the paperwork.

T-Buddy is not giving up on breakfast. Oh well. T-Buddy's a little rough around the edges, but he's turned out to be a great guy, with a big heart. On Valentine's Day he asked me to be his girlfriend. I told him sure, I was a girl and I was his friend. He said, "I know that, but I want you to be my *real* girlfriend." I said okay. After being a widow for almost twelve years, and a few jerk encounters, it was nice to get to know a good guy.

On March 27, 2007

28 percent of day diarists gossiped at work.

●

aircraft mechanic, timco aerosystems ....

Ladies, Start Your Engines

7:45 a.m. Next challenge—find a parking space within close proximity of the school uniform sale. Finally it pays to have a ten-year-old Nissan Sentra. I scoot around chubby mini-vans and stocky SUVs, spy an opportunity and go for it, impressing the car line and even myself with my parallel parking skills.

7:50 a.m. Now I'm perched on a bench outside the principal's office feeling like I'm in detention. Five other mothers are sitting, standing, pacing, waiting patiently—or not—for a sign (perhaps a black-and-white checkered flag?) to signal the start of the uniform race, er, I mean sale. I can identify other working moms instantly by the wild look in their eyes. I glance at my watch and allot roughly ten minutes to shop.

7:52 a.m. *Finally* someone sets up a folding table and unloads stacks of tan and navy blue uniform pants from giant Rubbermaid containers. I resist the urge to take a flying leap and dive in like a hungry squirrel hunting acorns. One of the stay-at-home moms begins sorting piles into size order. Puh-leeze! Step aside, Martha Stewart, and let the squirrels dig. I somehow manage to collect four shirts, two pairs of pants, and one sweatshirt—without compromising my dignity or my budget.

—*Cheryl Wolf, 48, Deerfield Beach, Florida;*
copy editor, Day Jet Corporation

Blogger, Go Fug Yourself

HEATHER COCKS, 29, SHERMAN OAKS, CALIFORNIA

It started as a lark, blogging with her friend Jessica about the famous and fashion impaired. Now the site—renowned for the barbed wit of its creators—gets 3.5 million visits a month, and even *Vanity Fair* "can't get enough" of their "fugging." Her take on the blog's appeal? "We're the Internet equivalent of hanging out with your girlfriends and passing around a copy of *Us Weekly*, wondering why in God's name Jessica Simpson wouldn't have worn a bra with that dress, or why anyone thought hot pants and leggings were attractive."

9:05 a.m. A telemarketer wakes me up from a fitful sleep. I can't tell if it's a recording or a real woman, as there are pauses for me to answer, but they seem overlong. I end up hanging up in the middle of her spiel about TV ratings systems, because I'm feeling fuzzy-headed from the flu I have, and I'm not in the mood to politely disengage myself. She's just paying the bills, I tell myself, yet I still hit "off" on the cordless.

9:25 a.m. I decide to settle into bed with *Harry Potter* and a granola bar. Usually by now I'm at my computer in the office, looking for images to put up on *Go Fug Yourself*, along with some snarky commentary. But today my head is spinning, my body temperature still isn't quite right, and I know Jessica, my friend and writing/blogging partner, won't hold it against me if I take half an hour to adjust to being awake. We almost always work from our respective homes (about twenty to sixty minutes apart, depending on traffic), so no major schedules were altered by my sudden contagion.

9:55 a.m. Kevin, my husband of almost one year, leaves for work as an editor for the TV show *America's Next Top Model*. But first he hooks up my laptop and plops it on the bed. I grumble that anything I can think of to write is nothing I would want to read.

"Maybe the fever will make you extra mean for *GFY*," he suggests helpfully. "Or maybe it'll be complete nonsense, which would be kind of fun, too."

10:10 a.m. The first thing I do these days is check for an e-mail from our book editor to see if he's finished reading our manuscript. Nothing yet. (We had sold the editor a book proposal based on the site, then turned in a draft at the beginning of March.) This is easily the thing about which I'm most neurotic these days. The book is new material. We invented a bunch of goofy "award" categories: the most tanorexic, or the most inexplicable style icon, then we list the nominees and pick a winner. We're proud of what we turned in, but we also know there's a long road ahead.

10:21 a.m. Jessica has already set some stuff to post on *GFY*. She found a photo of Melrose, a former *Top Model* contestant, in a crimson cape, and wrote that perhaps Melrose *allowed herself to become a child of the night, feasting on the blood of humans and occasionally turning—when appropriate—into a bat.* Since Jessica's posted something new, we're instant messaging each other now about other business, while I casually poke around our image provider's Web site for some pictures that speak to me.

Jessica and I bandy about ideas for the column we write for *New York* magazine's Web site. We write the column on Wednesdays and it runs Thursdays, so we need to pitch our idea today. The brainstorming process is a bit stressful because the column is a pretty open format, but it also has to walk the line between being about celebrities and being about people who matter to readers in New York (where, we imagine, they pay way less heed to low-level celebs than we do in L.A., because the scene there is so different).

10:46 a.m. It is a slow news week and we're not finding an easy peg for a column.

water cooler diaries

As far as we can tell, nobody got arrested or caught in any scandalous photos. No one mouthed off to the press. And it's the same old B-list people in the news. I mean, there are only so many times you can write about what Rosie O'Donnell said on *The View* to make Elisabeth Hasselbeck cry. Jess and I have devolved into more and more jokey submissions because we are flummoxed. I'm also still working from bed.

10:48 a.m. Lindsay Lohan, a regular on our site, has been seen around town with, like, five different older men recently. In this photo, it's a very sweaty and unstable-looking Robbie Williams. She makes it harder and harder to watch *The Parent Trap* without becoming depressed. I feel like Jessica and I make that comment to each other almost daily, usually followed up with, "But that Dennis Quaid sure is aging well." Today, I can't wrap my brain around how to scold Lindsay for her various offenses, so I bypass that photo and keep perusing our photo sources and scouring other gossip sites for celeb news.

10:58 a.m. I start noodling with an entry in my personal weblog, a fascinating treatise on a TRESemmé commercial that really chaps my hide. It shows a girl with curly hair that's a tad frizzy going to a stylist who "fixes" her with smoothing shampoo and a straight iron. All better! As a curlyhead myself, I resent the idea that curly = ugly, and straight = perfect. It's such a silly thing to react to so vehemently, and it's not like I don't ever straighten my hair for variety. But don't try to tell us that we should hate our genes, people. Bah, humbug. Maybe I'll write an angry letter.

10:59 a.m. No, I totally won't. And I don't feel like finishing this entry—not exactly incisive commentary—so I'm saving it as a draft and moving onto something else. Having a personal blog is great, because it challenges me to fill a blank space with some regularity, but the more I blog on *GFY*, the less I find time for my own longer-standing chunk of cyberspace. That feels wrong, like being a manicurist with bad nails.

blogger, go fuq yourself

11:05 a.m. My Internet connection keeps coming and going in the bedroom. Please don't make me get up like a real person. Wallowing in self-pity about my death flu isn't nearly as satisfying when I'm not bedridden.

11:12 a.m. Damn, it's a slow fug day. Why is no one leaving the house in anything insane, like gold lamé leggings tucked into Ugg boots, or a muumuu over jeans? We'd love to update more often, but we're a bit hamstrung by the narrowness of our subject matter. It's funny, we never set out for the site to fill a hole in celebrity fashion coverage. It just started with Jessica and me amusing ourselves, but then old co-workers from when we wrote for *Television Without Pity* were throwing us some links, and *Defamer* found us, and we started growing.

It's changed our lives. We quit our day jobs last summer to devote ourselves to the site and to writing the book, and we haven't had to go back yet, thanks to ad sales and our other freelance work. I hope we'll be able to keep it all going, because we love what we're doing and we love working together. Ha—and people think we hate everything. The reality is, if we hated *everything*, we'd post twenty-four times a day instead of just an average of four.

11:24 a.m. The countdown to lunch begins. I'd snack all day if I could, but I can't listen to every hunger pang or else I'd have food dripping out of my mouth 24/7. Which isn't to say that I'm a supremely healthy person. After all, I eat peanut butter for lunch every day, and while that is not as bad as, say, a lard sandwich, it's not exactly a salad.

11:36 a.m. I got an e-mail from a guy I was in ninth grade with, who saw the Web site and figured out it was me. He concluded with, *I hope I wasn't too obnoxious in high school.* It's funny how people not only remember others, but remember themselves. For instance, my reply would be something like, *I hope I wasn't too aloof in high school. I promise I was just shy*. Or, *I hope my eyebrows weren't too enormous. I hadn't discovered waxing yet*. But for all I know he remembers me an entirely different way, just as I don't remember him as being obnoxious.

Maybe this is why people fake their own deaths. They just want to hear what people say about them. Of course, I don't actually know anyone who's faked his own death, except maybe that dude Olivia Newton-John was dating, and we're not even completely sure that's what he did.

11:58 a.m. We may have hit upon some ideas for our column. One revolves around the tell-all book Madonna's nanny sold to Crown, only to have Crown change its mind. One is about Nicole Richie's many problems in anticipation of her April sentencing for her DUI offense. And one is about Heather Mills's fake leg, with which we are darkly obsessed.

Pitching ideas to editors is one of the times when I get the most self-conscious. It partly has to do with the push-pull of writing, where you do the work to make yourself proud, but at the same time you're tacitly asking for someone's approval. Your editor has to like it, your audience has to like it. And putting ideas out there every week to be picked up or shot down is an offshoot of that, a bit like laying yourself bare. Even if the subject matter isn't personal, the approach, the wording, the touches of humor, all that stuff is. Those are things that make your writing yours, so it's always hard to put it under someone else's microscope.

12:15 p.m. Panic! Our burglar alarm randomly went off, and because we just moved in two or three weeks ago, we don't have any codes. We weren't even aware that it worked. I was running around pounding on the panels to stop the beeping and screaming, and as I stood there in my pajamas with my matted, sick-girl hair, my first thought was, *I need to find a hat in case the cops come.* Suddenly, it stopped. Evidently, a quick power outage triggered the thing. It's an incredibly windy day.

12:35 p.m. No notes from the book editor.

12:42 p.m. Aha! Eva Mendes in dowdy, unhemmed jeans that hide her shoes, and a shapeless wrap/cardigan. Finally, I can post something today: *I feel like you can be comfortable at an event without* *looking as if you had been lying around the house in your too-big lazy-day jeans before realizing you are out of Diet Coke and Jif, throwing on a shawl to go run a really fast "I don't care what I'm wearing because I will only be outside for two seconds, so it doesn't matter that I don't have any shoes that go with these pants" errand, and then spontaneously deciding to drop in on Quentin Tarantino for some fun face time.*

1:06 p.m. And my entry is up. I'm not entirely happy with it, but my brain's not churning out maximum cleverness today, and sometimes, there's only so much you can say about a person who doesn't tailor her pants. Honestly, how many times can I crack that his or her feet were bitten off by a rabid dog?

1:17 p.m. We heard back from our editor at *New York*, who liked the pitch about Heather Mills's fake leg. People ask if we feel guilty about making such shallow contributions to society, but I say, I'm just as happy giving the world's altruists something at which to laugh. They need a mental break, too. It's the six-degrees-of-separation approach to doing good in the world.

2:15 p.m. We're now buried deep in hunting for stuff on the Internet about Heather Mills's fake leg, like clips of her appearances on *Dancing with the Stars* talking about The Leg, info about the special one she had made for the show, etc. Forget feeling guilty about what I do for a living—this is so entertaining that I can't believe we get paid for it.

2:23 p.m. I get an e-mail from my college roommate who is pregnant and having a baby shower on Memorial Day weekend. I'm hoping I can make it to see her in Wisconsin. She's my first contemporary to have a baby; when friends of friends or sisters have them, it's one thing, but when people you used to party with all the time become parents, it's a whole different kind of realization that you're all really, truly adults now.

2:52 p.m. My mother calls to let me know they're in Scottsdale, Arizona. My parents are currently driving a Penske truck out here with some furniture they've been storing for me: my piano and antique Bar Billiards table. It's amusing to me that my parents decided to road trip from Florida to California, given that we are not a family that ever did things like that. (When I was six, our first and last family car trip involved me vomiting all over my Cabbage Patch Kid, which, after a brisk scrubbing, got doused by my mother in her Chanel No. 5.) I'm looking forward to their seeing our first house. I admire and adore my parents, and find myself wanting to impress them.

3:13 p.m. *GFY* is mostly taken care of for the day. Bless Jessica for putting up three posts to my one, including a post about Julianne Moore—in a black-and-white dress with an explosion of feathers on the bottom—as an example of how clothes that work on a fashion runway often just don't look right in real life. Jessica said the dress made Julianne look a bit like a sofa. She was right.

Now we can turn our attention to our biweekly *In Touch* assignment, which involves writing commentary for photos the editor has chosen for the magazine's "If These Clothes Could Talk" segment. Jess and I instant message each other ideas. *How about, "We would suggest that she avoid any woodland cottages while wearing that cape, but it appears the Big Bad Wolf already [HILARIOUS ENDING HERE] . . ." How about, "What, is Mother Goose running a house of ill repute now?" No, hang on. We can't accuse Mother Goose of being a whore.*

3:32 p.m. Still no notes from the book editor. No, he hasn't promised any to us by a certain time, and we know he needs to go through it with a fine-tooth comb, but I always get uneasy when something I've written is met with silence. I always assume the worst.

3:51 p.m. The Man-Wife calls to check in on me. I wish he were coming home sooner. Yesterday, when I was cruising toward the nadir of my illness, Kevin's arrival from work cheered me up immensely. Calling him "Man-Wife" started when a friend of ours blurted it out in place of "house husband." She was referring to the brief period after we first got married, when I worked in an office and my husband was on a monthlong break. Unfortunately for Kevin, it stuck, but he's too good-natured to mind.

4:43 p.m. I am taking a very important break from Web surfing to see if I can locate Q-Feel's *Dancing in Heaven*, so memorably featured in the fine Sarah Jessica Parker film *Girls Just Wanna Have Fun*. It's for my friend Jen. We all need a little more eighties New Wave in our lives.

5:41 p.m. No notes from the book editor.

5:55 p.m. As the CFO of our little company (for real; we incorporated for tax reasons and had to pick titles), I have to be meticulous about keeping a ledger of any ads we sell, any invoices due and payments outstanding, and deposits that need to be made. I decide to handle all the computer-based stuff now and deal with faxing printouts tomorrow. Jessica keeps vowing (threatening?) to get me a World's Best CFO mug. I usually respond that I'm going to retaliate with a T-shirt for her that says "Madam President."

6:44 p.m. Just got off the phone with my sister, who is deploying to Iraq soon with her husband. They work for the government and are going voluntarily as civilians. It's a tough thing. I'm proud of them for serving the country, but it's certainly scary to think about her being there. Even though she lives in Washington, D.C., and I'm on the opposite coast, my sister and I are very close, the best of friends. Her departure to somewhere potentially dangerous doesn't feel real enough yet to cry about it, but I know the tears are coming.

6:58 p.m. I have found a silver lining—coming up with ideas for care packages I can send her. One of them is clearly going to include a lot of hair products. That kind of desert heat is not good for curls.

7:07 p.m. Jess left a while ago for a Lakers game and I am holding down the fort, so to speak, which basically involves checking our e-mail obsessively and surfing to see if there are any images coming in worth fugging tomorrow. We average 150 e-mails a day and like to respond to as many we can, even if it's as simple as writing, *Thanks!* Generally, we don't write back to any nasty e-mails. It's just best not to engage with the haters.

Today we got an e-mail that had the word "brilliant" pasted over and over again, which was nice to hear. Of course, we also got the typical e-mail from someone who thinks we're connected to Britney Spears, just because we post about her. The note encourages the pop star to take refuge in her home. I file this e-mail in the "Intern George" folder for our beloved fictional employee (George Clooney) to answer on the site.

8:00 p.m. I hate housekeeping. Okay, *fine*, I'll get out the broom.

9:48 p.m. Weary of straightening up and sweeping, and grateful that Kevin is home, I decide to take a break and have a very late dinner, courtesy of my Hot Diggity Dogger hot dog and bun toaster. This thing is heaven. My sister's husband bought it for her when they started dating. We ribbed her about it incessantly, so she bought it for all her bridesmaids. I'm telling you, this thing cooks a perfect hot dog.

Kevin and I talk a little bit about my sister going to Iraq. We're both at a loss. We want to be supportive, but we don't want to act like what she's doing is no big deal. Mostly, I want her to know how much we admire her and are going to miss her. Fortunately, we know from experience (her husband has been to Iraq before) that they have e-mail over there, so I plan to inundate her.

11:35 p.m. We recently got new carpet in the bedroom, and I am walking around on it slowly, digging in my toes. Then I lie down on it, just to do it. Being a homeowner is ungodly expensive, but it's definitely taught me to revel in stuff like this. It's *our* carpet. We chose it. We put it there (by which I mean we paid three men to do the job). The walls are painted our colors; the changes we made belong to us. I miss consulting a landlord anytime something breaks, but I love the satisfaction of the house being our canvas.

11:59 p.m. Kevin flops down on the carpet next to me, just as I did, and heaves a satisfied sigh. He asks, "Did you manage anything exciting today?"

"No," I say. But in a solitary home office, I guess that's kind of how it works.

Fan Mail

9:40 a.m. We got an e-mail from one of the readers who somehow thinks we have contact with Britney Spears. She has offered Britney a relaxing weekend at her house in San Bernardino, just to get away from it all. The sentiment in this e-mail is actually very nice, but the spelling is atrocious—*then u can have a weekend to be like me. home and eatting playing with my sisters kids i love. email me let me no* . . . She claims to be twenty-three, and the fact that an adult can't figure out that our Web site is not at all affiliated with Britney makes me sad.

—*Jessica Morgan, 31, Santa Monica, California;*
blogger, Go Fug Yourself

•

School Custodian

GLORIA STERRETT, 57, DELPHI, INDIANA

Six years ago she got laid off from her factory job, so she started working as a school janitor, the 3:00 to 11:00 p.m. shift. She's been trying to switch to days ever since. "The money's about the only good thing I can think of about being a night custodian." She's also a professional clown, part of the Smiles Unlimited Clown Ministry. Her costume includes an orange "Silly Boy" wig and big fake teeth. She performs at nursing homes, company picnics, and kid parties. "If people don't have a smile, I give them one of mine."

5:00 a.m. Husband, Danny, got me up. Had coffee fixed for me. He's a sweetie most of the time. I leave for work about three miles away, but I wouldn't mind driving farther for better conditions and peace of mind. I'm thinking and praying about my job interview this afternoon. It's a custodial position for a United Methodist church (big church). Forty hours, eleven dollars an hour, five days a week, Monday through Friday on days. And a block of insurance. I'm sooo excited about it.

I hate this job at the middle school. I'm so tired of cleaning up after those kids. They just see how big a mess they can make, or how much stuff they can tear up, and they say and think it's the janitor's job to clean up after them!!! Which we do, but sometimes it's really rough. It totally wears you out. And it's second shift.

Now things are starting to fall apart on me. First, shoulder spurs two years ago from repetitive motion, and now I have plantar fasciitis. That's the breaking down of the arches, and it hurts like hell. I went to the Good Feet store, then I got a foot bootie thing, then another pair of insoles way cheaper than the others, and I think they work better! When you are in pain, you'll about try anything.

6:05 a.m. I'm putting my stuff in the fridge. My co-worker, Trica, comes in and says, "Hi, Twila." I say, "Hi, Twila." For some reason she just started calling us nicknames. At first I was Shaniqua and she was Twila, but before it was over we were both Twila.

Trica and I get along okay, but I kind of have resentments. She was on nights with me, then the girl on days died last year, and our boss (a bully who has the principal wrapped around his little finger) says to me, "We're interviewing for the day job if you and Trica want to put in your letter of interest."

I've wanted days for years now, back when the girl who just died got the job. Trica didn't want days, so she said, but she put in for it anyway. So waah! Here's where the resentment comes in. Trica got the job. I asked the principal why and he said, "She had the better interview!" So I said, "I just want to let you know I am very hurt about it!" He asked, "Are you going to stay tonight?" I said, "Well, yes!" Duh. What is wrong with people? I think he thought since I didn't get the day job, I'd either quit or get mad and go home.

Today I'm working days with Trica 'cause it's spring break and the kids aren't in school. She just told me that our boss didn't come in yesterday. Conveniently, he had stomach flu. (Bad bout, he says.) We think he just wanted a three-day weekend. He's done this over and over again. He's taken off eight sick days since November, but who's counting?

I go to his office to get my radio. He tells me he's sick. I scurry out and say, "I don't want it." I got my cart and to work I went.

6:30 a.m. Get water ready to clean chalkboards. First room— cleaned desks, TV and PC screens, shelves, and chalkboards. The work is more laid back on these days of deep cleaning, as we call it. We do the things we don't normally have time for during the regular week. We don't have to hurry, or put as much strain on our muscles and joints. I eat an apple and sip my second cup of coffee.

7:15 a.m. Next room—wash windows, TV and PC screens, chalk-boards, desktops, and legs and backs of seats.

8:00 a.m. Break time. I sit at the picnic table in the outdoor lab. Have a banana, pretzels, and, of course, coffee. I listen to the birds. The weather is great. Still overcast some. Trica goes to her truck to smoke. Glad I quit almost nineteen years ago.

I'm thinking about going to visit my daughter and two grand-sons who are almost grown. They live about twenty-five minutes away. All three of them have had some personal problems and really tough times, almost to the point of no return. They weigh heavy on my mind. I can't even be there to try and talk matters through, being as I am on second shift. I feel I am robbing them of our precious time together. Lord help me!

See why I worry all the time? But I don't act like it. I don't talk about things a lot. I just take deep breaths and pray a lot. There's a cardinal six feet from me in a tree, chirping so sweetly.

8:15 a.m. Mark, a sub who worked nights with me last week, comes in to pick up his check. He has experienced our boss for himself, but we fill him in some. We have had three custodians quit since November. You guessed it, because of the boss. He's a real piece of work and does not respect women. He tried to get me fired twice in November but it didn't work. I'm still here. I'm leaving, but on my terms. He doesn't scare me.

Trica is also looking for another job, after taking days and knowing how badly I wanted it. (She said she heard they were not going to let me have it anyway, but didn't or wouldn't say where she got the info.) So now I have to go somewhere else to get days, and she says she's quitting, too, maybe before me. Not. I'm leaving first.

Break's over, back to work.

8:30 a.m. Washed double doors and the foyer, washed a couple of sets of lockers. This is another job we don't have time to do thoroughly

school custodian

in our daily cleaning. There are grimy fingerprints all over them. We sanitize them with this stuff called Quat and use Workout for tough dirt.

Kids are so disrespectful these days. They throw spit wads, paper clips, you name it. They use pencils and erasers to mark up the lockers, and grind pencil lead into all the tile floors. The toilets—let's don't go there. Some kids are nice, don't get me wrong, but lots of them are just plain bad. They get called into the principal's office and it just does not bother them at all. I have heard the principal yell at them through closed doors. Still, they don't care.

10:30 a.m. Lunch. Mandarin chicken salad that I got the night before at Pizza King. Trica and I eat in the outdoor lab. We talk about job interviews. She had two at a factory, both in Monticello, where her sister and a friend work. She thinks one interview went well but has to wait for an opening.

We talk some more about how our boss says he's sick. He didn't look or act sick to us. Trica worked alone yesterday at the middle school. She says when the boss has to do the same job and she's not there, he complains. I think it's not as hard as working nights alone, doing all the vacuuming, getting all the trash, cleaning six restrooms, including locker rooms. Night shift also has to make sure all the doors are secured, lights off, and the building is all clean and ready for the next day.

11:00 a.m. More windows. We clean the upper set of windows only over spring break because we need to drag out a ladder to reach them. Next, I wash down more lockers. I'm thinking and praying about my interview this afternoon. Hope I didn't jinx it by talking about my boss like that! Wouldn't that be the pits, having to put up with his abuse longer? My feet are killing me. Am tired, but got to keep going until break. Then it's just a half hour until we can go home.

1:00 p.m. Break. Trica and I go to the outdoor lab and chitchat some more. We talk about her mom. She and I used to work together in the assembly department at a furniture factory and got to be friends. Trica's mom and dad are snowbirds in Florida. They will be returning around Easter. Trica smokes, and then we go back to work. I finish up another classroom and it's time to go. Yeah!!! We empty our cleaning water, put away our dirty towels, turn out all lights, and make sure all doors are locked.

2:00 p.m. At home I float my two turtles. They are the size of a half dollar (so cute). By floating them I mean I take them out of one of my aquariums and fill a container with warm water and a couple of rocks. I have a fifty-five-gallon tank with five of my babies I took from my pond last year (two algae eaters, two fancy-tail kois, and a striped Raphael). Plus I have three other tanks with fish.

Danny and I made the pond our own selves—about a thousand gallons with a top pond that goes into a little stream, and a waterfall that goes into a bigger bottom pond thirty-one inches deep. I think this spring when we open the pond, I am putting all the fish I can into it and getting rid of the tanks. I'm really tired of messing with them. But I'll keep the two turtles and Lilly, my albino frog, and maybe one other tank. Here I go again. Ha!

3:10 p.m. After resting in my recliner about twenty minutes, I pick out what I want to wear to the church interview—a nice shirt and a pair of capris. Danny gets home from work. He had a good day. We kiss and talk a few. Then he takes my car and fills it for me. He is so good to me.

3:45. I'm getting anxious. I get to the church and wait my turn. Two before me. Three guys are doing the interviewing. One is the pastor. They all are real nice. Of course, what else would they be? They smile and say they appreciate my coming to apply. One question is, How well did I think the church was being maintained? "Very well," I reply. "It looks nice."

I ask how many applied? Sixteen. So if my ten letters from the teachers I clean for pull any weight, I may have a good chance. I've been praying and, Lord willing, this job will be mine. I even prayed in the sanctuary while waiting. I also took the opportunity to read the bulletin board, which may have been to my advantage. I saw pictures of senior citizens and captions about their activities. When they ask what I think would be an important part of my ministry here, I say that I would help do things for the seniors. Pastor Beaks says he'll get back to me one way or the other. Sounds promising, or wishful thinking.

4:30 p.m. Went to Curves for my workout. It has helped me to keep off the weight and tone up. Back home, change clothes, fix supper. Box meal. Chicken with veggies and topped with buttermilk biscuits. Yum. Very good for a box meal.

8:15 p.m. Nap. Not used to working days and getting up at five in the morning. Danny naps, too. He gets up at four thirty every morning.

10:30 p.m. For the past hour or so, I've been sewing seams on my new clown outfit. I am going to another International Clown Convention in thirty-six days and have been working on this outfit nonstop. Right now I'm sewing the jacket, which has tails like a Mickey Mouse suit. I've signed up for the makeup competition and balloon and face-painting comps. Last year, I was in the top ten for makeup, and in a group skit that got fifth place.

In July, I will have been a professional clown for nineteen years. Here's one of my lines—"My first name is *HeySeed* . . . my middle name is *But You Can Call Me* . . . and my last name is *Dolli*. But just call me, okay?"

A Perfect Fit

2:00 p.m. I interviewed for another job on campus. I have a lot of the skills they need, so I think I have a good chance. I also took a little luck with me to the interview. The shirt I wore belonged to my dad. He died suddenly last May. I was very close to him and he was a kind, gentle man. He was also a good businessman. The shirt was a little large, but I wore a navy blazer, so you couldn't tell. I think it gave me a little extra confidence.
    —*Jane Thornton, 51, Louisville, Kentucky; administrative specialist*

All in a Day's Work

8:30 a.m. The penguins swarm about me, demanding my attention. Then they "porpoise" away when they realize I come without capelin, herring, or smelt. However, a couple of the young ones still paddle around, trying to grab at anything that might be dangling—a zipper pull, a lock of hair, a thumb. I have been taught to fold my arms, ignore their advances, and follow the twenty-four-inch rule (that is, we try to keep the birds at least twenty-four inches from us). Because the water is chest deep in many spots, the penguins could get dangerously close to my face with their sharp beaks. I need to be vigilant. Spheniscus sticks right with me, gently nipping at the back of my wetsuit. She emits a curt, low "Hmm, hmm, hmm" that reminds me of the grunt my grandfather made over forty years ago when I almost beat him at checkers. I try to imitate the sound, just to see what it feels like.

—*Lisbeth Bornhofft, 54, Lexington, Massachusetts; senior educator,*
New England Aquarium

9:10 a.m. I get along with most of my co-workers but there's always one, isn't there? That one that just the sound of her voice sends your nerves on edge. Not only doesn't she work, she doesn't even try to pretend to work. I can hear her unpacking her daily mouth stuffings so she can later sufficiently eat and talk with a mouth full of food. I keep meaning to bring along a few socks to work.

—*Debra A. Williams, 45, New Haven, Connecticut;*
library technical assistant

10:00 a.m. I am not a fan of grocery shopping, so I usually do it in the mornings when there is less competition for aisle room. Today I make a couple of important phone calls while

school custodian

I shop. My cell phone plan is four thousand minutes a month and I use it up nearly every month. I'm a big fan of multitasking and have this strange knack for complete focus on the phone conversation while still doing other automatic activities. Once I made phone calls and sent text messages while in the stirrups at my ob-gyn. I recall him giving me this incredulous look and asking, "What do you *do* for a living?!"

—*Amie Chilson, 29, Campbell, California;*
founder and chief executive officer, Girl Powered Real Estate

4:00 p.m. I'm on the road to Denver. I switch on a Christian radio station to hear what's going on in that venue. Personally, it doesn't do much for me, but it's important to be in touch and honor what is meaningful to others, and I know plenty of folks who have felt truly saved and nurtured by this style of ministry. So I listen. A lot of the Christian pop music seems to "church out" the same simplistic themes over and over again—"vending machine faith." But isn't that what pop is about, I suppose? And the endless ads for transformational seminars—"God wants all of you, and you can have all of him." What does that mean?

—*Darlene Avery, 42, Colorado Springs, Colorado; hospice chaplain*

7:15 p.m. I have brought my daughter, Anna, to Little League softball practice. It is her first year playing, and some of the other girls on her team are very good. I try to catch up on work from earlier in the day and get ready for a big conference call on Thursday, while being careful to not miss a swing. I am the nice mommy now, with one-on-one girl time. Mean Mommy got the "I hate your BlackBerry" speech at dinner earlier, to which I replied, "Sometimes I do, too."

—*April Conrad, 39, Corinth, Mississippi;*
operational marketing manager, Coca-Cola North America

Owner, Avon Beauty Center

SHIRLEY EKBLAD, 50, ELMHURST, ILLINOIS

She's been with Avon for twenty-two years, first as an independent sales rep, then working at an Avon Beauty Center kiosk in the mall, then buying the store six years ago. A challenge only fuels her fire. "I've been known to warn people—'Don't let me do anything that involves a goal because then I have to achieve it.'" Way back when, the job helped her move on with her life after she divorced and became a single parent. "I told myself I'd succeed financially if it kills me. If it wasn't for Avon, I never could have done it!"

12:15 a.m. I just finished putting in an Avon order via the Internet. Up to take a quick bath. But do I take the time to put on any of the nighttime creams I sell to so many woman? No. Tomorrow I will. Do as I say, not as I do. Tonight I'm exhausted! I actually fell asleep in the tub. I think of how blessed I am that no matter how tired or stressed out, at least I am able to take a bath. How many people with horrible living conditions are not able to do what I just got to do almost every night of my life. Boy, I'm lucky.

The night, as usual, would not be complete without a few tosses and turns. Checking the clock. Hmm, great. It's only 3:00 a.m.

6:30 a.m. My son's alarm goes off. Thank God for the wall-installed ironing board in my bedroom—at least I get a few words with him while he irons his shirt. He's getting a real life awakening; first year out of college and he has a job with a well-known accounting firm. I couldn't be prouder of what a fine man he has become. Wow, I'm so blessed.

Okay, let me think. I'm closing at the mall today. So, as much as I shouldn't, I'll stay in bed until about seven forty-five. It's amazing how rarely I need an alarm clock anymore. If I don't naturally wake up between seven and seven thirty, there is my son or my twenty-five-pound cat, Norman, who comes in like clockwork each morning to sleep on my legs. Of course, I don't want to interrupt our bonding time, so I always let him stay there. He needs me! Who cares if he and his brother are the reason I am on allergy medication and an inhaler. Shh, don't tell my doctor.

7:45 a.m. Okay, Norman, let's go. It's time for me to do these darn foot stretches. I'm in therapy for some foot thing I can barely say and certainly can't spell, but it causes great pain on the bottom and ball of your foot.

8:00 a.m. Turn the TV on. *Good Morning America* is going to have on shoes you can wear all day long. Yeah right, on these feet? Get the tea going, feed the cats, put dishes in the dishwasher . . . I'll have a quick frozen Jenny Craig breakfast entrée. Boy, it's beautiful out. I really should work out. Okay, go downstairs for my list to add to it, start a load of wash, clean litter box, check e-mails. I'll read the one from my honey, the other 223 can wait. What did I come down here for? Shoot, forgot my breakfast in the microwave.

9:00 a.m. Holy @#$%. It's already 9:00!!! But I just started the wash and Oprah's on. I know what I'll do. I'll put Avon brochures in all my neighboring town homes. That way I can consider it working out. And I'll put my honey's new business flyers in each brochure. You *always* have to do more than one thing at a time! *Multitask, multitask, multitask.* Gosh, I love when that happens.

10:05 a.m. Cell phone rings. It's Cynthia, the Tupperware lady from the mall. "Uh, Shirley, who's supposed to open the kiosk this morning?" What!!! Try to think real quick. Start making phone calls to the girls who work for me, to see if they can recall who is supposed to be there. I rush up to my closet. What can I put on? I get another call. It's Jill, the missing employee. She's on her way. Her son was sick at school and had to be picked up. Cynthia opened the booth for now. Gosh, the joy of owning your own business!

11:00 a.m. or so. Start putting the Avon books out. This is great. See neighbors. Tulip butts are showing! Gosh, I love being outside. It's fun to see how everyone decorates their front doors. My favorite is the one with the "Cats Welcome" sign.

Almost noon Crap, where is this day going? Need to shower. What to wear? I heard that a woman spends eight years of her life getting ready. I think I've already spent that. While my hair starts drying, choose clothes (slacks with a jacket that can be taken on and off), jewelry, purse (I change my purse with every outfit!), and shoes. I grab three pairs—two [of] flats and some one-inch heels. I can last in the heels for about a half hour if I decide to go out after work. (God forbid anyone see the flats I wear to work!) Curlers come out at the last minute. Pack lunch to eat in the car, food for later, that to-do list. I can fit in four deliveries. Ready to go.

1:15 p.m. In the car. Damn, it's on empty! Okay, gas, bank, deliveries. Thank God my customers know my system—bag by the door, envelope with my address on it, send me a check. I don't bother them, not that they would be home anyway. We both don't have time for chitchat. I remember one time doing ten deliveries in one hour! I still have to break that record one of these days.

Okay, now toward the mall. Have to eat. Guess I'll have to floss my teeth on the way home. (At long lights; what else is there to do?) Call my honey back. Missed his call earlier. (I'm old fashioned and really try not to be the one to call. Sometimes I go crazy waiting.) It's been seven months since we've been dating. Gee, talking to him sure is a highlight of my day, but don't tell him that. I don't want it going to his head.

2:30 p.m. on the dot, at the mall. Phew. I really appreciate Jill staying until I got here. It gave me a chance to get a massage, read a book, and get my nails done. Ha-ha. Okay, where do I start? I wasn't here yesterday. Payroll, invoice questions, inventory, shelves not as straight as I like them. What were our sales compared to last year? Check deposits. @###$!!! What do I do first? Why did I take off yesterday? Yes, a lot of this gets done by my employees, but it's not exactly like I do it.

I turn around for my first two customers. "Hi, can I help you?"

The one says, "I would like to exchange this nail polish for one that is pinker." Her friend wants to see an Avon book. Page by page.

She asks, "What's the difference between the feminine hygiene spray and towelettes?" Forty-five minutes later, the one lady orders the feminine product (I did not have one on hand). And for the other lady, we find a perfect pink lipstick to match her new nail polish.

She says, "I'm just having a ball!"

The other says, "I don't get out much. I just don't have the energy. Now how long will it take for my order to come in?"

I tell them, "Like most people brush their teeth every night before bed, I usually place an order. So it will be quick."

Can't wait to see these ladies back again. They'll probably think I can do lunch with them. Ha-ha.

3:15 p.m. I really should have combed my hair when I got here. And I've needed to go to the bathroom for the last half hour. My feet hurt already. A customer just asked, "Do you sell Avon here?"

"Uh, yes." (If only I could say what I was really thinking.) More customers. Put away products. Check on orders. Start one thing then another. Forget the first thing I was doing. Go to make a call. Find out messages were not checked. Do that. Man, I'm going to pee in my pants.

Thank God I cut a deal with the store right across from me—*If you let me use your bathroom, I'll give you any Avon product you want at a discount.*

That way I don't have to go so much farther. One look in the bathroom mirror. Never did comb my hair. Come back to the Avon counter and a customer is looking at me like, *Where have you been?* I apologize for being gone and make the sale. We really do need a Port-a-Potty behind this counter. I try not to drink too much water when I'm here because if I have to pee, I could lose a sale.

5:00 p.m. Where is the day going? I'm hungry. I try to eat discreetly between customers. Glad we have a microwave. Heated up a frozen Salisbury steak dinner ten minutes ago. Oops, my girlfriend's birthday. I have to hurry up and sing her "Happy birthday" on her answering machine. Customer comes up and says, "Do you know how I could find out about becoming an Avon lady?"

"Oh yes, I do!" As busy as I am, that is one question I always stop for. I give her some info and the phone number of one of the girls in my group who can meet with her. Yes! Yes! I love when this happens. What a great opportunity this company provides, if you are willing to be dedicated, ambitious, and work hard!

6:00 p.m. Okay, done with dinner, pick the teeth with a toothpick, apply lipstick, comb the hair, piece of gum. Several customers say, "I'm so glad you're here."

I say, "I'm doing it for ten more years and then that might be it (Lord willing)!"

7:00 p.m. Where is the night going? I only have half of what I wanted done. Change my shoes. A mall employee says, "Will it ever be nine o'clock?"

I say, "Are you kidding me? I wish it was three!"

Customer says, "Did this store just open?"

"No, we have been here for almost nine years."

Another customer says, "Do you all just take turns working it?"

"Um, no. I am the owner and responsible for making sure it's open seventy-three hours a week."

Another customer says, "I think I'll do this." (I'm like, yeah, it's a piece of cake.)

8:00 p.m. I need to run to the stockroom. Where's my list? Let the other kiosks know I'm going so they can alert customers that I'll be right back. On my way, I'll put out Avon books at the food locations that let me. Of course, their employees will get a discount.

8:30 p.m. Stop the clocks. I haven't even finished inventory. Haven't started closing procedures. The other kiosk employees are standing in the middle, laughing and talking with each other. I'll never forget when I contemplated taking over this place. I was afraid I might get bored. Well, if so, I'd just do stuff like update my Christmas card list or sort coupons. Yeah, right. None of that has ever happened.

9:30 p.m. Mall closed at nine. I'm one of the few people still around. Put the tarp up. Hear stuff knock down. Oh well, whoever opens will have to do the usual setting up. Sure wish I had a storefront, but less exposure and more rent.

On my way home I call my daughter, who is in her second year of college. Of course I get her voice mail. (Yet, God forbid I don't pick up when one of my darling children calls!) "Hi there, I hope you're having a good one and behaving. Call me sometime, even if you don't need money. Hey, pay your parking tickets. I love you, Mom." She is another best blessing in my life.

I check my home messages. John Travolta still hasn't called me. Ha-ha. Delilah's on the radio. Gosh, I love her show. Kind of wish the ride home was a little longer sometimes.

9:45 p.m. Aw, there's one of my babies waiting for me in the window. I open the door. Mommy's home! Down the stairs comes running the other one. I missed you guys, too. Yes, I know you had such a rough day and need your bellies rubbed. Yes, yes, okay, let me feed you. Mommy needs a glass of wine. Check the mail. Not a sweepstakes winner again.

10:15 p.m. Check e-mails. Any orders? Time to place another Avon order. I work for about an hour. Paint my nails. TV on. News. What's Jay got on?

11:45 p.m. Bathtub is running. After all is said and done, I am one lucky lady. My family, friends, health, home, business that provides me with such pride—it is never boring or the same from one day to the next. My feet might hurt, but my heart is happy!

Ding-Dong

3:06 p.m. People in my line of work tend to be positive. We read motivational books, listen to tapes, and attend seminars that focus on overcoming obstacles. Well, positivity just went out the window. The construction team outside my house is making lots of noise again, right while my baby is napping. I feel like opening the door and yelling, "You are really pissing me off now!" But of course I don't. Respectable Avon representatives do not behave like that.

—*Rosemarie Kahn, 42, Levittown, New York; independent sales rep/executive unit leader, Avon*

Mine Geologist

CARRIE HEILING, 29, SALEM, MISSOURI

As a kid, she loved the family outings to tourist-type caves and old mines. She felt the same way on field trips in college. "I thought it was fascinating, to have all this geology right there in front of you, these rock specimens you could hammer out and take home." In the mine where she works now, her job is to find new ore and to make sure the miners are working the best areas. "It's a pretty neat job. I get paid to look at rocks, ride around on a utility vehicle, and get dirty. You can't get much closer to the earth than when you're in an underground mine."

6:00 a.m. "Ten minutes until we have to leave," my husband, Keith, tells me. I brush my teeth and comb my hair. "Five minutes," he says. I grab lunch out of the fridge. Crap, I left my big travel coffee mug at work yesterday. "Three minutes." I silently scream, I am *not* a five-year-old!!! Then I try to just let it go. I know I'm grouchy first thing in the morning. No sense in letting it ruin my day.

6:15 a.m. Keith and I have been carpooling for several months now, ever since our offices were moved to mines that are only about fifteen minutes apart. We both work for the Doe Run Company, with its six mines spread out over about forty miles. I don't like carpooling. I know it makes sense, but it means that I lose that half hour of alone time to wake up, veg out, relax.

6:45 a.m. At work early. I take a few minutes to reply to an e-mail from my friend Christian, a Peruvian geologist. He wrote that he is going on vacation tomorrow to an exotic sounding city. Wow, how exciting. I could use a vacation, too.

Christian and I met working together in Peru last year. Even though I work primarily in the mines, I was offered a chance to do fieldwork on a project there with our department's exploration geologists, who work on the surface of the land to find additional mineral deposits near our existing mines and all over the world. From January through March, I made three trips to the Andes. Every day that I worked there (at an elevation of fourteen thousand feet), I found a scenic place to eat my lunch and thought, *It doesn't get any better than this*. I hope I have opportunity to go back, or work on another exploration project at some point.

It has been a few weeks since I've written to Christian. I'm horrible about keeping in touch. That was actually my New Year's resolution, to stay in better contact with my friends. I've been doing pretty good so far. I only make a resolution if I come up with something reasonable and meaningful. I get annoyed by all of the people who resolve to diet in the new year.

7:13 a.m. Last week I filled in for another geologist, making maps of all of the active headings in his mine and recording the current grade at each location. Kind of like quality control; I needed to make sure all of the areas were still high enough grade to make our cutoff. Now he's calling to make sure this information had been entered into the computer system. Yes. I hate leaving work unfinished. And I always try to do my absolute best. I was raised to believe that my work is a reflection of myself, like an autograph.

7:20 a.m. I received a call from the man who coordinates the underground diamond drilling program. (The geology department here has three underground diamond drills that are shared among the six mines.) He lets me know the drill that I was expecting has arrived and been assembled. Good. I already have an area marked up and ready to go. The mineral deposits we look for here are galena (lead ore), sphalerite (zinc ore), and chalcopyrite (copper ore).

I have only been in charge of prospecting for ore at this mine since November, when the last geologist left. Not much prospecting has been done here in the past ten years and it desperately needs it. I am excited to have the drillers start. We core drill from underground to find more ore near our current mine workings. I think I have some good ideas of where to look, but time will tell.

7:40 a.m. Site team meeting starts, mostly supervisors and foremen. We review the calendar of major repairs, scheduled downdays, and large maintenance projects. I have to laugh that they always make sure the items on the schedule do not interfere with "major holidays" around here: deer season, turkey season, trout fishing opener, and, oh yeah, Christmas! As usual, the meeting gets off track around 8:00 a.m. I wish they would wrap this up.

8:30 a.m. Back in my office, I enter in my face grades (results) from yesterday's work into our archaic computer system. Part of my job is to monitor and control the ore that we are mining. I have to look at all of the active faces (headings) in the mine and estimate their grade, meaning the percent of ore minerals present in each face. Then I decide whether or not each heading still has a high enough grade to continue mining.

8:45 a.m. I wander to my boss's office down the hall to review and sign a pillar plan. We use a room and pillar style of mining. That means that every thirty feet there is a "pillar," which is a thirty-two-foot by thirty-two-foot unmined column of rock that we purposely preserve to support the rest of the ground we're working beneath. All of the "rooms" around each pillar are mined out. When we have mined all of the ore out of a certain area, we go back and extract the pillars. But first the area has to be assessed by the engineers in our technical services department and the pillar extraction is modeled in a computer simulation to predict any possible problems.

The biggest concern with releasing pillars is that once they are extracted, we can never go back into that area of the mine. It isn't safe. So, I really need to look at all of the information available and make sure that no ore will be stranded.

9:00 a.m. My boss didn't have any problems with the pillar plan and signed it. It is really nice that he just lets me do my job without looking over my shoulder every step of the way.

9:25 a.m. I enter data from the past several days into a spreadsheet. Since our operations have six mines and only four mills, I need to keep track of the tons and grade that the mines say they are sending. These need to closely match the tons and grade of the rock going through the mill. If there is a large discrepancy, I need to figure out why. Between haulage reports and mill analyses, I get all of the numbers I need for my spreadsheet. Good, everything seems to be matching closely.

10:14 a.m. Gross. I just opened up my locker in the change room and realized that I forgot to bring a clean pair of diggers from home to wear underground. The legs and butt of my tan pants are dark gray from several days' worth of mud and grime. I can picture my clean bib overalls folded neatly at the foot of my bed at home. I can't believe I forgot them again. At least I have a clean shirt in my locker.

10:41 a.m. Gathering my gear to head underground. My very fashionable (ha-ha) knee-high, steel-toe rubber boots are leaving a trail of dirt as I walk around my office. I forgot to wash them off before I came back up to the surface yesterday, and am often wading in calf-deep water and mud. I strap on my mine belt that has a metal tag engraved with my name and employee ID number. The belt holds a compass, rock hammer, the battery pack for my mine light, a spare flashlight, a can of white spray paint for writing instructions directly on the faces and ribs (walls) of the mine, and a self-rescuer. This last is a required device to be used in case of mine fire. It converts poisonous carbon monoxide into nontoxic carbon dioxide.

My mine belt weighs about twenty pounds. It used to leave bruises on my hips but doesn't anymore. I guess I've gotten used to it. I've got my hard hat, prescription safety glasses (So ugly! Who designs these things?), reflective jacket to increase my visibility so

mine geologist

I don't get run over by the larger equipment, my clipboard full of maps and charts, and a backpack that carries my spotlight and extra supplies. I think I'm ready.

11:18 a.m. I ring for the cage, communicating to the hoist operator that I need a ride down. The cage is like a huge elevator, fourteen feet by fourteen feet, with a capacity of thirty-five people. As I descend down the shaft alone, I watch the sunlight slowly disappear. I like to ride with my light off. I can hear the water pumps before I can see light coming from the shop area of the mine. They pump approximately five thousand gallons of water per minute up from the mine. Without them, the mine would flood relatively quickly. It's a little over a two-minute ride to the mine level. I am one thousand feet below the surface of the earth.

11:38 a.m. I signed in at the underground mine foreman's office and talked to the foreman about the places he needs me to look at. Now I've just finished my preshift inspection of my Kubota utility vehicle. It's like a four-wheeler with a bed on the back, or a really beefy golf cart.

11:59 a.m. I am sitting in the Kubota near the edge of "no-man's-land," the name for any area where pillars have been removed and the roof is not supported. At this particular area the roof is sixty feet above the floor. No one is allowed back in here because it isn't safe. I need to get a look at the rock pile from the two pillars that were just shot last night to determine if the grade of the rock pile matches the grade I thought it was supposed to be.

I can hear the area "working," meaning it is not stable and is making noise as the rock settles from having the weight redistributed. Crack, creak, knock. Then I hear small rocks fall. My pulse is racing. More rumbling, crackling noises, then a large crash as a rock larger than a truck lets loose and falls somewhere out of my line of sight. It scares the crap out of me. Several of my co-workers have had their vehicle squashed by falling rock, and others I know have been badly injured. I'll come back tomorrow.

12:16 p.m. I pull off of the main haul road. The approaching headlights are from one of our fifty-ton haul trucks. At only thirty feet wide, the road really isn't wide enough for the both of us. Down here, the biggest vehicles have the right of way. After I pull back onto the road, I can see the dust and grit that the truck stirred up swirling in my headlights. I feel it hitting my face. My poor skin. The grit gets stuck in my eyelashes, too. If I'm not careful to scrub it all off, it runs just like mascara.

12:29 p.m. My Kubota is getting low in diesel. Time to stop at the fuel bay, which is next to the parking area for the majority of the vehicles and equipment. I use a rag to handle the fuel nozzle because it is usually wet and sticky with diesel residue. I hate carrying that smell around with me.

12:54 p.m. I'm in a wet area of the mine where it is basically raining all the time from water dripping off the back (ceiling). The underground diamond drill operators aren't here today, but I check on their drill anyway to get a feel for it. This drill is about eight feet tall and mounted on a trailer small enough to fit just about anywhere in the mine. It has a round, hollowed-out bit that drills out a hole and leaves behind a cylindrical-shaped rock called core. The actual core is a little over an inch in diameter and is usually broken into two-foot lengths to fit into our storage trays.

Everything looks good. The trailer with the drill is pulled up parallel to the rib (wall), with the drill aimed directly at the spot I had painted a few days ago. I have a specific direction and angle that I want them to drill—the targets most likely to intercept ore, based on my available geologic information.

1:10 p.m. As I drive around the mine (about six miles from north to south) I can't find any headings that need to be graded. It's amazing how diverse the various parts of the mine can be. In the areas that have equipment actively working in them, the air is dusty and smells like diesel exhaust or explosives. It's so loud that I can't hear myself think. I prefer working in the deserted areas. There you can hear even the smallest noise and are surrounded in complete darkness when you turn off your cap lamp. It really is peaceful, that is unless the back or pillars aren't stable and start "working." Then there isn't anywhere scarier.

I guess I'm all caught up. I find several ore rock piles that I marked "Pb" to signify that they are lead ore and not waste rock. I put the location of the ore rock piles onto my map.

1:20 p.m. Leave it to a geologist to spend her time collecting rocks! Whenever I'm underground, I always keep an eye out for mineral specimens. I don't see any today, but sometimes I find perfectly formed galena cubes, beautiful calcite crystals, or just a piece of ore from a rock pile that is absolutely full of galena and chalcopyrite. I have samples sitting on the windowsill in my office, and like to have some on hand to give away to tour groups and visitors. They love it!

1:37 p.m. I'm ready to go, but the cage is being loaded with full trash Dumpsters going to the surface. While I wait, I watch a haul truck dump in the grizzly (a big grate on the floor that covers a hole leading down to the crusher on the next level, eighty feet below). The rock needs to be crushed into smaller pieces before being hoisted to the surface. We're collecting very high-grade rock today. That should make the bosses happy. Since I have time, I take the water hose and spray off my boots.

1:47 p.m. I ride up in the cage with two other miners I've seen around the shop. They ask me about the places I visited today, and if I found any more lead. I really like being around the guys who talk to me like a normal person. There are only four other women who work underground here, even less or none at some of the other mines. So much of the time I get guys coming up to me, just so they can say something clever. I can't count how many times I've been told that I'm so much better-looking than the last guy they worked with down here. They have never been rude, but still it makes me feel like more of a circus attraction than a person.

2:05 p.m. My boss stops by to let me know that they are trying to hire another geologist to help out between here and one of the other mines. If all goes well, I'll be moving offices again (that would make six in three years). But this move will be to a bigger, nicer office with the map room attached. Cool.

2:14 p.m. I finally get around to eating lunch. Yum, leftovers of a tasty little Italian dish that I cooked up last night. I love to cook. Keith always tells me that his co-workers are jealous of the leftovers he brings for lunch. I check e-mail and am happy to see one from a friend I'd been thinking about. I start to write back, but just call instead. That made my day.

3:00 p.m. I go over to the tech services office to talk about an upcoming pillar plan. On my way out, I tease one of the engineers, making some joke about him needing all his fingers and toes to finish crunching numbers for his current project. He comes right back, teasing me about being a geologist. A "glorified tour guide," he calls me. Well, I am in charge of giving a lot of tours around here!

3:11 p.m. I make copies of the map that I made underground. These grade sheets will show the mine superintendent and captain, foremen, surveyors, drillers, and other geologists where we have ore available to mine. Today I only looked at ore rock piles, and hopefully they will get hauled in the next day or two. I also mark waste rock piles on the map so the foremen can make sure their crew keeps those separate from the ore.

3:24 p.m. Yes! I finally got a shower here without getting a single blast of scalding water from someone somewhere flushing a toilet. It must be my lucky day. I spray my diggers with Febreeze before I hang them back in my locker. It helps get rid of that diesel soot/mine smell. I better leave the diggers here overnight, just in case I forget to bring a clean pair tomorrow.

4:15 p.m. I'm here past quitting time (three thirty) and one of the few salaried people who hasn't gone home yet. Keith shows up and we talk about random things on the thirty-minute ride home. We live in a town of less than five thousand people. There

mine geologist

is not much to do there and little variety in shopping besides Wal-Mart. Tonight we will head into the next sizeable town forty minutes away to run errands and go to the gym.

We pass an accident of three pickup trucks. No one seems to be hurt. I'm very surprised I don't see more accidents on these narrow, curvy, Missouri "highways."

4:45 p.m. Home again. It is such a beautiful day, seventy-plus degrees. I love living in the country. I love this time of year, any warm time of the year, really. Having grown up in northern Minnesota, I do not miss those long, cold winters at all!

I notice some of my perennials starting to pop up in my flower garden. I wonder which ones are flowers and which ones are weeds. I do not have a green thumb, yet I still enjoy gardening. (I guess I should say, *trying* to garden. Numerous plants have died under my care.) My daffodils are still blooming. The air outside smells so sweet, like spring. That sweet smell of spring is one of my favorite scents.

Night Shift

12:55 a.m. Got a call from the supe that I need to get out and keep an eye on my drivers. It's getting to be that time of night when drivers like to hide out on the waste dumps for a nap. I'm off to check that all the kids are behaving. A mining engineering degree and two years' engineering experience to prepare me to be a babysitter. Work feels like home sometimes, but with cold food and twenty times as many children.
—*Julie Higbee, 25, Riverton, Utah; mining engineer/operations foreman, Kennecott Utah Copper Bingham Canyon Mine, and mother of four (with one on the way)*

Dragon Skin

8:20 p.m. I'm learning how to do stained glass, starting with something simple but lovely, beveled glass snowflakes that one could hang on a Christmas tree. Then I'll get adventurous and stretch my skills and imagination! I've been at it for about three months now. It's somewhat challenging, but I've got books galore, all the resources on the Web (which are legion), and determination. And I have a plan.

My son, Tristan, graduates college in three years, then he will be commissioned into the army as a second lieutenant. As I understand it, the Interceptor body armor that the army hands out isn't as good as something called Dragon Skin, which is a vest with "scales" that interconnect, and protects 44 percent more of the body.

As a graduation gift, I want to give him this, although it costs about five thousand dollars. He's my only child and someway, somehow I will manage this. So the plan here is to get to a point where I'm good at making stained-glass stuff, sell it on eBay or at local art shops, and put all of the profits into a savings account so I can buy the Dragon Skin. I would be happy if I could make five hundred dollars a year; then I should be able to take out a loan for the difference.

If Colonel McGee (the man who designed the Interceptor body armor) says Dragon Skin is better than the Interceptor, then that is what I want for my son. I've managed to raise a decent human being; intelligent, loving, actually uses his common sense, has a gift for writing, hardworking, at times charming, sometimes stubborn, occasionally too sarcastic to suit me, but always true to himself. It would be unbearably awful for the world if Tristan were to die because there was a better body armor out there that he wasn't wearing.

—*Susan McNeill-Hotsinpiller, 50, Whitehall, Ohio; executive assistant,*
Safe Auto Insurance Company

mine geologist

Stay-at-Home Mom

JEANNIE HINES, 35, PLAINFIELD, NEW HAMPSHIRE

After she had her first child (now age four), she went from full-time to half-time employment as a registered physical therapist. After having twins (now four months old), she still puts in eight hours a week—"Partly to keep up with my skills. Mostly to get out of the house." She purposely avoids figuring out how little sleep she's getting. She describes her life these days as, "Constant juggling. It's almost as if I'm living in a daze." The hardest part of caring for twins? "The four-year-old! She's used to having me all to herself. She can be rambunctious with the babies. And she can throw tantrums."

Midnight Baby crying. Walk across our bedroom to Laura's crib. Bring her back to our bed, prop up my pillows, and start breast-feeding.

12:50 a.m. I wake up, still sitting up in bed, sleeping baby on my lap. I ease her back into her crib.

1:25 a.m. She's crying again. Husband, Rick, is going to try a binky (pacifier). Can't find hers so he gets one from Kyle's crib. (These babies share my boobs, so we figure they can share bottles and binkies.) She won't take the bink, so Rick brings her over to me for more nursing. This little girl just cannot soothe herself to sleep.

2:45 a.m. Now they're both crying. Binkies for both (Rick had to run downstairs to get a second binky). Neither of them want their binkies. Rick takes Laura to the bathroom for a diaper change and I start nursing Kyle.

2:50 a.m. Nurse both babies using my cool EZ-2-Nurse breast-feeding pillow. It's flat on top so it supports both babies while they nurse in a "football hold." Very handy.

3:00 a.m. Both babies fed and burped. Kyle's asleep. Laura's still crying. She's Rick's mission now. He takes her for rocking, bouncing, walking. At least our four-year-old, Keira, hasn't come into our room yet. I'm hungry, thirsty, tired. Rick returns to bed and starts pressing against my back. He's horny. There's just no way I can muster up any energy right now for romance. Poor Rick.

4:00 a.m. Laura's crying again. I nurse her.

4:50 a.m. I feel Rick lifting Laura from my lap. I had fallen asleep nursing again. Kyle is crying and Rick brings him to me. I nurse Kyle.

5:00 a.m. Kyle's now asleep, I lay him in his crib. Laura's now crying. I bring her to our bed, lay her on my pillow. She's content. I'm thirsty. Ah, there's still some water in the water bottle beside my bed. Laura's now asleep like a little cherub on my pillow. I'm not moving her! Back to sleep.

6:45 a.m. Rick gives me a kiss good-bye and we both complain about how rough last night was. I need to get up now though. Lots to do to get all of us ready and out the door by eight thirty. But I just want to sleep. Rick resets the alarm for seven. Hopefully, he has started the coffee.

7:15 a.m. Sitting in bed, in a daze, both babies lying here kicking, cooing, and smiling. So cute! Keira came in, all proud of herself for sleeping in her own bed all night. She's on the floor now with our chocolate Lab, Maggie, pretending she's Maggie's puppy. Okay, get moving. Wet and mousse my hair so it stops sticking straight up. Try to convince Keira to put on clean underwear from her drawer, not her favorite Little Mermaid underwear from the dirty laundry basket. Unsuccessful. Oh well.

7:30 a.m. Babies crying now. Hungry. Bring everyone down-stairs. Quickly pour my coffee, turn cartoons on, pour cereal and orange juice for Keira. Omigod!!! I open the refrigerator and see a large bowl of pasta with shrimp and red peppers and aspara-gus! I thought I'd heard someone come into the house when we were all upstairs. Wow. Wonderful neighbors. Plop onto the couch and feed both babies.

8:00 a.m. I am dressed. TV is off. I've asked Keira three times to get ready and she's still just playing with her doll. Time to get the diaper bag ready and extra booster seat in the car. Offer to Keira that she can bring her doll to her friend Camille's house if she gets dressed *right now!*

8:15 a.m. Wow, Keira's actually dressed. Pack bagel and OJ for her in the car. Running out of time. Entice her to go brush her teeth, toothbrush is already set up for her, while I strap the twins into their car seats and plug them with their binkies!

8:30 a.m. We're in the car. Ah, breathe.

9:00 a.m. Drop Keira off at Patty's house for preschool art class. Patty will have her for two hours of art, then has offered to keep her for a playdate and lunch with her daughter, Camille. Oh, joy! Yes, please! Keep her! Keira, too, is so excited over this plan.

Now, to decide what to do. I have a long list of errands. I'm semi-free right now since I'm minus one child, but do I dare go shopping with the twins, who will need to be fed again soon, and probably will poop sometime in the next couple hours? Hmm. Let me look at my list. Kmart for some large items? No way. Maybe the Powerhouse Mall? Yes, I can do that I think, if they are open this time of day.

9:20 a.m. First stop: Egg McMuffin. How I hate unhealthy McDonald's, but *love* Egg McMuffins! Why can't there be a chain of healthy, fresh food drive-throughs? And I'm not talking sal-ads. Drive-through salads just don't do it for me. Who can drive and eat a salad, anyway?

9:30 a.m. That's lucky. Powerhouse Mall opens at nine thirty. Time to unload. The babies' car seats snap right into this awesome double stroller, one in front of the other so it's like driving a tractor trailer. Let's hope they stay asleep a little while longer. Wow! I just watched a woman hop out of her car and trot into a store. So carefree. And here I am, muscling and lugging.

11:11 a.m. We did it! We shopped. I got a sweet little white outfit with blue trim for Kyle's christening. (I already have a white eyelet dress for Laura.) Then it was diaper changes, and an outfit change for Laura, who shat all over the place. We visited the hair salon so I could introduce the twinkies to my hair stylist, Tanya. That's where I breastfed them one at a time. (Twice at once would be way too obscene for public.) It was very relaxing nursing in the hair salon. Nice comfy chairs, a glass of ice water, and friendly hair girls happy to hold babies!

Next, it was a successful trip to L.L.Bean for a pair of shoes for work. I still work as a physical therapist two afternoons a week for my sanity. Merrills. Love 'em. So comfy.

We're in the car and ready to head home.

11:20 a.m. Quick stop at McDonald's drive-through. Hate McDonald's. Love McFlurries.

11:24 a.m. Oh, I just remembered. I've got to stop at the craft store for Sunday nursery school supplies. I offered to cover the nursery during the service, since the same mom has been stuck with it for weeks. I want to make flyable butterflies. Need semi-stiff paper and small dowel rods. Here we go. Turn right instead of left. I don't get out much since the twins were born so I'm kind of going crazy with errands today!

11:55 a.m. Most of mission accomplished. The craft store doesn't sell dowel rods, but I found paper and all kinds of scrapbook stuff that I just had to buy. Plus some spring flowers to hang on our door. I just love being out and about with the twins (when they're not hungry and not crying and not poopy). People just love seeing them and go goo-goo ga-ga over them! Gotta get

stay-at-home mom

home. Gotta pee. Gotta feed babies. They're awake now. Driving home to the tunes of the Dixie Chicks. Love 'em!

Noon Oh no. They're fussing. Fifteen more minutes to get home.

12:15 p.m. Home. Leave everything in the car for now. Gotta get these twins inside and feed them. Kick off my muddy shoes (it's "mud season" in New England). Shove part of a corn muffin in my mouth on my way through the kitchen. Quick pee. Wash hands. Play a phone message. Unstrap the babes from their car seats. Get them latched on for Mommy's milk. Let's see, Kyle was on the left breast last feeding, so he'll be on the right. I do my best to switch sides every time since Kyle is the bigger eater. Maybe this keeps me from being lopsided!

Relax. Slow down. Breathe.

The phone message was from Maura, our friend up the street. Can she drop off dinner tonight and her two girls (ages four and five) at 5:00 p.m.? Her babysitter called in sick and she has to work tonight. I called Rick and left a message to see if he's okay with this plan. Me and the twins will be out tonight, socializing with some of my old work buddies from the VA Hospital. The babies just smiled at each other on the mega nursing pillow. So sweet.

12:40 p.m. They're done nursing but now are a bit cranky, needing to burp or fart or something. Will try burping and diapers. It also look like Kyle needs some boogers sucked out with the bulb syringe. Rick calls me the "Nose Nazi." I know they're glad, though, to have those pesky boogers outta there.

12:55 p.m. Laid the babies on their play mat. I'm feeling really tired now. Heavy eyelids, and an achy body that really needs some exercise. Keira will be home in about forty-five minutes. I think I'll try to eat something healthy and then rest.

1:10 p.m. Munching on a carrot while heating this morning's mystery pasta delivery! Let the dog out. Telephone: it's Maura.

I tell her, yes, bring the kids over tonight, even though I have not yet heard back from Rick. She tells me her five-year-old, Audrey, would like us to come over this afternoon. I tell her Keira's not here right now, but apparently, it's not Keira that Audrey wants to play with; it's the babies! I have to decline. I really want to try and rest. Maura conveys the message and I hear Audrey sobbing in the background. I promise to bring them over Thursday morning. She sniffles an "okay."

1:20 p.m. I'm standing at the counter eating this fabulous pasta. A white wine and pesto sauce (I think) over what appear to be homemade thick noodles, tossed with roasted red peppers, asparagus and huge, tender, perfect shrimp! It's gotta be from our gourmet cook neighbors, Bob and Ida.

1:25 p.m. Went back to the car. Got my purse, got the diaper bag, got the McDonald's trash, got the four shopping bags, got the mail, and got Maggie inside all in one trip. Wow. Time is running out for a rest. Oh my gosh! The babies are holding hands on their play mat! Sweeties they are. It must be pretty cool to have a twin.

1:30 p.m. Telephone. It's Rick. He'll take the kids tonight, no problem. I tell him about the awesome pasta and he says it is indeed from Bob, who sent an e-mail letting us know. Check e-mail. Good thing. The dinner with my co-workers tonight is postponed. Too many people can't make it. I call Rick to let him know, and fire off an e-mail thanking and praising Bob.

1:40 p.m. Lay Laura in her crib with binky. Minimal fussing! Put on some soft classical music. Nurse Kyle one more time. He falls asleep. Lay him in his crib.

1:55 p.m. Keira should be here any minute. Hopefully when she arrives, the barking dog won't wake everyone. That reminds me, I've got to fill Maggie's water dish. I saw her drinking from a mud puddle outside! Its tough work taking care of everyone and Maggie, too!

There's not enough of me to go around, though today's been pretty easy just having the twins and not Keira as well.

2:10 p.m. Keira's home. Thank Patty profusely! Drink for Keira. Tell her it's time for Quiet Time. Babies are already sleeping. She can lie in my bed with me as long as she's quiet.

2:15 p.m. Keira's playing quietly under the covers. Laura's eyes are open and she's experimenting with her voice. Move her to my bed for easier "binking."

2:30 p.m. Kyle's fussing now. Negative sniff check of the pants. Let's try a bink and his Winnie the Pooh mobile over his crib. I would just really like a short nap!

2:40 p.m. Crying escalates. No rest for the weary. Mix bottles. The twins get two afternoon bottles of formula a day. Since I work two afternoons a week, I've "trained" my breasts not to need to feed them from 2:00 to 6:00 p.m.

2:50 p.m. On my bed, Kyle in my lap, Laura lying up on a pillow. Feed bottles. Keira announces she has to go poop. I tell her she needs to try and wipe herself since I'm stuck feeding babies. I hear from the bathroom, "I'm done!" I try to verbally coach her from my bedroom on how to wipe. She reports it's been a hard poop, not a soft one. Can't be too messy, I hope. She says she's trying but she just can't reach.

Okay. I extract the babies' bottles, eliciting loud crying from both. I barricade them with pillows. I go and wipe Keira. She starts goofing off putting both of her legs in one pant leg. I don't have time for this. The babies are screaming. Keira cries, too, saying she needs help with her pants. I tell her, "No, you know how to put your pants on." Now all three kids are bawling. I wash my hands and try not to lose it.

"Wash your hands, Keira." She doesn't. She goes into my bedroom and lies beside the hysterically crying babies, covering her ears with her hands. I physically assist Keira back to the bathroom. I help her hands find the water and soap. She takes a large scoop of water and throws it at me. That's it. I tell her she is not welcome back in my room. The twins are still crying at an ever-increasing volume. I remove Keira's blanket and two stuffed animals from my room. I escort Keira out as well, and close and lock my door. Screaming. Crying. Fists pounding on my door.

Being a SAHM is so joyful. With clenched jaw, I try to soothe the babies and get them calm enough to take their bottles again, while Keira tries to bust my door down.

3:30 p.m. Bottles are empty. Laura is asleep. Kyle continues to fuss, burp, and fart. I can hear Keira playing with her Legos and her dollhouse. If I can get Kyle settled, then I can give Keira the attention she so desperately wants. (You'd think she'd like to help me feed babies, but, no, that got old fast for her.)

3:40 p.m. Game of Chutes and Ladders with Keira, and a Cheerios snack. Kyle in my lap.

3:55 p.m. Laura crying. Going to get her.

4:00 p.m. Babies on play mat. Keira and I play Uno.

4:10 p.m. Laura crying. Will hold her in my lap while Keira and I play third and final round of Uno.

4:30 p.m. I just finished reading *Cinderella* to Keira with both babies on my lap. I really need to pick up this house but it's so bad I don't know where to start. Telephone. Rick's leaving work and will stop at the grocery store. I put in a movie for Keira. She chooses to watch *The Nutcracker* ballet. Excellent choice, if I do say so myself!

4:45 p.m. Quick snack for me: three scrambled eggs with lots of salt. Breastfeeding women have to listen to their cravings, right?! *Shit!* I burned the eggs while moving the now-sleeping Kyle from the living room floor to the Pack 'n Play. Oh well, the eggs are

stay-at-home mom . . . .

still delicious. Keira's lying on the couch, mesmerized by the movie. Ah! I just realized it's almost five. Not too early for a glass of wine. Hopefully this SAHM gig won't turn me into an alcoholic. I'm not drinking alone; there are three others here, and a dog!

5:15 p.m. Maura and her girls just arrived. The four-year-olds immediately change into dress-up clothes, put on music, and start dancing all around. Five-year-old Audrey's sole mission is to take care of the babies. The extra hands, though overly enthusiastic, are welcome right now. Both babies are crying again.

I mix bottles while Maura hands over the girls' pajamas and a box of mac-and-cheese for dinner. And she's gone. And Rick's home. Audrey and I feed babies. Grace and Keira dance and pretend. Rick puts away groceries and starts prep for dinner. Audrey and I change diapers together. Rick mentions that I never got around to emptying the dishwasher! He's teasing, of course. He knows how overwhelming it is to be a SAHM.

6:00 p.m. Help all the girls in the bathroom and wash their hands. Rick just laid out mac and hotdogs and fruit for them. Now to heat Bob's dish for us.

6:10 p.m. Put Laura in the swing. Kyle crying. Nurse him away from the noisy crowd in the kitchen. I forgot to put ointment on his face so now his eczema looks awful.

6:15 p.m. Save Laura from overzealous Grace, who was vigorously shaking a teething toy right in her face. Let's eat. Two bites. Called to help Keira in the bathroom. Eat again. Chat with Rick. Girls playing on their own. Breathe.

6:30 p.m. Dessert time, one Thin Mint Girl Scout cookie for everyone and fresh fruit salad (thanks to Rick). Start to put away leftovers one-handed while carrying a crying Laura. Can't get too much done. Got to feed her.

7:00 p.m. Laura asleep. Ease her into crib. Bribe Maura's girls with leftover Valentine's candy to get ready to leave. Their adult brother is here to pick them up. Fifteen minutes of getting them out the door, and that's better than usual!

7:15 p.m. Kiss Keira good night. Rick's taking her up for her bath and tuck-in. Hook Maggie to her indoor leash so she doesn't get into all the food and dirty dishes still left out. Go upstairs to change Kyle and nurse him. Tuck him in.

8:15 p.m. Both babes are now in clean dipes, clean jammies, they're fed and asleep in their cribs. Please, please, please sleep well tonight.

8:20 p.m. Laura crying. Give her some Infant Motrin in case all this fussiness (and drooling and chewing on her fingers) is teething. Rock her back to sleep.

8:30 p.m. Rick and I finish cleaning up the kitchen. Quick telephone call from my parents. Very quick. No time for idle chatter these days. Laura crying again. It's Rick's turn. He reappears, holding Laura and says they're going to watch TV. I'm getting in the shower and hopefully going to bed.

9:00 p.m. I feel refreshed and relaxed and ready for sleep after that shower. Face moisturized. Zoloft taken. Coffee ready for automatic brewing at six forty-five tomorrow morning. I look in on Keira, then Kyle, and Laura. So sweet. So angelic. Nothing better than sleeping children! Please sleep long into the night!

10:50 p.m. Baby crying. Nurse Kyle. Drink water. Good night.

11:50 p.m. Laura crying. Nurse Laura. Back to her crib. Check on Keira. Wow, she hasn't kicked off all her covers yet. Back to my warm, cozy bed. Good night.

Helping Hands

2:00 p.m. On the way out of the main aquarium building, I am stopped by a mom with three small children who is trying to get them on the escalator. They all want to hold her hand, but she only has two to offer. She sees me behind her and asks if I can hold her daughter's hand. I do, and I ham it up, too, trying to seem like I'm good with kids. "Have you seen the sheep-headed fish yet?" I ask my traveling companion. She nods no. I tell her about its enormous head, and where to find it. And the end of the escalator I say, "One, two, three JUMP!" And she does. But when I get back to the building, I wash my hands. Good with kids, huh?

—*Hillary Bates, 27, Baltimore, Maryland; media relations manager,*
National Aquarium in Baltimore

●

Long-Distance Truck Driver

PATIENCE BOURNE, 64, CARROLLTON, MISSOURI

She became a trucker about three years ago, after spending most of her working life as "an office drone," then later creating (and losing) a small empire of rental properties. "I love to travel and drive so I decided to start a new venture." The cons? "Short days with too much down time, and long days when you collapse in your bunk." Oh, and the fact that truck driving has been rated one of the ten most dangerous jobs. The appeal? "A sense of freedom. It's not a job or a career; it's a lifestyle. Anybody can do truck driving. It's not limited by height or build or age."

4:53 a.m. Spent the night at a truck stop in Plainfield, Wisconsin. Turned out to be a nice one with lots of parking, but not many trucks. Truck stops can be hit-or-miss in quality, except for the chains, which are fairly uniform. This one has roads on two sides and fields on the other two. Just back from a walk to the convenience store to use the restroom. It rained during the night and the air feels soft and smells clean.

Almost all the trucks have their engines off. I do, too. Slept well. I'm used to the sound of truck engines running at night, and the refrigerated engines, too, so either way I am able to sleep regardless of the noise and vibration when my own engine is running. Since I have a late start today, I am going back to my sleeping bag. My truck's sleeper berth has a twin bed with fitted sheets, but I also use a sleeping bag for warmth; plus it's easier to remove for laundry purposes.

7:58 a.m. Make a second trip to the c-store for restroom, milk, and coffee. During the two and a half years I've been driving, I have noticed a marked improvement in the quality of the coffee! Some stops have three or four brews, including a heavily caffeinated version. After I eat breakfast (last of the cereal I packed), I check my truck for safety. I hit all the wheels with a hammer to make sure none were flat, check all the lug nuts to make sure none were loose, check the lights, including flashers and turn signals, and check everything under the hood.

I need to unload, so I drive about five miles to the muddy yard of a potato warehouse. I had picked up 45,000 pounds of potatoes in Montana on Friday afternoon, spent all day Saturday stopped at a truck stop in that area because of Department of Transportation requirements, and then drove 1,200 miles Sunday and yesterday.

One thing I don't like about my job is having to obey Department of Transportation hours-of-service rules, which sometimes necessitate sitting out when you have the energy to drive, or rushing to get in the extra miles before the clock stops. Truck driving is one of the most heavily regulated jobs, but to my mind the regulations do not encourage safety. The more rules, the more people break them.

8:35 a.m. There is a trailer being unloaded ahead of me, so I chat with its driver. Although I have lived in America for most of my adult life, I was born and raised in England (the daughter of a British army officer and a stay-at-home mom) and my accent is still fairly strong. This seems to intrigue many people. This other driver is older and tells me he had spent time in England after World War II, and how much he had enjoyed being there.

My turn to unload. The trailer I am pulling is a standard dry van, 13 feet, 6 inches high (watch those bridges!) and 53 feet long, making a total length of about 70 feet. When loaded, it is sealed with a small numbered plastic or metal strip through the door latches; easy to break but impossible to reuse. The loose potatoes were loaded by conveyor belt. Now they are being unloaded the same way, but with a scoop that picks them up from the floor of the trailer. The trailer will be a mess when it's done.

10:00 a.m. Back to the truck stop to have my trailer washed out. It was clear other trailers hauling potatoes had been here, too, from all the potatoes already on the ground! The pressure washer cleans the inside roof, walls, and floor of the trailer. The young guy who does the wash out is also interested in my accent. It's usually a good conversation starter.

10:45 a.m. On to Milwaukee for a load of beer; again a live loading, which means I'll have to wait while the product is put on the trailer. As an over-the-road trucker, I have two kinds of days. Like yesterday, when I just drive all day, with stops for restrooms, food, and a nap. Or days like today, loading and unloading, changing trailers, scaling. It's all just part of the job.

1:15 p.m. I check in with the shipper, only to find out that the load for today is, in fact, for Thursday. I call my dispatcher to sort it out. Sometimes I get very frustrated with the nondriving aspects of the job, and mentally write letters of complaint to dispatch, company bigwigs, the DOT, radio stations . . . But then I get over it, and remember again why I am on the road. I love to drive. And, on the whole, I am loving this life. One of the other tough parts, though, is leaving my cats after I have been home, whether for a day or a week. I have two cats that are officially mine, and two or three others that I have trapped and had neutered, and that have discovered the food supply.

2:00 p.m. My own food supply is low and the choice is pitiful; brown bread, my last slice of cheese, the remnants of a package of salmon, and a tangelo. Mainly I bring my own food, though at the truck stops with delis, I'll buy hard-boiled eggs and salads. Just as the coffee has improved, so have some of the deli selections! I eat out at restaurants about once every three or four days, usually breakfast.

3:10 p.m. It was my error. My dispatcher had sent me the load information on the satellite but, when I copied the info into my

long-distance truck driver ....

notebook, my handwriting was not clear, so I had given the shipper the wrong pickup number. I apologize and the shipper sends me to the right dock.

Before loading, I successfully pull the pins holding the tandems (back wheels) and move the wheels further to the rear of the trailer. This makes for a more stable transition between the dock and trailer during loading. It also raises the rear of the trailer, which is sometimes necessary if the dock is high. While the truck is being loaded, I take a nap.

6:45 p.m. After being loaded, it takes a number of tries to pull the pins out again and move my tandems to where I hoped they should be. It can be really frustrating, needing to move the rear wheels of the trailer backward or forward depending on the weight of the load, particularly on old, rusty trailers that don't slide easily. Sometimes rocking the tractor back and forth loosens the pins. Other times, you need to attack them with a hammer. There have been days when I have been reduced to tears as I climb into the cab, rock, climb out, and try to release the pins again and again and again.

I beat the rush-hour traffic out of Milwaukee by about five minutes, and drive fifty miles to Beloit, where I scale my truck. The total gross weight of a tractor-trailer combination cannot exceed 80,000 pounds. The weight on the steers (front tractor wheels) cannot exceed 12,000 pounds, and neither the drives (rear tractor wheels) nor the tandems can exceed 34,000 pounds. This time I am overweight on the rear wheels, so have to pull the pins again, and move the wheels further back. Thankfully, I luck out on the second weigh.

I buy myself a Taco Bell burrito for supper.

9:20 p.m. I am parked at a rest area on I-80, just north of Davenport, Iowa, where I will spend the night. Rest areas come in two varieties—easy pull-in-type spots, or those where you have to parallel park. This one is the former, and I parked at the end of the row. Other than the sound of engines, it is quiet. In general, rest areas are much calmer than truck stops because there is nothing to do there; whereas at truck stops you can go to the c-store, shower, watch TV, play video games, do laundry . . .

Today I drove only a total of 369 miles, which is not too bad given the other factors of the day. (On Sunday I drove 667 miles, and yesterday it was 559 miles.) Tomorrow I will have this haul unloaded in Cedar Rapids, Iowa, and get reloaded at a different location in that city, and then head to Hannibal, Missouri, where I need to be before midnight (only about 260 miles).

I like it when I know my next day's work and can schedule my time. Within the perimeters of pickup and delivery times, I can stop when I want or take the route of my choice. This is an incredible country and the varied scenery can be quite spectacular. Even the flat plains have their appeal.

10:00 p.m. Leave a "happy birthday" message on my eldest daughter's phone. Also talk briefly with my trucker buddy. We work for the same company, but our different routes mean that we have met only six or seven times in one and a half years. He has helped me with logbook and weight/tandem questions, and has given me insights on the best way to get to certain stops, or how to dock if he knows it's a tricky situation. Sometimes we just chat to relieve the aloneness, and yes, the loneliness, of the road.

Some days, I meet a lot of friendly people at truck stops and rest areas and delivery points. Other days, I barely interact with anyone. Since I am a soloist as a rule, this works for me. Still, thank goodness for cell phones.

Heavy Lifting

2:14 p.m. Our next stop takes us across a little bridge to the customer's house. He's at his barn and motions me to drive the van over there. He seems surprised to see not one, but two women in UPS uniforms. His packages are pretty heavy, about sixty pounds each. He says it's something for his tractor. We make sure to use proper lifting techniques, and each put a package on the four-wheeler at the customer's request. Some men have underestimated the weight I can carry. Gentlemen will reach to take packages from me and I'll say, "It's heavy," then their arms drop and knees bend. This has trained me to release the weight of heavy packages to customers a bit slower.

—*Veronica Reisinger, 28, Flowery Branch, Georgia; UPS driver*

•

All in a Day's Work

7:00 a.m. Go in to the bedroom to get dressed, realize I didn't do laundry and will actually have to wear a skirt to work . . . I change my outfit twice before finally settling on a black skirt and off-white shirt. I also wear bike shorts under my skirt because, nine times out of ten, I'm going to end up under a desk fixing a computer or something like that.

—*Ginger R. Gosselin, 37, Kenosha, Wisconsin; office manager and*
"uneducated intelligent person" (according to her boss)

7:30 a.m. I decide to index the editor's introduction and the first chapter today. As I progress my expectations as to topic are confirmed. I can see I'll need to divide "morality" into "morality, principles of" and "morality, progress of," and cross-reference them. I work through the text, chunking off the main lines of argument as discrete sections, creating entries for each, picking up important elements. Hmm. The author's got a whole section on how we can tell which animals are the same species, and there's a wonderful bit here about zebras being clearly a type of horse. He writes, "To say a zebra is not a horse! You might as well say to me that a whale is a mammal and not a fish!" Someone will want to find that bit again. I write entries for speciation, zebras, horses, and whales.

—*Kate Mertes, 51, Alexandria, Virginia; editor/indexer*

10:25 a.m. Helped troubleshoot the zigzag machine. At least once a day when I'm at the sewing machines, I daydream about the what-ifs and life and home. What if we hadn't lost the pregnancy? Would I be sitting here now, sewing? Or would I be out shopping for nursery things? What if my husband, Scott, hadn't been laid off? The what-ifs only last as long as the bobbin thread . . . not long.

—*TaMara Gayle, 35, Burbank, California; creature fabricator/puppeteer, Stan Winston Studios*

10:45 a.m. Janice just got to work. She had a dentist appointment this morning so she stopped at Sprinkles and brought us cupcakes. (Yum!) She sent out an e-mail and everyone gathered at the "eating cubicle" and got half a cupcake (a whole one would be too much). They are wonderful. We have a saying here, "When you come to work, watch out for the Novation fifteen." That is how many pounds you put on from people bringing sweets to share.

—*Sherry Maffia, 56, Carollton, Texas; adminstrative coordinator, Novation Healthcare Contracting Services*

12:30 p.m. I did a quick walk-through of the company. It is fairly big—150,000 square feet, or thereabouts. My staff is keeping it clean and organized, and I like doing the walk-through. Even so, I always see things that could be better. Maybe they just think I come down on them? I need to get back to saying two or three really positive things each day to the best staff members. I am thinking about the old trick of having three pennies in one pocket and transferring one penny to another pocket each time you say something positive. It doesn't work for me. Most of my suits don't have pockets.

—*Hannah Kain, 50, Fremont, California; owner, president, and chief executive officer, ALOM Technologies*

Paint Tester . . . for Now

EMILY GAARE, 23, CLEVELAND HEIGHTS, OHIO

She got the job through a temp agency—testing the quality of car paint systems on panels and parts. It's only for one year, then she starts medical school. She's tired of coasting, eager to move on. "My whole life is currently in flux. I'm married but my husband and I haven't yet settled down. I'm working, but my job is in no way relevant to my goals." What's something she'll remember from this stage in her work life? "Having the world's worst health insurance through the temp agency. Hoping, hoping, hoping I won't have to go to the ER because I won't be able to pay for it."

6:05 a.m. In the shower, I realize that I have a job interview tomorrow evening, to be a bartender in a wine bar. I will have to shave my legs today to avoid having razor burn at the interview tomorrow, but there's no time! I compromise and shave half of each leg. I need a third job because my first two are poorly paid.

6:22 a.m. E-mail check, still dripping from the shower. I don't have Internet access at work, but my second job (as a test prep teacher) communicates with me largely via time-sensitive e-mails. Students send me essays from their practice exams so that I can give them a score and feedback. Nothing today, which is a relief. I love helping them, but this morning I'm already late.

6:32 a.m. I fish through the laundry bags (with clean laundry in them!) until I find a shirt, underwear, socks, and an undershirt. I put on yesterday's jeans and bra. Who has money for tons of jeans and bras? And who's got time to wash them more than once a week? The sniff test does well enough for me today.

6:36 a.m. Check the weather online while brushing my hair and dispensing my coffee from our coffee machine. I am a super multi-tasker! Flex my toes and flinch. The steel-toed boots I wear all day seem to be slowly destroying my feet. Only five more months until I start medical school . . .

6:45 a.m. I'm out the door of my apartment building and on the way to the bus stop. My bus friend, Russ, shows up and we chitchat. He works in a library in one of the universities downtown. When I get on the bus, I remember that my monthly transit pass has stopped working. Again. I stick it in the machine, let the machine misread the card, and get waved on by the driver.

6:56 a.m. Off the bus and on the train. My transit card misreads again, and I am again waved on by the ticket person. There are signs all over saying that the transit authority WILL NOT HONOR misreading cards, but the ticket checkers all know how crappy the cards actually are. If you show them a valid monthly, they will always let you on.

While I wait for my train friend, Janet, I read the news ticker. The incomplete headlines never make much sense—*Police Dogs . . . One of the Chicago Police Force's most useful crime-fighting units since before the days when Al Capone corrupted much of the Force has become the source of embarrassment . . .* I spend a few moments trying to understand what has happened, then give up.

6:59 a.m. Janet arrives. We talk all the way to her stop downtown, mostly about her job with the federal government. Today she gives me a lesson on the eighteen levels of supervision at her work, and how people whose backs need scratching are typically promoted into bogus positions, usually with a couple of underlings to corrupt. The two people behind me are train friends as well and I get a brilliant idea. What if everyone got together in a big public transit friends party? It would be sort of like Woodstock on Valium.

7:48 a.m. I walk through the gates to the plant—a series of squat, brown buildings linked by an umbilical cord of exhaust tubing on each roof. To get to my building, I dodge trucks and tow motors in the shipping area. Someone I don't know says hi to me, but I say hi back anyway. This happens a lot at the plant. I am one of maybe twenty women here under the age of thirty, and probably the only one who does not work in an office. And I'm kind of cute.

Our lab is a single room, sealed off from the rest of the second floor by a door that keeps the temperature in the lab standardized. Besides me, there are three employees: Bob (the boss), Ed (a temporary, like me), and Javier (a real employee). My desk is right behind Bob's. None of us has even the semi-privacy of a cubicle. We all sit facing the walls except when we talk to one another. Then we all face the center. Watching us switch from working to talking is like watching synchronized swimming.

7:53 a.m. I'm chatting with Javier when my other co-worker, Ed, arrives. I spend three minutes putting up my hair, delaying my work until my boss arrives. If I do not stretch out my work, I run out of work and then I am expected to sit at my desk and stare into space, or perhaps doodle incessantly. My strategy for avoiding severe boredom is to do my work very slooowly.

8:00 a.m. Some of the tests we run are "cycles," which basically check how a paint system handles changes between heat, cold, and humidity. Ed and I move our panels from the humidity chamber to the freezer. Our boss still isn't here. Ed, Javier, and I all agree that we won't bring up the subject of cleaning out the boxes of old panels and parts that clutter the storage area just outside our lab. Bob wants to get this done right away, but we're all hoping he won't remember and we can put it off for another day. Standing around while Bob agonizes over which box to keep is like watching a train wreck in slow motion.

8:10 a.m. The panels on my desk are about four inches by twelve inches, so shoddily painted in a spectrum of reds and blues that they make me question the quality of the entire automotive industry. Huge globs of dirt and smears of other paint colors make them worthless to us. And these are the panels that my company wants to show to automakers to get their business!?

8:17 a.m. My boss, Bob, finally arrives, taking a seat at his desk directly behind me. He immediately begins talking to us about his son, who has recently been accepted into college. We all stop pretending to work and give him our undivided attention. Bob has tried to get my advice on how to get into college for months now, partly because I also work for a test preparation company. His opinion: the ACT college entrance exam is obviously an invalid test because his son didn't score well either time he took it. I have long since stopped sharing my real opinions about this subject; for example, that Bob's son was lucky to be accepted anywhere because his test scores and grades were awful.

8:32 a.m. I pull a water-resistance panel from the water bath and check it for blisters or any color changes. Nothing has happened to this panel so it passes the test. I mark "no change" in my book. Bob leaves to get water from the only water fountain in the building, which is downstairs in the shipping department. I immediately stop what I am doing. It's all part of my Work-Saving Plan.

8:51 a.m. Ed and I talk, stopping just before Bob gets back. Luckily, we can hear him coming, so we can time this perfectly. This is our usual routine. If Bob ever figured out that there really isn't enough work, one of us would be out of a job. The trouble with being a temp is that it's very easy to be fired.

8:57 a.m. Bob comes back and says, "We gotta get rid of some of that shit out there," pointing at the storage area outside the lab. "Okie-dokie? Hunky-dory? Appleroonie?" Appleroonie is a word Bob invented one day, a word I mistakenly laughed at. Now it is a word I cannot escape. He thinks I want to hear him say it three times every single day. Mostly I manage a feeble smile and look away so that he can't see the suicide wish in my eyes.

Today Bob goes on to talk about something else he likes,

James Bond. He shares with us his Bond preferences: Pierce Brosnan and Roger Moore. Ed replies, "Those old ones are kind of corny, though." Bob then repeats what Ed has said, which is his way of claiming to have said it in the first place.

"Kind of corny, huh? Corny. To a certain extent. To a certain extent."

9:00 a.m. The Rolling Stones are declared the fourth greatest band of all time by our radio station. Bob starts clicking his pen in and out, in and out, just slightly out of time with the Stones song on the radio. "You guys ready to do some dumping?" he says, referring to the boxes in the storage area. Fortunately, Javier has some tests in process so we are able to postpone the cleaning until later. I go back to texting my friends. With my back hunched over my lab book, Bob can't see my phone, but even if he saw me playing with it, he has yet to figure out exactly what a text message is.

9:09 a.m. I've stuck a fresh batch of panels in the water bath to soak for a few hours. Now I have nothing to do. "When the cleaning person comes," Bob says, "tell him he can't leave his cleaner outside the door. It doesn't belong there." Javier says that the cleaning guy (who is new to the job) probably just forgot the vacuum accidentally. Bob replies, "It's 'cause they don't want to haul it up and down the elevator."

I think Bob has something against the cleaning crew because they are mostly Hispanic. He makes plenty of racist, sexist, and homophobic jokes, but the last time I asked him to stop he just switched to talking about "doze people," refusing to tell me which "people" he meant because I would be "insulted." If I reported him, I'd be pulled from this assignment by my temp company and it would take weeks to find another job. I can't afford to care.

9:30 a.m. The janitor arrives to clean. We stand just outside the lab on our "vacuum break," our excuse "to get out of the way."

paint tester . . . for now

10:15 a.m. Snack break. We are as regular as kindergartners with our snacks—one piece of fruit each for Ed and me. But today I've brought an apple and some raisins, both of which are very good snack break foods because they can be savored for an extended period of time. Raisins are especially good because they can be eaten singly.

10:21 a.m. Bob is on the phone with one of his friends at the company, clicking his pen. In and out. Out and in.

10:24 a.m. We hear a fire alarm, which is a fake fire alarm, according to the announcement from security over the PA system. We stay in the lab and work.

10:30 a.m. The fire alarm finally stops.

10:32 a.m. Bob decides to vent his frustrations about people in the panel-spraying section of the plant, "Doze people don't do dick anymore." He begins to ramble, informing us that we should not give our money to the government any sooner than is absolutely necessary. I head to the band saw located outside the lab door to cut panels into testable pieces, and to avoid getting sucked into a conversation.

11:00 a.m. Bob goes to get more water. No boss. Heaven.

11:20 a.m. I've entered zombie mode, counting down the minutes until lunch. I take a bathroom and water break, then return to the lab. One breath and I know—The Smell is back. The Smell is something we get from an exhaust pipe that goes right by our lab. It's caused by sewage or rotting leaves or something else unpleasant. I've stopped caring what causes it because it has become obvious that it's not going to get fixed anyway, after three reports to maintenance and multiple complaints to security that the fumes could be toxic. The Smell is bad enough today to make me nauseous. I even stop looking forward to lunch.

Noon Bob comes back into the lab, takes a whiff of stinky air and says, "Mmm, smell the fresh air!"

I joke, "Was that 'air' or 'ass'"?

12:07 p.m. Now Bob is tapping his box-cutter knife on his desk. He is, as always, off-beat.

12:10 p.m. Bob goes to lunch, so I go back to texting my friends, most of whom live far way. Since getting out of college I have fallen out of touch with a lot of people.

12:28 p.m. Ed and I decide it is twelve thirty enough, so we go to lunch. We like to go to lunch at twelve thirty because, when we get back at one thirty, we have only three more hours of work to go. The afternoon can slip away when there are only three more hours.

1:15 p.m. We sit in a booth in the plant cafeteria, studiously ignoring Fox News in the background. Ed is working a sudoku and gets stuck. I get him unstuck and go back to my book. We avoid talking because we like each other better when we don't actually talk. Usually, we scavenge newspaper sections from around the cafeteria, but today we only have the Friday section from four days ago. I'm glad I brought a book.

1:32 p.m. We can no longer ignore the fact that it's after one thirty. We stagger back to the lab.

2:07 p.m. Lo and behold, I actually learned something new! Bob explained why the accelerated weathering machines destroy panels so frequently. Evidently UV light breaks the integrity of a paint system. This bit of knowledge was good for fifteen wasted minutes.

2:30 p.m. I am ready to destroy my co-worker Ed. He has just said that the name "Planned Parenthood" does not make sense because the focus of the organization is birth control. I am reminded that this is why I don't talk to him at lunch.

paint tester . . . for now

3:15 p.m. I am texting again. Bob is clicking his pen, as if his mind is on solving world hunger instead of the weighty problem of unit conversion (between kilojoules and megajoules) so that he can put a set of panels into the weathering machines for the correct length of time. Solving this problem takes him thirty minutes.

3:50 p.m. More texting. I'm at the end of a gasoline resistance test (where you sit panels in a gasoline bath for an hour). One of my panels has completely failed. All the paint fell off! I love it when my panels fail because it is the one exciting thing that happens at work. I always feel like I have actually done something when I cause a real change in the paint.

4:00 p.m. I am getting desperate for things to do. Oh, look. My glasses weigh 13.5 grams on our scale. I go on a mission to discover rough equivalents in weight from common lab objects. It turns out that two and a half paper towels, one small panel piece, and one medium-size breath blown directly onto the scale all have the same weight as my glasses.

4:06 p.m. Bob has left the lab for his regularly scheduled pre-commute pee break. Ed asks me a question about how Nissan tests heat resistance. I say, "Cannot respond to that inquiry!" This is a joke between us, mimicking one of Bob's favorite responses to any question he doesn't want to answer.

4:12 p.m. I've recorded all my results for the day in my lab book. Another total waste of eight and a half hours. Did the automotive industry gain anything from my day? Not really. But then again, I'm barely paid anything for my time anyway, so it's almost fair. I take a quick bathroom break to waste time.

4:16 p.m. I ceremoniously cross off the day on my desk calendar, taking my time making the X. I've almost made it to April. In August, I will leave this job and never look back. Bob starts clicking the damned pen *again*. Click Click *Click*! Fourteen more minutes until I go home.

4:30 p.m. I leave work as quickly as I possibly can, speed-walking to the gate. I hold up my bag with the ID somewhere inside, letting the magnetic scanner read it. I am free! Hooray!

4:38 p.m. At the train station, my transit card misreads again. I will have a new card next month, hopefully one that works. I walk up to the platform and sit outside. I breathe. I hear the absence of clicking pens. When the train arrives, I am in a happy daze.

On March 27, 2007 . . .

46 percent of day diarists did personal activities
on company time.

●

paint tester . . . for now

Principal Clarinet, Nashville Symphony Orchestra

LEE CARROLL LEVINE, 50, NASHVILLE, TENNESSEE

She started playing when she was twelve, on her sister's hand-me-down clarinet (she was the fifth of six kids; her parents didn't want to buy yet another instrument). In junior high, she joined the band to get out of gym class, but found that she loved making music in a group. "When I was fourteen, I knew I was going to be a performer." She's been with the Nashville Symphony for over twenty years. Why the clarinet? "I like the sensation of blowing through that big wooden tube, the vibration under my fingers, the sound in my ears. It's a very a physical experience."

6:15 a.m. The first thought of the day is not a happy one. I have to drive The Son (age fourteen) to school today, and that will cost me a precious hour of preparation for today's Classical Series rehearsal. But I cannot trust him in the car with The Daughter (age sixteen) until they understand that it's dangerous to get into a screaming fight while she's driving in morning rush-hour traffic. About whose music they'll listen to, for heaven's sake.

6:16 a.m. Wake up the kids. They ignore their alarms just like they ignore me.

6:25 a.m. Extra points for The Husband for buying Mexican fair trade at the local coffeehouse. Now I can caffeinate with a clear conscience. While the coffee brews, I take a look at the music I have to play in three hours. There's a guest conductor this week, unfamiliar repertoire, quadruple woodwinds, and lots of extra (noncontract) musicians on the stage. My job is to play the clarinet solos beautifully; make sure my section uses the same articulation, note length, and style; and work closely with the other woodwind principals to establish and maintain good intonation. In other words, today I need to be the leader I'm paid to be.

I've heard it said that women dress for women. The same could be said about us—musicians play for musicians. There isn't a newspaper critic anywhere who is more biting than a classical musician sitting on stage. Our heads are filled with a running commentary, most of it negative, about what we hear coming out of our own instruments, and others'. We play for the conductor, for each other, and maybe for an audience.

6:30 a.m. The dog joins me on the sofa, warm against my bare feet. My blood pressure drops instantly while I study the music score and scratch her ears. This is the 1910 version of the ballet *The Firebird*, not the 1919 version we usually perform, nor the 1945 version. I've never played the 1910 version, which was the twenty-eight-year-old Stravinsky's first major work. I should download a recording of it from iTunes. I need a shortcut to learn how it goes. Why did I spend so much of my preparation time last week on the other programmed pieces?

6:45 a.m. Round up the kids, throw 'em some Frosted Flakes. Is this the best I can do? What healthy snacks can I send with them to school? Rummage for carrot sticks, yogurt, nuts, and cheese, all of which The Son spurns.

6:50 a.m. Glance out the window at the hedge I trimmed yesterday. The clippings are still on the patio because I couldn't get the leaf-blower started. Is there time to get that repaired today? Sigh.

7:00 a.m. Leave for school. Boulez's recording of *Firebird* (1910) will be waiting on my computer when I return.

7:05 a.m. The Daughter's car is ahead of us, and I use this opportunity to observe her new driving skills. Wait, why is she taking the interstate to school? We're not *that* late. This is frightening. People drive like maniacs on the interstate during morning rush hour, cutting in and out of lanes, tailgating, putting on makeup, driving like me. Don't they realize she's a new driver? God help her.

7:23 a.m. The Son gets out of the car at school. Why does he have his new Sony Digital VideoCam with him? He tells me he and his buddies want to shoot some "sick footy" (skateboard videos) after school. Will the five-hundred-dollar camera even make it to the skate park? How long before it's stolen or lost? I must be out of my mind for giving him such an expensive toy.

7:45 a.m. I need a plan for dinner. The quick-stop grocery store? Or the one with the all-natural beef? Wow, check out that bicyclist! I wish I was doing that right about now. This spring weather is perfect for a workout, but a power walk is not looking likely. Another shortcut: sucking in my stomach with conviction will be my abs workout today.

8:45 a.m. Supper is in the Crock-Pot. I've made three meals—breakfast, lunch, and dinner—and it's not even 9:00 a.m. yet. I've been listening to the Boulez recording of *Firebird*, so now I'm a little more confident about rehearsal, but I'm feeling a little dizzy because I haven't eaten yet today. I fix my favorite breakfast to go—cottage cheese with fresh blueberries.

9:00 a.m. Kiss The Husband good-bye. I'm unhappy with how long it's taking me to get out the door. The clarinet is packed in a hurry. Every reed that was under consideration is tucked into a side pocket. I'll soak those in warm water once I get to the hall. The music folder is shoved into the sleeve of my instrument bag. I nearly forget to pack the things I need for the orchestra meeting between rehearsals: our collective bargaining agreement; the comparative wage chart from the International Conference of Symphony and Opera Musicians; and my brown-bag lunch. We're discussing negotiations for our next contract.

My anxiety level is growing. What makes me more nervous, the negative attitude of my colleagues in the section or my own level of preparedness? My biggest critics sit directly to my right, and their opinions are delivered through body language. As clarinetists, they know the instrument's pitfalls. When I execute a passage skillfully, there is a shuffling of the feet—universal orchestra code for "Great job!" But, if I should happen to goof (a misplaced accent, or—God forbid—the errant squeak), I could get anything from a flinch to an audible snort. You need nerves of steel for this job. Studies have shown that orchestra musicians experience the same level of stress as air traffic controllers.

9:27 a.m. I don't want to alarm other commuters, so I apply my makeup while driving on side streets when the coast is clear. I slap on some cover-up, blush, and lipstick, just to hide the wear-and-tear of being a working mother. I wish I had left ten minutes earlier, but if there are no delays I'll be at the hall on time. Breathe deeply, slow down my heart rate. I've had excellent training; things will be fine. It's not brain surgery, for crying out loud.

9:40 a.m. The last few blocks in the car, I clean out my purse. The mess in there has really been bugging me lately (receipts, shopping lists, gum wrappers that I'll throw away on my way into the hall). I pop a piece of sugarless peppermint gum into my mouth—nothing worse than playing the clarinet with halitosis.

9:47 a.m. According to the contract, I must be in the building ten minutes before the tuning note, and seated five minutes before the tuning note. I make it with three minutes to spare. When I walk into this brand new concert hall—the Schermerhorn Symphony Center—I am filled with a sense of awe. The architecture resembles something from Berlin or Vienna—very "old world" and appropriate for classical music. But the interior design makes use of ultramodern technology to achieve near-perfect acoustics.

Through the stage door, I pass the 24-hour security guard and proceed to the backstage area, entering the "sound lock." Our concert hall is actually a building within a building, separated by a foot of insulated air space. The sound engineers are in their state-of-the-art booth, preparing to record this weekend's performances. Orchestra musicians are unloading their cases in the very comfortable lounge, and hurrying to their lockers for last-minute necessities such as pencils or rosin.

I enter the stage and go directly to my seat, which is elevated in the center-back of the orchestra, behind the strings and in front of the brass. From here, I look out into one of the most beautiful single-purpose concert halls in the world, with its rare use of natural light through the high windows. I feel like I'm finally at home. I put my instrument together, join in the cacophonous warm-up, and wait for the orchestra manager to introduce the guest conductor, who happens to look like Elliott Gould.

11:20 a.m. The first rehearsal break comes within ninety minutes, and I'm relieved at how well everything is going. The notes are flying across the page, and the guest conductor is navigating through them fearlessly. His choice of tempo indicates that he is comfortable with the rapid music, even if we are not. He's not the greatest I've ever seen, but he has a thorough knowledge of the score, he corrects faulty balance among instrumental groups, and his baton technique is pretty clear. I'm not sure he captures the emotional power of Stravinsky's music, and I wish for a more inspiring leader. Still, this guest conductor is better than the male diva we had on the podium last week. At least this guy doesn't stop us 5,879 times an hour to micromanage the music.

During this break the five negotiators are given our info for the lunch meeting, painstakingly prepared by the union shop steward, who has no children, no spouse, and therefore more free time. Each of us will be seated at a table with sixteen orchestra musicians who will give us their ideas for proposed changes or improvements in the contract. I was elected to this position by my colleagues and serve without pay.

11:25 a.m. When can I get my leaf-blower fixed?

11:30 a.m. Before the end of the twenty-minute break, my colleague from the bassoon section brings me to tears in the ladies room. We are washing our hands side-by-side, and without provocation she looks me in the eyes and tells me that she admires my playing and that she's glad I'm here. It's an unexpected compliment, and I find myself full of embarrassment and gratitude, since my own inner critic tells me that—given my level of preparedness—I'm faking.

12:30 p.m. First rehearsal ends, and all the musicians head to the meeting room. It's clear almost immediately that the biggest issue on everyone's mind is higher salaries, followed closely by health-care coverage. The collective bargaining agreement already mandates that management cover 80 percent of our health insurance, but not our dependents. I'm relieved that my husband and kids are covered separately through a less expensive policy, but not everyone has access to outside family coverage.

Other issues of concern are overuse or repetitive motion injuries, work-hardening following an injury, maintaining high artistic standards, and the orchestra's financial health. The bass player makes a good point when he says, "Sure, I want the highest salary possible, but not if it leads to another bankruptcy." The flutist suggests we pool our sick days, or contribute them to colleagues who suffer chronic illness or injuries. I try not to roll my eyes when a violinist insists we should never allow management to program physically challenging music immediately after a week off.

2:00 p.m. I'm in my seat five minutes before the A sounds and we tune for the second rehearsal. For the first time I understand the musical connection between the ascending string tremolo at the end of "The Death of Katschei" and the ascending scales at the beginning of the finale. The first figure represents the evil monster's death, the departure of his soul, and the broken spell that dissolves his enchanted castle. The second figure underscores a heroic French horn solo of quiet joy, the slow steady rise of hope, and the dawn of a new day, with a crescendo to an explosive celebration.

With this in mind, I try to control the crescendo more carefully, holding on to the piano (soft) dynamic for longer, and delaying the peak of the forte (loud) climax until the last moment, since only at the last moment is hope allowed after a long oppression.

I really love this job and, sitting on this stage, I think I may have died and gone to heaven.

4:00 p.m. Rehearsal ends for the day. The orchestra librarians gather music folders, while the sound technicians adjust microphones, and the stage crew adjusts the chairs for the next rehearsal. They are preparing the stage for an award-winning guest soloist, who will dazzle us tomorrow with the much-loved Tchaikovsky piano concerto. I love to hear a guest soloist's unique interpretation. Many of them do not expect much from this orchestra, given Nashville's reputation as the capital of country music, and it's great fun to consistently surprise them with sensitive and accurate accompaniment.

4:30 p.m. Make a bank deposit of freelance studio work payments. You're not going to hear a lot of clarinet on the average country artist's records, but there's good work in gospel publishing, jingles, or an occasional movie soundtrack. Now time to pick up The Son. If he's still not ready to end his skate session, I'll go next door to the Mexican restaurant for a margarita. I am mentally and physically exhausted, and distracted by the homeless man asleep on the sidewalk and the inner-city kids playing basketball in a parking lot.

I straddle the most diverse worlds. I play art music for the elite in a $125 million concert hall, written by a struggling composer, in a neighborhood of the poor. The truth is, I'm not sure I could afford the tickets to hear my own orchestra play, on the salary I earn. But this music expresses universal human experiences, and at least my orchestra does strive to make it available to everyone through free public concerts from time to time.

4:45 p.m. The Son is not ready to leave the skate park so I head to the Mexican joint. A stranger wearing impossibly high heels invites herself to my table, asking permission only *after* she has already plunked down next to me. She's got to be in her sixties, not drunk but a bit off center, and I feel like this is some kind of test. I try to be nice, "Sure you can join me!" though I just want to drink my cocktail and read the instructions I brought with me from home for planting rose bushes.

5:30 p.m. On the way home I get into an argument on the cell phone with The Daughter, who has planned a date with her boyfriend for the fourth night in a row. She is furious with me for saying she can't do this on a school night. I had planned on a meal we could eat together, but instead, everyone eats tonight on their own schedule, and the atmosphere in the house grows sullen. I'm furious that the sink is full of dishes. Why am I the only one who seems to be able to load a dishwasher?

7:00 p.m. The Daughter and I take a trip to Target to shop for her digital camera, and I have a perimenopausal meltdown. I just don't understand why she cannot decide between a Canon and an Olympus. Any suggestion I make, she immediately dismisses. I leave the store feeling terrible, thinking I'm just not cut out for the really tough job of parenting after all.

8:00 p.m. We come home to find The Son violating the no-TV-on-a-school-night rule because he left his algebra book at school and therefore can't do his homework. This means we will have to leave the house earlier than usual tomorrow. Sigh. Isn't this how I started the day, earlier? The Husband is in his own home office, obviously choosing to direct his energy elsewhere at this particular moment.

8:15 p.m. My friend Zen calls and we talk on the phone for almost an hour about work-related issues. As a violinist, she has a slightly different perspective on the guest conductor and on the sound of the orchestra, by virtue of her position at the front of the stage. She is a good bit younger than I, with more idealism and energy, which I find inspiring. We exchange ideas about what kind of artistic leadership this orchestra needs and agree that this week's conductor is not a viable candidate for the permanent job, which is disappointing.

9:30 p.m. I realize I haven't turned in the overdue summer mission trip registration for the kids at church. The Daughter has an opportunity to join thirty-five other teens on a trip to Ecuador to work on a construction site at a home for the elderly. This is something she wants to do, and I only need to assist in a little fund-raising—provide music for the talent show?—to make it possible. I also realize I haven't typed up minutes from today's lunch discussions. And the leaf-blower still isn't repaired yet.

Security

6:00 p.m. My husband, Karl, is home after playing his afternoon concert with the New Jersey Symphony. He is so supportive when I go away, sometimes for weeks at a time. We are trying to decide whether I can take our five-year-old son, Zachary, with me on a tour of Northern California. He'll miss some school and it's expensive because he's full fare, but I think we're going to go for it. Zach loves coming with me, although he can be a nightmare traveling sometimes. I'll never forget the Houston airport when he was almost four and wouldn't cooperate at the security screening. The airport cops were advising me that I needed "the nanny" from TV! I was so depressed. But when things go well there is nothing like returning from a concert to your hotel room and seeing your sleeping child.
—*Erika Nickrenz, Denville, New Jersey; pianist, Eroica Trio*

Hurricane Relief

1:00 p.m. At the volunteer housing center, I am feeling somewhat discouraged, thinking about the thousands of trailers and mobile homes that still remain in our area, and the more than three thousand known households still in case management and in need of assistance to recover from the hurricane.

The construction manager and I spend the next few hours reviewing fifteen needs assessment forms, completed in our door-to-door efforts to identify those still needing assistance. We decide on three households that need urgent attention.

The first case involves a household of two adults and one child. Their house was first damaged by the hurricane, and then damaged further by a fire caused by an electrical problem as a result of the storm. The family is living in one room, the electricity is turned off because of the fire, and both bathrooms are damaged. Neighbors have been helping, and the family has been alternately staying with relatives and friends. The family does not have any resources available at this time. One person is on a fixed income and another works, but only has an annual expected income of less than $20,000. The construction manager estimates that the needed repairs will cost $15,000.

The second case involves a household of three, a single parent with two children. The homeowner took all the resources received from FEMA and insurance to begin repairs on the inside of the house, and to replace furnishings such as beds and appliances. There are some resources left to buy materials to fix the roof, but not enough to cover the necessary labor.

The third case is a household of two, a grandmother who is over seventy, and her grandson who is mentally challenged. Their house had just been remodeled before Hurricane Rita but was greatly damaged by the storm. Now only one part of the house is habitable. There are little or no resources available, as the grandmother is on a fixed income. She has been trying to fix up the house a little at a time but is getting very discouraged.

As the construction manager and I map out next steps, we express our desire to "fix things" for these families, but we recognize we should be careful not to give the family any false hope. We are not able to do all the repairs or rebuild for everyone with whom we work. Often the families, and sometimes the volunteers, lose sight of the fact that our resources are limited. Recovery work is often disappointing, frustrating, and almost always tiring, but for those impacted it is always an opportunity for a new way, and a new beginning.

—*Catherine D. Thomas, 55, Lake Charles, Louisiana;*
disaster recovery specialist, United Way of Southwest Louisiana

Etiquette Columnist

DIDI LORILLARD, 60, NEWPORT, RHODE ISLAND

Her Web site is newportmanners.com, offering classic solutions to everyday etiquette problems. For every rule, there is a reason—"Even 'elbows off the table.' Families were bigger in the old days, and tables were set with lots of glasses and candles. It was a matter of safety and keeping things tidy." For relationship issues and how to behave, she grounds her advice on core principals—compassion, consideration, compromise, and kindness. "But then there is the issue of being kind, but also honest. And sometimes you can't be both."

6:00 a.m. The birds chime in with the alarm clock. After making a protein drink, I settle down to read the nine questions that have appeared on my Web site while I was sleeping. The author of the most interesting one (*How do I break into the office clique of women who have lunch together most days?*) did not leave her e-mail address, which means she won't see my answer unless I list it in my site's archive. I post the most interesting questions under one of four categories: Codes + Conduct, Entertaining, Relationships, and Wedding Etiquette.

Every once in a while I wonder, why am I doing this? Especially after my Web site was hijacked and I had to get it put back in my name. (My husband said, Hire a lawyer and get it back. He is my rock.) But there is usually one thank-you note a day that makes me realize the site is useful to people all over the world, such as the one I received this morning: *We have shared your response with several people. The feedback is that you are creative and gave solid advice. We appreciate your input.*

I just got a personal e-mail from a friend whose husband

died several months ago. She wants to know if she should send invitations to his memorial service in May. My many friends are how I got into this business in the first place. They would often come to me for help solving social dilemmas, and have told me I have a gift for this. I was looking for a project I could do at home for the rest of my life, and now this etiquette Web site has become my own little cottage industry.

7:00 a.m. By now I've had a chance to read over all the latest questions. I like to think about them when I am chugging away on the elliptical machine. On my way to the gym, an art dealer and I exchange cheerful greetings.

7:30 a.m. My personal trainer of two years meets me at the elliptical machine. The father of three children, he inevitably has concerns, and talking things over is par for the course. It is a kind of therapy that makes both of us feel good. Today we discussed his fourteen-year-old son and why he is failing so many subjects in school. I tell him about the challenges I had, teaching my then nine-year-old Little Sister (through the Big Sisters of Rhode Island program) the importance of numbers and making math fun. Now, at the age of thirteen, she gets A-pluses. We're still working on science, and I am determined to make her as curious about this subject as I am, if not more.

After my half-hour workout with the trainer (free weights, machines, and balance ball boosts) I hop back onto the elliptical machine for another forty minutes. While on the machine, I have a discussion with the local hot dog vendor for an upcoming outreach event hosted by the Newport Democratic City Committee, which I am co-chairing. We are hosting a family picnic to thank all those who voted in the last election.

While I stretch out, I talk briefly to the island's most famous landscape architect, an elegant older woman who is my role model for fitness. She is an amazing master gardener.

9:00 a.m. On the way home from the gym, I always take a slightly longer route just to look at the ocean. On the island, if the sun doesn't break through the clouds by noon, chances are it will be gray all day. But the sun is shining brightly, crocuses are budding, and the tide is going out. No high schoolers today playing hooky and surfing any jacked-up waves.

I pick up my *New York Times* and the *Newport Daily News* off my front porch. Last night's *Newport Daily News* headline is, "Impeach President? War Foes Mention It," which reminds me that I promised a friend whose son just enlisted that I would go to the next peace rally with her. I call her and leave a message. There is a voice mail from my daughter in business school in Philadelphia who, after traveling the world and being the most independent of children, now phones me every single day on her way to classes.

9:35 a.m. I log on to my Web site for the second time this day. On the home page, the Tip of the Day is *Wake at dawn with a winged heart and give thanks for a day of loving. —Kahlil Gibran.* There are now fourteen questions and I go to work.

The first question reads, *My daughter recently broke off her engagement. Should she offer to return the engagement presents that she has received?* I answer, *Your daughter needs to return all of the engagement presents, if possible, in their original boxes along with a heartfelt thank-you note that states that she and her ex-fiancé by mutual consent have decided to call off the wedding. . . .* The kindest way to handle this delicate situation is to tell people that both parties have decided that they should not get married.

I e-mail the answer to the person who asked the question. I do not post this Q&A on my Web site because I already have an answer archived that addresses this particular dilemma. All of my responses are tailored to the reader. The only time that I refer readers to my archive of Frequently Asked Questions is if, say, the question is about wedding etiquette and I assume that the groom's or bride's family will have more questions during the wedding planning process.

The next question is one that I also have answered, about whether the host has to put a stamp on the envelope of a reply card to a dinner event. *Yes, as long as you have gone to the expense of having a reply card and envelope printed up, you might as well spring for the postage. . . .* I post the entry in "Entertaining" because it does not specifically mention whether it is a reply card for a wedding invitation, private party, or charity event.

I now still have fourteen questions to go because two more have come in while I was answering the first two. *When a gentleman is escorting his lady, which arm should he offer her?* This is archived under Relationships: Dating Etiquette. *The escort should always walk on the side of traffic, so this will determine which arm he offers the lady.* The same person e-mails a follow-up, *Is there any difference for formal military affairs?* My first answer still applies, and I respond to him accordingly.

12:30 p.m. I have been working all morning and now have only two more questions to answer. One is from the wife of a middle-aged man whose intestines are deteriorating. She wants to know how to tell him that he has very bad gas when he sleeps, and that it makes her sick to have to lie awake smelling him at night. In clear medical situations such as this, I suggest the person make a doctor's appointment for the loved one, and in this case, I assure her that this is a common problem easily controlled with medication and proper diet.

The last question is from a consultant who travels a lot with his boss who uses prostitutes. *Last week he made me lie to his wife for him about where he was while we were on this trip. I did it, but now I feel guilty for helping him lie. How can I deal with this?* I spend a good twenty minutes giving him an answer and then post it under Relationships. As part of my response, I tell him to politely tell his boss about his discomfort over the call girls, and I assure him that being honest will only make his boss respect him.

The last e-mail turns out not to be a question but a compliment from another etiquette consultant. *I was raised to be a Southern Lady at all times, and am consequently writing a book about manners. I always enjoy reading others' take on etiquette and I have to say that your website seems to be one of the few that actually has a knowledgeable person manning it. You are also the only person who seems to agree with me about the proper way to eat with your white gloves on!* This is a first. I have never received two compliments in one day before. I also rarely delete a question by mistake, which I did just now.

1:50 p.m. My youngest daughter, Savannah, calls. She is excited because they had two feet of snow in Squaw Valley where she works as head of media relations for a ski resort while studying to take the bar exam.

My family, bar none, are the best. Plus, they are always on call. My children, for example, advise me when I need to tell a reader on which toe he should wear his toe ring. My mom here in Newport and my aunt in Boston are primary sources for the old-fashioned answers—*Where does the expression "mind your P's and Q's" come from?* or *What is a knife rest?* From time to time, I also rely on friends from around the country and in Europe to verify my answers. But it is my copy editor, Nancy, who watches my back. Everyday she logs on to the administrative side of the site and edits the Q&As before they are posted.

Now I am off to play tennis for an hour, a challenge I took up last June after a friend gave me a book for my birthday about getting younger every year. The writer suggested that, after a certain age, it is good to take up something you've never done or thought you would never do. I had always supported my kids, playing tennis to the extent that I might have been called a tennis mom, so now the tennis mom plays tennis three to five days a week. I am by far the worst in the group, if not one of the oldest, and no matter how many women join the clinic, I am still the worst, but I am improving slowly.

3:45 p.m. After tennis and errands, I am ready for a lovely bath with Jo Malone's Blue Agava & Cacao scented oil.

4:30 p.m. Logging on to my Web site for the third time today, I find the Tip of the Day is, *Treat a compliment as a gift.* The first new question is from a guy who shares an office with another guy who makes lots of personal calls about the problems he is having with his girlfriend. *Can I say something to him?* This is a common complaint. I advised him, *Say something such as this: Can we talk man to man for a moment? You might want to lower your voice when you're on the phone because the rest of the office doesn't need to know about your personal life.*

Another young man asks if he needs to wear a tie to Easter brunch if he is not going to church before the brunch. *Yes, wear a tie because you can always take it off if you find that the other gentleman guests are not wearing them* . . . As a guest, it is always best to overdress slightly out of respect for the hostess.

Other questions and issues: Is it right for the mothers of the bride or groom to wear black to the wedding; cruise ship etiquette; women shaking hands; how to monogram for a newlywed; how to seat twelve guests at a dinner table; do you send out-of-town guests invitations to the bridal shower; and the most popular question of all—*How do I invite friends to dinner at a restaurant to celebrate my spouse's birthday and politely tell them that they have to pay for their own meal?* As part of my advice related to this last letter, I suggest including a line under the RSVP that reads, *In lieu of a gift, dinner is "Dutch Treat."*

Many of the answers to these questions I have down pat and can personalize in a matter of minutes. (I try to answer all questions within twenty-four hours.) My book *Newport Etiquette and Modern Manners* is taking shape through these questions. Every hit to my Web site is recorded by a stats program inside the underbelly of the site, so that when I eventually go to publishers with a proposal, they can log on to my stats to see how many hits I have received, which areas of the world the readers come from, and how long they stay on the site.

6:00 p.m. The local news is on but I need to make some calls in order to prepare for an interview tomorrow with the mayor of Newport, who is talking to four possible candidates about the one opening on the Waterfront Commission. My problem with being an activist is that if you speak out too often, you are not taken seriously, so I work through the Newport Democratic City Committee. As the chair of the third ward, which covers the waterfront, I will, I hope, be able to keep further development in check. It is not that I am opposed to developing, but I strongly believe in building green, while keeping the historic integrity of the harbor.

My eldest daughter calls again. Planning and producing her upcoming wedding has been a learning experience, and considerable help with the Wedding Etiquette section of my Web site.

8:00 p.m. My dinner guest arrived at the same time I received a phone call from a well-wisher about my interview tomorrow night with the mayor and the City Council.

10:00 p.m. My dinner guest has gone after helping me sort out a moral dilemma. I was asked to write a letter in support of a young woman, an old family friend, who wants to join a prestigious women's club in New York City, which I felt uncomfortable writing. Our dinner conversation confirmed that, with etiquette, there are no rules carved in stone, but in most cases honesty wins out over kindness.

Going on to www.newportmanners.com. The Tip of the Day is, *If you have nothing good to say about anyone, come and sit by me. —Alice Roosevelt Longworth.* How timely. There are now six new questions on the site, all of which I have answered before. A stepparent asking how to set boundaries when her adult stepdaughter and husband come for a visit; an aunt asking if it is proper etiquette for her niece to invite just the husband of a couple she knows to her wedding (she doesn't like the wife); a father wanting to know what to do for a friend whose teenage son had just committed suicide the night before . . .

11:00 p.m. I finally get to watch the news of the day.

Ask Amy

11:30 a.m. I settle into my cluttered office, pull my chair close, and start attacking the mail. Every envelope, every e-mail, brings with it another issue—and opportunity. I build my advice column out of letters such as these and I try to choose issues that will interest, entertain, educate, or resonate with readers. People are amazing. Sometimes, on bad days, I prefer the technical term that Marge Simpson uses, "cuckoo bananas." I open envelope after envelope. Their stories spill out. Adultery. Addiction. All over asshole-i-ness. And that's just the A's.

—*Amy Dickinson, 47, Chicago, Illinois, syndicated advice columnist ("Ask Amy"),* Chicago Tribune

•

Celebrity Chef

SARA MOULTON, 55, NEW YORK, NEW YORK

A seasoned chef with seven years' restaurant experience, she has served as the executive chef for *Gourmet* magazine since 1987 and hosted two cooking shows on the Food Network. Her foray into television started behind the scenes, helping Julia Child teach French cuisine to PBS audiences. Now she's got a new show in development for public television called *Sara's Weeknight Meals*. She prefers doing live TV over taped—cooking, answering questions, a producer talking in her ear. Her best training for the job? "Being a waitress and a mom. In those jobs you never do just one thing at a time."

6:50 a.m. In bed, thinking about a dream I had about Julia Child. We were at some event and she was making some kind of ground meat pie (not very Julia!) and an asparagus salad. We used to make asparagus all the time. I think it was on my mind because in real life the folks at the James Beard House wanted me to cook that as my first course at its upcoming media awards dinner, in place of the arugula salad (with spicy pecan praline and aged Gouda) that I had suggested. They said my arugula salad was "boring," not "sexy" enough.

Made me sad to think about Julia. She would have given me good advice about the James Beard debacle.

7:15 a.m. Finally got out of bed. My incentive is that pot of coffee I make first thing. French roast in a French press. Noticed that my husband, Bill, had put a few pots that I had cleaned the night before back into the sink. They were greasy, he said. I had cooked a roast duck on Sunday (a rare treat) and it gives off a lot of fat. The pan and rack I roasted it in are nonstick (not my favorite material) and almost impossible to get clean.

7:30 a.m. Started organizing materials for my husband and sixteen-year-old son, Sam. Directions, Avis rental info, a review from the *Fiske Guide to Colleges* . . . They are going to check out a college for Sam in Madison, New Jersey.

7:45 a.m. Made bed. I don't usually but my housekeeper, Magda, who normally comes in Tuesdays and Thursdays, has put her back out. Also, I like to listen to my lite jazz station, which I can only turn on when I am alone in the bedroom. My husband, the music guy, hates it. After a few tunes the jocks talk about liposuction and how it can now be done by laser. It is a pretty gross description and makes me think all over again, *What is wrong with people? Why can't they just go on a diet and exercise to lose all that fat? Why always the quick fix?*

8:00 a.m. Decided it was time to get Sam up. So I made him a hearty breakfast, egg sandwich on English muffin with melted cheese. He is extremely nervous about getting into college and I wanted to start his day right.

8:15 a.m. My twenty-year-old daughter, Ruthie, calls from Boston with her usual eleventh-hour panic about an impending exam. I tell her all my usual stuff—"Don't panic. Don't be negative. Focus on what you know." This philosophy has always helped me in crunch situations like exams, or live demos, or even doing live TV.

The husband and I bicker about directions to the college. He wants MapQuest, but then thinks it is too complicated. I tell him to figure it out himself then, and remind him that Sam is nervous so he should calm down.

8:45 a.m. This is normally when I am already at work at *Gourmet*. I have to put makeup on today, something I hate to do, because I am having lunch with the magazine's travel writer at a nice restaurant, Esca.

9:05 a.m. Walk to work and it is a beautiful warm day, the first in a long while. Everyone seems to be in a good mood. My office is in the Condé Nast building in midtown Manhattan, home to many magazines, from *Gourmet* to *Vogue* to *The New Yorker.*

9:35 a.m. I take the elevator up to my tiny office on the fifth floor, which *Gourmet* shares with *Self* magazine. Then I head downstairs one floor to the cafeteria to toast a mini bagel (my usual) and top it with scallion cream cheese and sliced tomatoes. Every time I put those tomatoes on top I hope nobody (culinary) is looking. I should not be eating tomatoes out of season. They are pretty awful but for some reason I like their texture and mild acidity. Second cup of coffee, hooray!

10:00 a.m. Have decided to explain to Catherine, our marketing director, why I am not going to be one of the chefs for the James Beard media awards dinner. Normally, I do not cook for 350 people, but they talked me into it because they originally told me my arugula salad would be just fine. Then, a couple of months down the road, they changed their mind and wanted something with asparagus. Asparagus does not excite me. I should just have said no to begin with. Lesson learned. Catherine is interested because it would be a good event to bring clients to.

When I first started as executive chef here, my job consisted of cooking lunch for clients (potential advertisers). The idea was to "make the magazine come alive" by preparing recipes from *Gourmet* and serving them in our elegant dining room. After the meal (accompanied by exquisite wines) we would hit up the client with big ad pages. Over the years, my job here has expanded to include testing and developing recipes for clients, teaching cooking classes, consulting, doing demos, and just about anything else that convinces the client to give us some money.

10:30 a.m. The one thing I must get done today is to figure out my speech next week in Boston. I'll be speaking at the Northeast Foodservice and Lodging Expo to all sorts of restaurateurs about "My unplanned career and how things have changed since I went

celebrity chef

to cooking school." I figure I should throw in some food trends, to make it more meaty. To do that I have to go through and organize all my files, which is a big undertaking but which makes me happy. I feel like I am always striving to get more organized. Most people say I already am, but I don't agree. There is too much clutter in my life.

10:40 a.m. Long chat with Brian Maynard, mucky-muck at KitchenAid and a good buddy for years. I ask him to be a sponsor of my PBS show, and explain the concept. The show will be about getting dinner on the table during the work week—all entrées. It's about rethinking dinner, so I'll do a show on preparing breakfast for dinner, soup for supper, the substantial sandwich, etc.

Brian tells me that the fact that Cuisinart is already a quarter sponsor could be a big problem, since they both make small appliances. We have a nice chat anyway, and I am going to get a proposal together, just in case.

11:00 a.m. Call Jennifer, my chef de cuisine, and remind her to try out all the kitchen gadgets we got in to test for a *Good Morning America* spot: an egg separator; silicone rubber bands for trussing chicken; a new super-duper jar opener; a garlic crusher . . . I'm getting nervous because there are only two I like so far: the sugar dispenser that dispenses half a teaspoon at a time with the press of a button; and the nesting flat measuring spoons. I've been the food editor at GMA since 1997 and do a segment every year called "Gadgets, $20 and Under." I also cover GMA's "fancy food" show, eleventh-hour Thanksgiving help, Christmas cookies, taste tests, and useful household info, such as what food items you should wash.

For the gadget segment, we need about eight total. I hope we can find some more. Jenn is cooking a dinner tonight for one of our clients, so I figured she could just incorporate testing them into her prep.

Talk to Ellen, one of my publicists at Bullfrog and Baum, about the *Gourmet/Golf Digest* outing, a culinary/golf weekend for our mutual client, South Carolina tourism. The idea is to bring new tourists to the area by luring them with demos and golfing with top chefs. Ellen volunteers to pursue some of their firm's celebrity chefs for this event, such as Bobby Flay or Marcus Samuelson, but I'm not sure Marcus golfs.

11:15 a.m. Organize my files and try to separate them into health issues, equipment, product info, useful tips, and ideas for my new TV show. One interesting new thing I add today—an article entitled, "Butter Becomes a Surprising Victim in the Fight over Trans Fat." Who knew butter and meat had natural trans fat in them? How depressing!

11:30 a.m. Get a call from Maria at GMA, saying she's sending over two more gadgets to test: a food cuber, sort of like a giant ice-cube tray that is used to freeze leftover chicken stock, tomato sauce, etc.; and an oil-and-vinegar cruet.

11:35 a.m. Emily Luchetti (another chef, and one of the two people who flattered me into doing the James Beard Awards dinner in the first place) calls and talks me back into making the ("boring, unsexy") arugula salad for the event. She agrees with me that less is more, and that sometimes the chefs make dishes that are way too fussy for these kinds of events. Phew!!! What a lot of energy has been wasted on this. I know the salad is good and will hold up, but all these other people are making me doubt myself.

11:45 a.m. Bite the bullet and call the publicist for Tom Colicchio (head judge for Bravo's *Top Chef*). She is so nice! I didn't expect to get any kind of response, since he is such a busy guy these days and I don't know Tom that well. It looks like there is a chance he might consider joining us for this *Gourmet/Golf Digest* event. The publicist likes my idea about his not doing a demo, just talking about his show. She doesn't cut me off when I say there is no money, and apparently he loves South Carolina and golf.

Noon Call Bill on his cell. Sounds like they spent most of their time lost this morning. Finally they are there and going on the tour. I have gotten no work done this morning! Too much time on the phone.

12:30 p.m. Just finished going through all the Diet Coke recipes. Readers entered their own appetizer recipes that are supposed to be paired with Diet Coke on Oscar night. The Oscars are over, but that is the premise anyway. I discard, as usual, all the ones that use pre-prepared ingredients such as cans of soup or taco mix. We are looking for a from-scratch recipe, not just a bunch of processed ingredients thrown together. We need one winner and ten runners-up. I hope we have them! There aren't that many entries that I like enough to test. I keep hoping we will learn something new from one of these home cooks. Sometimes we do.

Chat briefly with Natalie, my creative partner and co-producer on the PBS show. She is just back from Napa, shooting Michael Chiarello's show for the Food Network. She is very excited to hear about Cuisinart agreeing to be a quarter sponsor of the show. They were the first company I talked to last fall about sponsorship, but they had originally said no. I was proposing a different show at the time, which I had to abandon because my original partner and I weren't working well together.

Just three more sponsors to go to produce the new show! My current show, *Sara's Secrets*, is still airing on the Food Network, but my contract is up and I don't know how much longer they will run it. I need to get back on TV.

12:45 p.m. Choose a recipe from my friend Jean Anderson for the "Gourmet Scoop" article in the May Web site update. It is a Southern recipe to go with the interview I did about her new Southern cookbook. She writes a great story to go with the recipe for butter beans her mom used to make. People always write best when they write about their own experience.

1:00 p.m. Off to lunch with Bill Sertl, *Gourmet's* travel editor. We went to Esca because we both love fish. I fully intend to eat light, but then I cannot resist the pasta with mussels and greens. We chat about the magazine and people we both know in the industry. He also tells me about a great source for rental apartments in Paris, where I have been trying to go for a special occasion with my husband.

3:00 p.m. Long lunch! Hear back from the boys. Sounds like Sam liked the college but thinks it might be too close to home.

4:00 p.m. Almost done sorting out my files. Have not found all that much trend info for my speech, but I have found great tips, food facts, and health info, all of which will be useful for my new show. I want to make sure the show is packed with info, so I'm not just making recipes but educating at the same time. I love to teach; that's the reason TV is so fun for me.

4:15 p.m. Long phone chat with the guy who manages a mall tour I have gone on, and also a new project called Food University, a hands-on cooking class at Wyndam Hotels around the country. We did our first demo in March and it was successful, but not well enough attended. He is trying to get additional sponsorship and is very hopeful. We'll see. Right now, he cannot pay me my usual fee so I am reluctant to get involved. Until I have my new show on the air, I must focus on making money.

5:00 p.m. Time to head downtown to my publicist's office to sign copies of each of my cookbooks for charity events. I'm very proud of my books; they are like my kids.

5:30 p.m. The walk downtown is crowded; it reminds me of that movie *A Thousand Clowns* with Jason Robards. I call Sam on my way to the publicist to tell him to scrub and put a baked potato in the oven for me. I am on Weight Watchers (and have already lost eight pounds out of twelve). A baked potato with a little Parmigiano-Reggiano, olive oil, and 2% cottage cheese does it for me. I do not feel deprived.

My publicist has already opened up the four boxes of books and set them to the right page. I sign away and we catch up on other business. She hasn't received the missing info regarding my

Naples trip this weekend for the fund-raiser for the Naples Philharmonic. This is definitely a bummer. I already know what I am demo-ing (the "boring, unsexy" arugula salad, creamy cauliflower soup with chorizo and greens, and green chile and zucchini quiche), but I am going to see an old college friend on my second day there, which is why I need the news about my flight, hotel, and itinerary.

I hate traveling, although I need to do these trips. They bring in good income and I always meet some interesting people. It is important for me to be out there while I am not so much on TV. I need to write up a "while-I-am-gone" document for the boys regarding what's for dinner, what they need to do, and where I can be reached. They barely read it, but they still count on it and it makes me relax.

I talk to Ruthie on the way home. Thank God for cell phones while you are walking. She doesn't think her test had gone that well. She always says that.

6:15 p.m. I arrive home just when the boxes of groceries are delivered in the hallway. I always order the groceries for Tuesday because my housekeeper unpacks them, but I had to switch it to a later time today because she was sick. I need to put the food away and unload the dishwashing machine so I can load in the new dishes. And then there are those greasy pots from the night before. And all of this has to happen before I can start dinner.

Bill comes home and makes the mistake of asking how I am. When I respond that I am stressed out by all of the above, he says he would pitch in after the first minutes of the six thirty news, which we watch religiously. So I calm down (I have a hard time with clutter) and cook dinner, which tonight is a prepped stir-fry shrimp dish from FreshDirect for the boys. I ordered that kind of food this week, knowing I was going to be late. I always try to get dinner on the table by seven on the nose. Otherwise Bill turns on *The Simpsons* and I have a hard time peeling him away.

6:30 p.m. Sam heads off to Brooklyn to hang out with friends. I make him clean up his room before he goes. When he argues, I point out that I haven't asked him to do all that much around the house, just his own stuff. I think it was sort of a rough day for him.

Bill agrees to sit down with me and review the day. He was disappointed by the students who showed him and Sam around the college campus. They didn't seem to have much depth. But he and Sam ended up having a great meal at an Italian restaurant, and an interesting talk about the world.

I tell him about Emily Luchetti's talking me back into doing the James Beard dinner. He thinks I'm doing them a huge favor, and they should have been more respectful and not second-guessed my choice in the first place. Magda (my housekeeper) calls and says she is feeling better and will be here tomorrow. Good news! We don't have to do the dishes. Bill tidies up and then heads out to work on his encyclopedia of hip-hop. Most days, he goes back to work after dinner, but he loves the project so it is okay.

10:10 p.m. I just finished reading a chapter in this new book recommended by a life coach I am working with. It's called *Now Put Your Strengths to Work.* Not a bad idea. I just wish I could figure out what exactly my strengths are. I am sure I will, but now it is time for bed.

Supper's (Not) On

5:38 p.m. Walk in the door to a disturbing lack of aroma. Discover I forgot to turn on the Crock-Pot. Dang.
—*Andrea Wenger, 42, Broadway, Virginia;*
marketing director, Eastern Mennonite University

●

All in a Day's Work

8:06 a.m. I look at my desk. It looks like the scene of a burglary. What a mess. Our annual budget was due to our associate VP today. It came down to a final mad battle to balance, enter, and publish the budget last night and still hit the road by 5:00 p.m. to fulfill my mom duties. I am so relieved that it is over. I stare at the mess. It feels like the morning after a big party, which would explain the headache. I have a budget hangover.

—Jeanne Krogen, 48, Cottonwood Heights, Utah;
accountant, University of Utah

10:00 a.m. I read an entire week's worth of slush. It's all bad, mostly because every one of the stories is a derivation of one of three clichés: a battered wife murders her abusive husband; a gold-digging, philandering wife tries to murder her husband, only to be one-upped by him at the last moment; or a hen-pecked husband murders his nagging wife. Out of each week's worth of manuscripts (a pile of about fifty stories), 95 percent of these typically fall into one of these categories. I realize that, as an editor, I'm privy to people realizing their fantasies through their fiction, but really. Doesn't anyone believe in divorce anymore?

—Nicole Sia, 24, Brooklyn, New York; assistant editor,
Alfred Hitchcock's Mystery Magazine

10:20 a.m. A reporter and cameraman for the local news station arrives. The president of National Association of Women Business Owners asks me to say a few words on UPS's behalf. The president, along with the director of the YWCA Women's Shelter, are going to be announcing a new women's empowerment program that UPS will be involved in. I'd be glad to talk about the program, but if I end up on TV I'm going to

water cooler diaries

wish I'd had these dark roots touched up last Saturday instead of next weekend.

—*Cindy White, 41, Oklahoma City, Oklahoma; UPS sales manager*

12:05 p.m. My students and I head to the lab. We are going to remove the sulfur from the by-product of our new hydrometallurgical process, which is a much cleaner and more efficient way to produce lead metal. Basically, instead of using lots of fossil fuel to melt the lead so it can be purified, we use solutions and electricity to do the same job, and the temperature never gets above 150° F.

It doesn't take long for us to get dirty and sweaty. The stuff we use is a lot like axle grease—jet black, slimy, and tenacious. It also makes a bad smell (like rotten eggs on steroids) so we stink, too. When I have to do this sort of work, I try to think of all the nice people at my company, ordinary folks with families and hobbies and worries just like mine.

If the project I'm working on can benefit the company, then maybe it can provide a little more security for all of those nice people, without the added worry of whether our jobs are going to be there for us next month or next year. At least this is the sort of stuff I try to think about when sweat runs in my eyes, and I stink so bad I have to avoid public places afterward so people don't think I have some sort of severe gastrointestinal disorder.

—*Vanessa Eckhoff, 34, Viburnum, Missouri;*
metallurgical engineer, the Doe Run Company

celebrity chef

Intake Counselor, Oregon Department of Corrections

JANET ROSS, 51, KEIZER, OREGON

Most of her day is spent reading about, writing about, and talking with murderers, sex offenders, thieves, and drug addicts. A lot of the people she deals with on the job are hardened, but she isn't. "I'm at heart a homemaker with a great love of creating." She recognizes the contrast between her professional and personal life, but her co-workers don't. "I have worked in four different institutions and for some reason I am eventually always referred to as 'Momma Ross' by most staff members, even if they are my age or older. What's up with that?"

5:00 a.m. Dang. What a long night. Tossed and turned since 2:45 a.m. And to think I was going to sleep in. I have a doctor's appointment and am going into work a little later. Oh well, get the coffee going and hop into the shower. Hop, right. I haven't hopped in a long time.

5:35 a.m. Man, I am bummed. HGTV took my favorite quilting show off the air. Let's see if they just moved it to another time. Well, DIY has it later in the morning when I am at work, but that would require me to actually get with today's technology and get a DVR or TiVo or whatever they call those recording devices.

8:00 a.m. Here I sit waiting to have an EKG and blood work to prepare for an upcoming hip surgery. The majority of the people in this very full waiting room are much older, and look very tired and frail. In the hip-surgery world I am considered young and active. *I love that!!!* A bad hip (from years of daily long walks) and migraines have been my burdens to bear the past three years. I'm starting a new type of migraine drug today. It has many negative side effects with hopefully two positive effects: less migraines and, for some, weight loss. Oh, please let me be one of the some.

8:28 a.m. Still waiting. I'll be getting to work later than I had planned. Today is day one in my brand-new office after a long-awaited construction expansion. No more cubicle world. No more absolute lack of privacy. No more trying to concentrate on some horrendous police report while my co-workers are cutting up. No more being assaulted by my male co-worker's gaseous habits.

On the other hand, no more daily sharing of each other's lives. No more listening to Jon's little ones over the speaker phone detailing their latest adventure, like "going pee-pee in the potty." No more spontaneous laughter when one of us goes manic. This, I will miss the most. Good-bye cubicle world, hello privacy. Sad thing is, my life is filled with privacy.

Man, this gal sitting next to me stinks. Oh, thank goodness they just called her name. Oops, mine, too.

9:00 a.m. Home for a quick change and off to work on this rainy Oregon day.

9:59 a.m. Wow, what is normally a thirty-five-minute drive to work took almost an hour due to a wreck. Big surprise! In the three years I have lived here, there have been six or seven wrecks in that exact same spot. Hopefully, no one was hurt. I think what I like least about my job is the commute.

10:00 a.m. I have worked with the Department of Corrections for over twelve years and am *almost* comfortable with the constant security measures. Seems I no longer notice the oddity of the high fences topped with razor wire. Or that the friendly person driving the perimeter patrol vehicle is fully armed and ready to respond if needed. Perfectly manicured lawns and roses line the walks to the first series of locked gates and doors.

From the moment I step foot on the prison grounds I am more than likely on camera. (Out of habit, I now find myself incessantly checking for cameras hidden at the tanning booth, public bathrooms, and even the ATM.) Getting from point A to point B is not as fast as I'd like, as I go to my office through a series of twelve locked doors. Travel through the institution requires ID presentation visible to all staff. Of course, mine has a picture that makes my driver's license look like a glamour shot.

10:10 a.m. Finally in my new office. Wow, it's not much bigger than a prison cell. No windows. Blasé color on the block walls. And it's a mess. I have to get busy moving furniture around and rearranging my computer setup so I can get to work.

11:35 a.m. Okay. I think I am finally happy with the furniture arrangement. I also took the time to hang up the pictures of my favorite people, and my poster from the world-famous Pendleton Round-Up Rodeo. It feels like the first day of school. My coworkers and I all keep running back and forth between our new offices, trading equipment and checking things out. But now that I am settled in, I better get to work.

My job is to evaluate information about an offender's criminal history from police reports and rap sheets, his prior parole and probation officers, and his own self-report. Then I enter the data to determine the inmate's initial custody classification level. This identifies both public and institutional risks, and the appropriate facility to serve his sentence. I also interview inmates to develop a corrections plan, which may include cognitive, drug, or alcohol programs.

All of this is summed up in a criminogenic assessment report that staff across the state, community corrections, and the parole board can review. For offenders, knowing that I've done my homework about their case before I interview them usually helps them come to the conclusion that they can either help themselves make better choices, or they can learn to be better criminals.

Bottom line—if my role in an inmate's incarceration helps a few of them make some positive change in their lives, then it's all worth the not-so-fun things of my job.

12:20 p.m. Finished up a criminogenic report from last week. I just had to wait until our Security Threat Group staff interviewed the inmate to determine if he had any gang association. By golly, it was determined that he does, as much as he claimed otherwise. This time around, the guy is in for sex offenses and, *again*, he did not do it. Of course not. Right. Interesting, those two things usually don't mix too well—being a gang member and a sex offender.

Time to have a bite to eat. A Lean Pocket and a large glass of water with lemon and Stevia mixed in. I'd rather have a huge Diet Coke, my lifelong addiction, which I am trying to break.

12:48 p.m. Let's see. What do I have in the way of files? Looks like today will involve nothing more than drug-related offenses. Somewhat boring, but at least not as emotionally taxing as person-to-person crimes. Most cases do not have too much of a negative effect on me, but there have been some interviews that have left a lasting impression—the mentally ill male rocking back and forth as he described beating his girlfriend to death with a hammer. The guy who slit his seven-month-old son's neck because he said he was trying to save him from demonic forces. Or some of the horrendous child sex offenses that always leave me with disgust.

1:10 p.m. All our office doors are open. I think we are having cubicle DTs. I am enjoying the commotion going on in the hallway—the very thing I whined about in the past—but I'm having a hard time concentrating.

2:00 p.m. Off to interview an inmate, an older repeat offender who is back in for another drug-related offense. It's only me and the inmate in a small room. I sit closest to the door, just in case, though nothing's ever happened. During the interview, I pay close attention to body language, tone of voice, etc.

You would think, after working in this environment for twelve years, I'd quit feeling naked in front of these guys. It wasn't so bad when I worked as a transport officer and wore a uniform. Funny, I could always check my mood after restraining a chain of thirty-plus male inmates, and all of them muttering how tight the restraints were. If indeed a second check of the restraints revealed I had unconsciously caused them to be a little snug, I'd ponder if anything was secretly bothering me.

2:30 p.m. Boy, did this guy want to talk and talk. Thirty-year addiction to heroin, cocaine, and alcohol have all played a role in his numerous prison sentences. Too bad. He says he is a talented artist. Many criminals are. Sometimes a person's criminal history will indicate that I will be dealing with one bad hombre, so to speak, only to find a person who has experienced things in life I can only imagine. I have to try to put myself in that person's shoes and ask, "What would I have done in those circumstances?" But having very clear boundaries is key to working in a prison, not only for myself but for the inmates, too.

3:19 p.m. So far, I am not liking this new migraine medicine. Feeling a little woozy. Not the best of conditions to be in when talking with convicted felons.

3:30 p.m. One of my co-workers who proclaims an affliction of OCD is crawling out of her skin. Another co-worker across from her office has taped a piece of paper on the outside of his door and it is crooked. She is going nuts looking at it. I wonder if he did it on purpose?

3:38 p.m. Yep! I was right. He hung it up crooked on purpose.

3:40 p.m. Wouldn't you know it? Right when my co-workers and I were chatting, my supervisor strolled by chanting, "More productivity. More productivity." On to another file to prepare for another interview. At times, it seems routine, kind of like herding cattle. I discover an escape incident in this inmate's past. This will slow the process way down. I wonder what I am going to have for dinner?

4:10 p.m. Just got a call from my daughter. She didn't want anything, just to talk. She, her boyfriend, and his two adorable little girls are moving four hours away. This will be their last weekend living a short eight blocks from my house. I think we are both beginning to feel the ache of missing each other.

4:19 p.m. My son, who is thirty, called to tell me what day his college graduation will be held in May. He, my daughter-in-law, and my eight-year-old most perfect granddaughter live six hours away. Man, I'm glad I took the time to hang up my pictures today. I love seeing the happy faces of my loved ones. I miss them.

4:54 p.m. Another file prepped for tomorrow morning. This file involved a stolen vehicle, identity theft, and methamphetamine possession. Nowadays, identity theft and meth use seem to go hand-in-hand. I'm pooped and want to go home. Out the same twelve locked doors and gates I go.

6:15 p.m. Home sweet home. I stopped by the most awesome grocery store and picked up some perfectly barbecued tri-tip and vegetables. I think this medicine is making me hungry. Please let me be one of the some that lose weight!

6:33 p.m. In my recliner watching HGTV and eating dinner, still upset that they moved the time of my favorite quilting show. Oh well, maybe I'll learn how to knit. That show is on early in the mornings. Today has been a long day. I wonder if I can stay awake long enough to watch *American Idol*. I love that beat-boxer boy. What talent.

intake counselor, oregon department of corrections

The Limits of the Law

3:50 p.m. Now the warrant unit has an issue with a domestic violence restraining order that needs to be served on an eighteen-year-old member of the Bloods who just sexually assaulted his girlfriend. The search warrant only allows us to look for his gun in a backpack behind the couch in his parents' house, so if someone's moved it, he's home free. I'm all for protecting individual rights but sometimes it gets ridiculous.

—*Jean Stanfield, 49, West Hampton, New Jersey;*
sheriff, Burlington County Sheriff's Department

•

Voice Actor

KARA EDWARDS, 30, PINEVILLE, NORTH CAROLINA

She has a "tiny" voice, perfect for cartoon characters and younger roles. Fans know her best as the voice of Goten, one of the main characters on Cartoon Network's *DragonBall Z*. She's also the green puppy, Razzles, on the new PBS kids' show *Raggs*, and has recorded commercials for hundreds of products, from Clinique to the local chicken shack. "I'll voice anything that pays my standard fees and doesn't include adult content. I refuse to have my voice heard one minute on a show aimed at six-year-olds, and the next minute at your local XXX shop!"

7:30 a.m. I can't sleep anymore; I'm still on East Coast time. The very first annual voice conference begins today. Voice actors from all over the world have converged on Las Vegas, networking and praying that this will be the week that changes their career. I am the one doing most of the praying. After five years as a radio cohost, I made the decision to quit my job and chase my dream. I became a full-time voice actor six months ago.

Agents will be here, big-name voice actors will be here, clients will be here. Bob Bergan, the voice of Porky Pig, is scheduled to do a presentation. There is even a rumor that the big man himself, Don LaFontaine, may show up. He's the highest-paid voice actor in the world, famous for his movie trailers and GEICO's "In a world . . . " commercials. It's scary that I almost missed it.

Mom is in the shower. As much as I love spending time with her, I wish I could have afforded to stay at the other hotel with all the other voice actors. The flight price and conference fee were very high. Fortunately, my mother was scheduled to be here at the same time with her company for a computer convention, and I

voice actor

was able to bunk with her here at the Marriott. March turned out to be a very good month for me and I could have afforded it after all, but that's part of being an actor. Money comes, money goes. Thank God for my husband and his regular paycheck.

7:49 a.m. Time to find some work for next week. I have several Web sites I belong to: Voices.com; Voice123.com, etc. Clients post jobs on these sites—everything from a company that needs its voice mail recorded, to small private jobs, to a new cartoon series—and the race is on to put together an audition and proposal that stands out. Voice acting is one of the most competitive fields to get into, second only to runway modeling.

Possible job #1:
> I need this by 1:00 p.m. Central on Tuesday, March 27. Obviously, MP3 is perfectly fine. Plan to use the voice-over for a church service. I am looking for male, female, American English, British accent, and James Earl Jones style . . .

I go to church. I like church. But, I'm in a hotel room in Vegas, Mom is in the shower, and I can't record audio right now. My mic would pick up the sounds of water running. Besides, I don't like the sample script they attached for the audition, poor grammar. And a female who speaks American English with a British accent? Um, then it wouldn't be American, now, would it? A female that sounds like James Earl Jones? Boy, would I kill to hear the winning audition on this one! According to the "answered by" section of the site, forty-three people have already sent in auditions! Well, ya gotta pay the bills.

Possible Job #2:
> We're looking for audio made up of animated sounds— boing, wheee, yaaay . . . It's got to feel important and strong but NOT corporate. So a boing is not a usual boing, but more character filled and weird-ish . . .

I have no idea what this client is talking about, but I want this job! Plus, the budget is around $750 for a minute of whoops and whees! When Mom goes to her meeting, I am auditioning! Of course, about two hundred other voice actors will also audition for it. I remember when I got my first voice-over agent ten years ago. She said I would book, on average, one out of every fifty auditions. I read yesterday that the new statistic is one out of every four hundred.

10:25 a.m. Just finished breakfast with Mom and her co-worker. It's funny. I built a studio in my house (really just a microphone in a padded walk-in closet, with a ton of equipment) and started my own business. But my mother has been a strong business-woman for a couple of decades, and it wasn't until this morning over breakfast that I understood anything about her job as the regional manager of a major corporation. Wow, I'm a business-woman now, too! And I also have to worry about marketing, net-working, profit, expense . . . I feel like I've grown more in the last six months than I have in the last thirty years.

11:03 a.m. I just got a call from Liz, a professional voice actor I have never met. Most times when voice-over actors work together, it is usually through ISDN, which is like a satellite that lets you hear a person in real time, while not being in the same city or even country. So one of us came up with an idea for a voice-over bulletin board, now a family of about four hundred voice actors. This is what makes today so special. We are all meeting for the very first time.

On the phone, Liz is bubbly and fun. We make plans to meet this afternoon before the official meet-and-greet at 6:00 p.m. The actual conference doesn't get under way until tomorrow morning, but we are all getting together this evening to register and reveal ourselves! I am so excited, yet completely terrified. I am thirty but I sound sixteen, so I'm sure everyone is expecting a teenager! Plus, I look really young so it is going to be difficult to convince people to see me as a business-savvy professional, and not just some kid playing around with cartoon voices.

11:38 a.m. Just got off the phone again. (My phone has rung more in the last two hours than it has in the last two months, since 99 percent of my work correspondence is done online.) This time it was my friend Jen, who lives in L.A. She called to catch up and remind me that I am terrible about calling people back.

I had no idea six months ago that I would be this busy! I thought, *Gee, work from home; that means I'll be able to finish that scrapbook, do some painting, sit around and relax in my organic gardens . . . not!* I'm either in front of the computer or behind a microphone about twelve hours a day. I'm passionate about creating voices and characters, so it's very hard to walk away from potential work.

11:57 a.m. Job Possibility #3:

> We are looking for a strong voice for our climate change documentary. We are on a tight deadline and need someone who can do this TODAY. The earlier the better.

Climate change? My husband, a morning weatherman for the local CBS station, would love that. Goodness! These people need to plan ahead! While I can audition from Vegas, I don't have the proper studio setup to record an actual job. Last week, I bought this MacBook with a low-quality backup mic to bring with me so I could still be in touch with clients. But some of the people here have portable studios. It won't cost me much more to get one. I just need to buy a large plastic padded box to fit my mic in from home, to deaden the sound and stop any echo. But I also need some time to put the proper editing software on the laptop. Then I can record and edit MP3 files to be e-mailed directly to clients from anywhere in the world!

12:49 p.m. I take a break to walk down to the lobby. A man asks me, "What are you here for?" I tell him, "A voice actor's conference." He stares at me blankly. Most people don't understand my job at all. The average person never thinks about the voices they hear on a daily basis. For me, it's all I think about. I sit on a plane and study the in-house safety video. I listen to the radio for the commercials, not the music. I spend quite a bit of time online listening to my competitors' demos, trying to figure out how to make mine better, different.

12:58 p.m. I am losing my mind. I should have stayed at the Palace Station, the hotel site of the convention. I feel like I am missing out on some great networking opportunities. In fact, I am going to call there and see if I can get a room for the next few days. Hey, it's a tax deduction, right? The lady on the phone said she would call me back in two hours. Ugh. I should call my husband and see how his day is going.

2:02 p.m. I am sitting in the closet of room 303 at the Marriott. I have hung all the clothes I can inside to absorb sound reflection. It's time to record auditions and send them out. This first one came through my personal Web site, which is how clients often find me. It's a radio commercial for a local homebuilder. He included the entire sixty-second script, but I will only record a small section of it. I don't want a client to be able to use my audio without paying me. This hasn't happened to me, but I know other voice actors that were victims of this scam.

Job Proposal #1:

> Hello, my name is Kara Edwards. If you are looking for a fun voice with lots of energy, then I have the voice you are looking for! I hope you enjoy the custom demo I've attached! My fee for this project is $200, however all fees are negotiable . . .

The second audition request is on Voices.com and is open to all voice actors. I better hurry! Job Proposal #2:

> Hello, my name is Kara Edwards. I saw your listing for a female voice talent for your computer adventure game. I have several years' experience voicing video games for computer and console. My standard fee for video games is $300 to $500 per character, depending on the length of the script . . .

voice actor

Looks like I'll have to wait to record the "boing! whee!" audition until I get home. You have to record the sounds to an attached video and I can't do this on my laptop. Fortunately, the deadline for entry is after I return.

2:35 p.m. All done! When I e-mail a proposal, I always forget about it right away. If I sit and wait for an answer, I will go crazy. Rejection is a daily part of my life. I've gotten over it by now. It occurs to me just now that a large part of my career is spent in closets. Hmm. The fact that they are usually padded closets is pretty funny.

3:11 p.m. Just got a phone call from the Palace Station. They have no rooms available. Oh, well. It just means I will have to get to the conference early and leave late to make the most of this networking opportunity. I feel a tremendous amount of pressure to make great contacts and absorb a ton of information. Voice actors don't always get chances like this.

3:45 p.m. I've decided to head over to the other hotel and wait for the meet-and-greet in Liz's room. It's a chance to make a friend beforehand, someone to walk in with me so I won't feel so alone. She says she is nervous also. Whew!

4:30 p.m. Cabdrivers in Las Vegas ask a lot of questions. I really do cringe when I have to explain my job. No one gets it. In fact, the word "voice-over" can be deceiving. I don't just place my voice "over" a piece of music. I act. I interpret. I have a gift and I try to use it to the best of my ability. I take care of my voice. I do not smoke, I drink in moderation. I consume tea by the gallons, and I do not scream. I work on my breathing. I warm up every morning by singing my favorite songs, from "Lord, I Lift Your Name on High" to anything by Aerosmith. I also sing scales in all pitches to get the vocals going. I brush my teeth before walking into my studio each time. Clean teeth mean less noise and smacking sounds.

5:25 p.m. Liz and her roommate, Amanda, are both very sweet. They are getting dressed for the meet-and-greet. It's casual attire, but I still tried to pump up the wardrobe with some skirts and nice shirts, and it seems the other ladies did as well.

6:00 p.m. It's time to go and meet everyone else. I can feel the excitement soaring through this incredibly crappy hotel. Boy, am I glad I didn't get the room here after all! It stinks like smoke and urine. The walls are actually yellow. Suddenly, I am more nervous about the damage that is going to be done to my throat and lungs than I am about meeting all these people! My hands are shaking.

10:27 p.m. This is going to be the best week ever! There were about one hundred people at the meet-and-greet, and two hundred are expected overall. A few looked nothing like I expected! I'm guessing they thought the same of me. I do some on-camera work, so they may have thought I should have been much more beautiful! Oh, well.

The best was finally meeting Bob, an amazing voice actor also in Charlotte, although we've never met. When I saw him, I wasn't sure he was the right guy so I waited until I could read his name tag. The kindest soul alive! And Dave is so much better-looking than I expected! The pictures online don't do him justice. (Guess that explains why he is also a news anchor on TV.) And Deirdre wasn't nearly as intimidating in person as she is online! (She's the creator of the voice-over bulletin board and "Mom" to the rest of us.) We all told each other how talented we think the other person is—a virtual love fest.

The biggest surprise of the evening was how many people wanted to meet *me*! Not just because I've chatted with them online, but also because they were actual fans of my work, or wanted me to share my expertise. One guy was kind enough to request an autograph for his kid. It really flipped me out! I spend so much time thinking I'm not worthy. I hope this conference will be a big boost to my confidence. I hope I make lifelong friendships, and that a big-time agent decides she can't live without me! I hope I leave Vegas a better voice actor and a better person. This is a week that will change my life. I can feel it.

News from Lake Wobegon

9:45 a.m. Help! The wax remover stuff has now completely plugged up my ear. Now, it's no longer like I'm hearing through a tunnel. It's like I'm stuck deep down in the darkness of the tunnel, way at the bottom, covered with leaves. Shoot. I've got a meeting today that I can fake, but what if I get called for an audition? Or worse, what if I get a voice job? Or, what a minute, what am I saying? This could be much, much worse. This could be a Saturday and I could be somewhere on the road with *Prairie Home Companion*.

I can't hear anything. How I am supposed to get through the show doing all my goofy character voices if I can't hear what I'm doing?! But wait. Just wait. It isn't Saturday. It's Tuesday. I rarely do anything *Prairie Home Companion*–related on a Tuesday, and whatever is going on with my ear is temporary anyway, so just relax. I've always assumed that the worst thing that could happen to actors would be to lose their voice, but now I realize that losing your hearing wouldn't work well in my profession either!

—*Sue Scott, 50, St. Louis Park, Minnesota;*
actor and cast member, A Prairie Home Companion

●

Reading the Signs

12:45 p.m. Take out new client's natal chart. She runs a nice little shop where she makes her own soap. I spread out some paper so I can take notes, and get my ephemeris (showing the locations of the planets) and a couple of reference books if I get stuck.

Felicia has a T-square: Neptune on her nadir, opposite her midheaven, squaring Venus on her Ascendant. Cézanne had Neptune on his nadir, I discover online. Saddam Hussein did, too. Will she think that's funny? I think it's funny, but it's her life, not mine, and this T-square looks like a bitch. All my clients have T-squares lately. I tell them, it makes for a hard dynamic in life, but it also gives us the energy to push past it. Ultimately, people with T-squares may go further than people with Grand Trines. (A grand trine is when a large equilateral triangle appears in the chart—it's lucky, but you have to get off your butt to truly take advantage of it. Like being born with great talent, it's nothing if you don't use it.)

Back to Felicia. She's all angles, which makes this dynamic more pronounced in her personality, and tougher. Something from her childhood pulls at her, makes it hard for her to stand with confidence, especially in her career. The solution is her Venus in the twelfth house, the most sensitive, compassionate placement for Venus. Her way out of this lifelong lesson? Don't shut off, don't harden or fight it, just tap into that compassionate, universal, detached love, without becoming a rescuer or a rescuee. Everything is on the left of her chart—she's a total self-starter, has never had anything handed to her in this life. At the same time, she doesn't need people to get started.

Neptune in the fourth. Denial about one of the parents, probably the father, who may have been dreamy and artistic, maybe addictive. Her inability to see her childhood for what it was may be her self-undoing. Fucking Neptune, it's such a pain in the butt. Oops! Should I say that? I don't want to piss off Neptune.

Moon in the third. Intuitive about communication, about short interactions. This moon is probably why she is such a natural at running her business. People come in to her shop, she senses what they want, she focuses her emotional energy into these little daily interactions, and they appreciate it.

2:00 p.m. Get up and stretch. God, I love this job. I get to peek into people's souls and, in an hour and a half, sum up their soul path, their life journey for them. Every chart is like solving a code to something mystical. I see the enormity, beauty, and complexity of the tasks someone has volunteered to take on in this life; the energies they have come to balance. I feel enormous responsibility to share with my clients as much wisdom as I can during my readings. Lately, I am realizing that most people can't take all of it in at once. I have to be content to offer what they can handle.

—*Carole Gaudet, 43, Woodstock, Vermont;*
astrologer, CompleteAstrologer.com

Government Worker,
United States Department of Agriculture

TAYLOR COLLINS, 57, DOVER, DELAWARE

She's a farm loan specialist—"One of those horrible bureaucratic jobs,"
is how she puts it. "I'm the liquidator, primarily. When a farmer defaults
on his loan, I help get the government money's back, after making sure
the farmer has exhausted all his rights. Basically, my job is the reason
Willie Nelson started Farm Aid." A creative spirit and artist, she planned
to only work until her midforties, but then her husband got multiple sclerosis. "After John got sick, I was kind of forced to be the breadwinner;
I needed benefits. It's tough being creative and being stuck."

6:30 a.m. Oh, crap! Why did I turn the alarm off? A quick flip
of the remote to check the weather forecast. The local broadcaster
finishes a news story about a murdered family: a missing mother,
a hanging father, and four children found dead in their beds. I
only wanted to know if it's going to be forty or sixty-five degrees,
spring weather being so unpredictable. Now all day I will ponder what beasts live among us under the guise of delivery men,
day traders, postal workers, students . . .

I'm really late now! I didn't shower, but I blow-dried my dry
hair and it's poufy enough to pass for clean.

7:15 a.m. Drop grandson off at the sitter; I have guardianship of him.
Long story, but suffice it to say that my son and daughter-in-law
are not in the marriage made in heaven. I think Aldous Huxley was
right when he said that earth is probably another planet's hell. And
just why is he crying? He's started doing this recently and it's driving me crazy. Doesn't he know that he was supposed to be terrible

at two, not three? I don't know a thing about raising a child these days. Time-outs and self-esteem and keeping them entertained? Things are so different now than when I had kids.

Crap, I forgot my aspirin. I'm always forgetting to take that pill. The five others—no problem. But no time for that now. First thing this morning, I'm off to a breakfast for an advisory board meeting at Delaware Tech Community College. I don't know why I agree to serve on so many things.

7:45 a.m. Sat beside Edna. I like her. She became a nurse a couple of years ago at age sixty. That's the great thing about community colleges; the people here are real. Edna is on the nursing advisory board, I'm on the business technology board. Progress is great. My degree in executive secretarial dropped from the curriculum about the same time disco died. Things just aren't the same without either of them.

Today the college president, George, asked us here to help with capital improvements for the school by supporting a real estate tax proposal (sixteen dollars per year for each household in the state). This will help the college meet the educational demands for all the health-related and other essential technologies that need to be offered, such as troopers, teachers, paramedics, etc. Money and taxes, is there anywhere on the planet that this subject doesn't come up? The stock market cost me plenty this month. And gas—over $2.50 again.

9:00 a.m. Chat with Dr. George after the meeting and assure him I'll advocate for the tax increase. It's critical that we get students trained in the health field, as I know I need their services more all the time now. I opted for long-term health care a while ago, and there had better be someone in a nursing home somewhere trained to take care of me in my old age. Next to cloning arteries for heart bypass, I can think of no better utilization of tax dollars. Cloning would have helped with my husband's MS, but today it's a local—not just personal—issue. So I will write to the governor and tackle the state and local representatives, too, asking them to support the tax increase.

Popularity—glad I got over that in college.

9:15 a.m. Arrive at work to an architecturally challenged structure, the contractor's take on the southwestern look for Dover. Thanks to 9/11, no unfurled U.S. flag these days on our building. My office on the second floor (I actually have an office with a door and a full-windowed wall, which is kudos for any bureaucrat) belies the fact that a government worker lurks here. It's filled with an eclectic mix of colorful paintings, things I collect, and eBay forays run amuck: the Taos rock that Natalie Goldberg touched; my friend Anna's dancing bovine figurine, photos of my late husband, John; the ticket (almost ringside, thanks to Lou DiBella) to Tyson's last fight in D.C. Just the right amount of scattered kitsch. If I didn't know better, I'd think this office was a happy place to be.

My desk is piled with unrelenting paperwork and the same old foreclosures that I've been working on for decades now. The laws covering our servicing and liquidation process involve many appeals and complicated checkpoints. Most of my duties involve reviewing case files to insure no discrepancies exist before proceeding to liquidation, as the last place you want to find out something was skipped is in court. The process is stressful enough for all parties involved, so when a case reaches my level, I give it a thorough, impartial review before I'd recommend it for liquidation. I have to sleep at night, you know.

The phone message light is on and there are e-mails. My fifth supervisor in the past six years (which speaks volumes about how high morale is under the current administration) drives me to distraction. She is more paranoid than I am, and her mood swings make my past PMS hormonal shifts seem like Zen moments. Micromanagement here now borders on an art form, and incessant multitasking spins even mundane minutiae into intense crisis mode. I'm two years or less to retirement—not that I'm counting.

10:00 a.m. Equal Employment Opportunity counselor calls and wants to know if I signed my settlement agreement yet. Months ago, I filed an age discrimination complaint. The whole process has been time-consuming and draining, as I'm trying to interpret tons of unfamiliar regulations. It's risky on multilevels, since I have heart issues and certainly didn't need the extra stress. But when you're mad as hell and decide not to take it anymore, you do what you need to do.

The agreement that's being presented indicates that management and I have reached an amicable agreement and that, in essence, we can go back to the playground and play nice. I told the EEO counselor that I will get back to him, after I have a chance to speak with my attorney. Over the years I have learned much about employee rights and management's responsibilities, and that having a federal job is no guarantee that you won't have to fight just as hard as anyone else if you feel you've been wronged.

10:30 a.m. The government loves regulations. I have to write them, read them, learn them, rewrite, reread, relearn, and ultimately file them. Plus, we have a form for everything. If I jumped out this office window, someone would be filling out paperwork for years and filing it in perpetuity. I remember when Phil, a co-worker, had an accident. It's a good thing he lived because I just don't know who would have done his paperwork.

Call hairdresser to change my appointment, as I forgot about the arts council meeting this afternoon. I try never to miss hair appointments since my heart surgery, having missed an appointment a week prior to that. A million tubes protruding out of me did not cause nearly as much concern as my stringy locks.

Ran into Sally, who works for a sister government agency. She, like everyone else around here, is rushing off somewhere. I am trying to fix the copier-from-hell, which is jammed, but isn't half as difficult to figure out as the mail meter. Having no support staff means I get to do all levels of jobs, all the time. Over my twenty-eight years as a bureaucrat, I have climbed up through the ranks from GS-3 clerical to GS-12 professional, yet I'm still filing. Sad that support positions went out with IBM Selectrics. What was management thinking?

Lunch Salad. Okay. I lied. I had Boston Market but if my thirty-three-year-old daughter, Kelly, ever asked, I would swear it was salad. Kelly helps out with her nephew—we utilize the "it takes a village" approach to our situation—which helps us all survive.

She wants me to live to be a hundred so she won't have to become a premature mother.

I read *The Writer's Almanac* poem for the day, and also my words for the day: "corrigendum" from Merriam-Webster; "ratiocination" from Word of the Day, "outre-mer" from OED, and "roborant" from *Doctor Dictionary*. In my battle to ward off Alzheimer's, I try to memorize four words daily.

12:30 p.m. The 1940G environmental regulation that I need to check starts on page 21 and concludes several unrelated subparts later on page 24. What I needed to know could have been summarized in one sentence. In 1995, the USDA streamlined from about fifty agencies to thirty-six. Ever since then, it has been promising that streamlined regulations will be "coming out soon." I am a folk artist and an aspiring poet. I am first vice president of the National League of American Pen Women. I don't want to sound dramatic here but, "Woe is me!"

2:00 p.m. I called my family attorney to have him look at the settlement agreement. I'm basically pursuing the action in a pro se (self-representing role), but won't sign anything legally binding unless my attorney says okay. He can see me Thursday at ten. It's only money, right?

3:30 p.m. Leave early for arts council meeting. Three hours of leave today for civic meetings. No wonder I don't have any annual leave left. The meeting proves productive. When I'm not working my thrilling job, not raising a grandchild, and not almost croaking from my heart condition, I try to paint and sell my limited-edition prints. Art and its advocacy rank high in my life and, when I retire, I will be able to create on a daily basis.

6:15 p.m. Leave meeting early. (You know you're overbooked when you leave work early to go to a meeting that you also leave early from.) Forgot that I have to pick up my grandson. As I arrive at the sitter, he's crying and doesn't want to leave. What's he crying about now? Isn't this where we left off this morning?

7:45 p.m. Grandson recites his prayers, "Now I may me round to seep . . . " Close enough. Amen! Two seconds later he's asleep. No nap today. No bath. Which reminds me—the dryer needs to be unloaded so I can put in last night's wet laundry.

9:30 p.m. eHarmony communicates that another match is found. That makes ten so far this week. There's Paul, Jeffrey, John, Larry, another Larry, earl with a little *e*, and Samuel. Samuel? Would a grown man actually go by the name of Samuel these days? What was I drinking the night I signed up for a year's subscription to this? Why would I even consider dating after thirty-five years of marriage? Widowhood. How I despise that word.

I guess it was the chill of nearing retirement that possessed me. I like money. And when I'm retired I won't have much extra unless I paint my arthritic fingers to the bone. So eHarmony seemed like a good idea at the time. What a bizarre way to find a date, but some swear by it. Anything would be better than my friend Juanda's date— dinner and Lowe's. Not dinner and dancing, not dinner and a movie, but dinner and the home improvement store!

So what do these matches from cyberspace ply me with? Hmm. John from OC is way too close to his mother. One of the Larrys spends way to much time hiking with his son's friends. But Jeffrey has carpentry skills. Why is that so tempting in a man now? Funny how priorities change as sixty approaches. Come to think of it, dinner and Home Depot might not be a bad idea.

On March 27, 2007

32 percent of day diarists reported they would quit their job if they won the lottery.

Fashion Designer

ANGEL CHANG, 29, NEW YORK, NEW YORK

She's teching up the fashion industry with her own line of women's wear in future fabrics with gizmo accents. Heat-sensitive dresses that change from orange to yellow. Vinyl raincoats with LED lights. Five-layered skirts with 3-D images and cotton embossed jackets with iPod controls. "My mission is to create pieces that facilitate the lifestyles of young contemporary women. We're working more, traveling more, always chatting on our cell phones, and checking e-mail. Clothes should reflect these changes. They should be a tool for the wearer, and fun to wear at the same time."

12:15 a.m. I wake up when my cell phone beeps. A friend sent me a text message for a party this Friday. Why are people calling me so late? I have a voice mail waiting, too. It's my mother, congratulating me on being selected for this year's *PAPER Magazine*'s "Beautiful People" issue that just hit newsstands. The magazine featured me, along with fifty other actors, designers, models, and other quirky up-and-comers. The profile they wrote on me lists all the things I've done in the last ten years and called me a "workaholic." Just reading it made me feel like I should go on a vacation.

I had taken a nap earlier while working on an essay for the PhD fashion studies program at Stockholm University. The deadline for admission is coming up. My father's dream is for me to get a PhD, just like him. But how can I continue my fashion business and be a grad student? My dream is to have my own fashion line and write books about the research underlying each collection. Maybe the PhD will help me write a book . . .

fashion designer

Still tired. Nothing's cozier than my big cashmere blanket I received as a perk during my days at Donna Karan Collection as a design assistant two years ago. Life was harder back then, but in a different way. My stress is more intense now because it permeates my entire life. I need to take better care of myself, work less, and lead a balanced life. That's hard for a New Yorker to fathom.

3:00 a.m. Wake up again and have missed a phone call from my boyfriend. He lives in Vienna, but is traveling on business right now in Brussels. It's not easy having a long-distance boyfriend, but New York is no place to find love. And in the fashion industry, I feel that work comes first and relationships come second. It's like how Anne Hathaway's character felt in *The Devil Wears Prada* when she's always got her boss calling, and she has to drop her own social activities for those of the company's. Her boyfriend says she has a choice, but the truth is, she really doesn't if she wants to keep pace with the rest of the people in the industry.

4:00 a.m. I can't sleep because I'm in a coughing fit. It also doesn't help that I'm thinking of all the things I have to do. Most importantly, find a studio to move into this weekend. My application for my preferred space in Tribeca didn't go through; my financials weren't strong enough because I'm a start-up company. I feel like it's only in New York where you have to give your financial statements, tax returns, and pay stubs before being able to rent a space. If I were a normal person, I'd have the sense to live out in the suburbs where life is easier. My parents keep trying to lure me back to Indiana, but I'd rather die of stress than boredom.

9:15 a.m. UPS delivery man comes. Since I'm moving out of my studio, I told the fabric mills to send fabric references to my home. He apologizes for waking me up. I give him a grunt. Why is it that whenever some important event comes along, something always goes wrong. Tonight I have to attend *PAPER*'s launch party for the "Beautiful People" issue, but I'm sick and not in much of a partying mood.

water cooler diaries

10:30 a.m. I brought my laptop home with me, so I'm working in my pajamas in my living room. I've got on an Alexander McQueen McQ gray tank top and brown Columbia University shorts—the same things I would've worn in college. In many ways, I feel like I've reverted back to those student days, living on a shoestring budget, still having a roommate. She's in Connecticut right now on a business trip so I have space to work at home alone.

I book appointments to view studio spaces. Then I order a FreshDirect delivery. With a click of the button online, I can have all the ingredients of a recipe delivered to me the next day. I also have a cookbook now that has made learning how to cook so easy, *Staff Meals from Chanterelle*. Tonight, I'm inviting my friend Sunny over for Mussels à la Provençale.

12:20 p.m. I'm developing fabrics and techniques for my next collection and am trying to find a place in the city that does machine embroidery. I want to stitch quotes into hidden areas of clothes so that they're only readable by the wearer. If I embroider them on ribbon, I can pair them with the waterproof shiny silk taffetas, jacquard chiffons, and stretch organza I'm ordering for the next season.

This next season will be inspired by female spies from the last century: the famous ones (Josephine Baker, Marlene Dietrich); the unknown ones (Limping Lady, Doll Woman); and those in the news today (Valerie Plame). These women all have an innate sense of adventure. They are independent, well traveled, educated, and multilingual. They embody the best assets of my ideal customer, and, funny enough, many graduated from my alma mater, Barnard College.

I'll be using my heat-sensitive color-changing prints in the way one would use disappearing ink. I could hide blueprints, maps, or important messages on the clothes of the wearer. (That's what Josephine Baker did.) There are so many options. It's both exciting and overwhelming!

1:10 p.m. I finally get dressed while simultaneously cleaning my apartment and eating some yogurt topped with flaxseed. I take

fashion designer

a multivitamin, too. I would normally pick up something at the deli, but this week I'm trying to balance my life. I'm wearing a tan, long-sleeved polo dress in a cotton velvet fabric. My friends at United Bamboo designed it. I've had it for five years because it's just so cozy to wear. I hope I design clothes that make people feel the same way.

I run to the fish store down the street to buy mussels for tonight but am tragically disappointed. The business has closed down. I keep seeing how hard it is to maintain a business, and it only gets me down. My showroom just informed me that another one of their fashion designers, Naum, is closing their line.

I ride my bike through SoHo to my studio to pick up some images for my appointment with the embroidery company, then hop on the subway to my next meeting.

2:30 p.m. I'm at Greg Mills Ltd., my public relations and sales showroom on West 39th, to go over my Fall 2007 collection with Greg. The collection, which is on display now in the showroom, was inspired by old-world travel mixed with communist military colors. There are lots of pleated georgette dresses, cotton velveteen tailored looks, and hand-beaded fighter jet waistbands. There are also jackets with hand-embroidered iPod control buttons so the wearer can listen to her music without having to take her iPod out of her pocket when changing tracks or volume.

Greg introduces me to Jenny Feldman, an editor from *Elle*. She mentions how much she likes the heat-sensitive disappearing camouflage print. The print disappears on the areas touching the wearer, so the subtle effect is quite beautiful. We show her the fur purses and cuffs that are imbedded with scents of different nineteenth-century vacation destinations. (It was a collaboration with Joel Leonard, a perfumer out in Copenhagen.) Jenny says the line looks great, but I'm always skeptical. When I look at my collection, all I see are the faults—the stitching, the fabric choices, the design . . . So much in design has to be compromised because of price and timing.

Greg and I meet for a postmarket follow-up, to go over the store sales. While I received plenty of press for the fall collection, sales were disappointing. Stores are more conservative and it's difficult for a new designer to sell in the first season, so I'm not shocked by the news. Velvet's hard to sell (who knew?). The line was too small (I needed to offer stores more styles). And grasping the tech element was challenging for some.

Fortunately, we will be selling in Kirna Zabête, one of my dream stores. They sell the best global trend-setting luxury brands such as Balenciaga, Chloé, and Gaultier, so they are definitely a great place to start. My pricing is in line with these companies ($500–$2,500 per item), and the target customer is the same as well.

Greg and I schedule a meeting next week to merchandise the Spring 2008 season, and to figure out styles and fabrications that the stores would like to see. They want a larger line from me, so this season I'll be aiming for twenty looks—about forty individual styles of garments. It's twice as much work, so I will have to get more financing and more people on my team this summer.

Producing in the factories in New York is expensive, so eventually I will have to look into manufacturing overseas. This is a daunting and annoying roadblock. I need an angel investor, but I don't know how to find any that would be interested in a fashion start-up like mine. So far, the collection has been financed through loans from family and industry sponsorships. The Italian wine company Ecco Domani awarded me $25,000 (through their Fashion Foundation) for my second season, so that was a tremendous help. Now, of course, the challenge is to do an even better third season in September. Expectations grow with each presentation. You're only as good as your last season.

3:30 p.m. I went to see another office space on 38th Street, between Eighth and Ninth avenues. It looked nice and I took some pictures. Fifteen hundred dollars per month for three hundred usable square feet, and I would share it with a studio mate. It's in the Garment District so it's close to all the trim and fabric stores. The problem with the Garment District is that it's noisy, polluted, and gross guys are always making lewd comments to women on the street. It's also too far away to ride my bike, so that would mean having to take the gross subway every day. It's an option, in any case.

4:05 p.m. I take the subway to Canal Street and pick up my bike. Getting around the city takes so much energy; a bike alleviates most of the pain and reminds me of the fun summer days of riding along the canals when I was living in Amsterdam, working at Viktor & Rolf. It also makes me feel like a kid. Random guys on the street sometimes try to pick me up and ask if I'm a student. Those jerks.

I'm down at 11 Beach Street in Tribeca checking out another studio space. The space is $700 a month, has no windows, low ceilings, and is the size of any normal home's walk-in closet. No thanks. My cutting table won't even fit in here. Why does New York have to be so expensive?!

4:25 p.m. I ride my bike home and pick up a baguette at the bakery on the way. SoHo has turned into an outdoor shopping mall, but my street still maintains a cozy neighborhood feel. And I love my apartment, even though it's so tiny and my bedroom is the size of my full-size bed. I eat lunch, vegetable soup I'd made the day before.

5:00 p.m. I ride my bike down to another space in Tribeca at Warren and West Broadway. The place looks dirty and is a share with three other photographers. No again.

5:30 p.m. I'm at my studio on 247 Centre Street—an all-white, industrial loft-like space with old wooden floors. The building used to be the home of A Tribe Called Quest and other hip-hop recording studios so it's got good creative energy. Right now, I share the space with two other artists, one of whom is Tom Sachs, whose DIY-looking work I really admire. Tom has ten assistants, mainly young art students who play loud music, so it's hard for me to concentrate.

I had cleaned my studio for my meeting with *Vogue* last week; they interviewed me for a story on future fabrics. But of course the place is a mess again with sketches, papers, and fabric all over the table. My dress forms and industrial Juki sewing machine are in a corner, taking a break right now after heavy use right before the show. It seems impossible to keep a design studio tidy.

My intern, Crystal, a student at my alma mater, is on the computer compiling bios of famous female spies. There is another person waiting for me, an NYU sophomore. She wants to intern this summer. Unpaid interns receiving school credit are the backbone of so many young fashion companies. Most companies at the designer level don't make much money, although they promote this image that they are superluxe. Fashion is all about selling a fantasy image. It amazes me that these college students have heard of me and want to work for me. She's good with computer graphics and Web sites, so she's hired!

6:10 p.m. Crystal is printing out a bunch of images I downloaded of Zandra Rhodes and Ossie Clark dresses. I want to silkscreen textiles the way that Zandra Rhodes did. Her stuff from the seventies was phenomenal. Crystal mentioned that she's unfamiliar with the names of fashion designers. Feeling obligated to teach her, I write up a long list of twentieth century designers that she should read up on: Coco Chanel, Cristóbal Balenciaga, Christian Dior, Lanvin, Comme des Garçons, Junya Watanabe, Hussein Chalayan, Nicolas Ghesquiere, Hedi Slimane . . . They are all, for various reasons, some of my favorite visionaries in the industry.

6:35 p.m. I ride my bike to the grocery store to buy mussels and other ingredients for tonight.

7:10 p.m. Sunny and I are getting ready for the Beautiful People party at Hiro at the Maritime Hotel. I'm walking around the apartment in a black unitard I bought from American Apparel down the street. It's amazing how convenient and simple it is to wear. As a designer, I take note.

Over it, I slip on my pleated white silk chiffon tunic that I designed for my first season. In the last two months, I've worn it to my Ecco Domani Fashion Foundation awards after-party, to the Grammy Awards in L.A. (where my classical pianist sister just won a Grammy), and to a fashion designer after-party at the SoHo Grand Hotel, where a trend-spotter shot my picture for the Web site Facehunter.blogspot.com. It's become a signature item of the line, and it's also the only sample that's big enough to fit me. (I'm normally a size six, inconveniently just one size up from the conventional sample size four.)

With no time now to make dinner, we agree to make the mussels and fries after the party.

8:30 p.m. In the cab to Hiro, I tell Sunny how my showroom meeting went this afternoon and how the collection didn't sell as hoped to large department stores. I also tell her I was invited to lecture at the Avantex Symposium in Frankfurt, Germany, in June. It is the largest trade fair for technical fabrics. They want to hear me tell them how to take a fashion/tech prototype to market. What am I supposed to tell them? How challenging it is to sell an innovative idea? Those companies (Philips, Gore, Schoeller Textil) are pouring millions into this field of wearable technology with conductive materials and wicking fabric. The last thing they want to hear is that their products won't work.

8:40 p.m. At Hiro, I say my first name at the door. They recognize me and let me in immediately, without looking at the list. It's weird having people you don't know recognize you. In the last six months since I launched my collection, I'll sometimes hear people whisper, "Angel Chang is here." For so long, I'd only heard discouragement from others. All I could do was follow my gut and pursue my dream. If people hated it, I wouldn't continue, but they loved it so here I am.

9:00 p.m. It's a strange feeling having a company throw a party in your honor and have your picture show up on a big screen. The same thing happened two months ago at the Ecco Domani Fashion Foundation after-party. How did I get so lucky? Does that mean I'm doing something right?

I see others at the party: Ladyfag, the female that looks like a drag queen; Fancy Nancy, who has her funny TV show; Carol Lee, the creative director who wrote my profile for the magazine; a male model friend of a friend who I last saw working as a waiter at Indochine . . . And I meet a guy in head-to-toe Thom Browne. I wrote a profile on the menswear designer last year for *Vogue Hommes*, so I chat with his assistant, Hans. He said his boss won't let him go out to any public function wearing any other label. It seems that everyone is working and networking tonight.

I also meet some guys from Evisu, the high-end Japanese denim line. There's their marketing guy, Chad, and their CEO, Nick. They work a few blocks away from my apartment, so I convince Chad to do breakfast tomorrow at Balthazar. I love waking up early, although it's extremely difficult for me. But if you're going to do it, you might as well reward yourself and go somewhere nice. Chad's convinced that it won't happen. I tell him to call me when he wakes up. Good, a neighborhood breakfast buddy!

10:15 p.m. Back in my apartment, Sunny cooks the mussels and we open up a bottle of chardonnay. Her boyfriend comes over and we watch season one of *Alias* that I Netflixed for my research. I love all the different costumes and wired-up devices the heroine, Sidney Bristow, carries with her on her missions. I'm trying to find inspiration for a piece in my next collection, an anorak that forecasts the weather. With global warming, we can never predict the weather on our own these days. This coat is something that Sidney would've worn.

Midnight I go to bed wondering again why I'm still so unhappy. Here I am, living the dream of having my own fashion label. After all the years of training and working with amazing people and going to fabulous parties, all it has done is raise my expectations.

I feel really jaded now, and it's hard to snap out of it. Those exciting events and interesting people have become part of my ordinary day, so the luster has faded.

I am doing exactly what I've always wanted to do, but I'd always envisioned the positive rewards and overlooked the negative challenges. How am I going to finance the next collection? How am I going to pay my rent? Where am I going to move my studio? How am I going to coordinate production? What if the collection doesn't sell? Pursuing the dream was easy; the difficult part is learning how to live it.

Wired

8:00 p.m. More e-mail. I'm always on e-mail. I once read a book about getting organized. It said you're supposed to categorize e-mail into those that can and should be responded to quickly, and those that are low priority and can be filed and answered later. That is totally ridiculous, as it requires way too much brain power that I cannot spare. Geez, who has time to analyze their e-mails? I also don't get why everyone is so in love with their labeling machines. That was also a harebrained recommendation in that book. I think I just need another assistant who can answer e-mail and do this stuff for me. I grab my calculator and try to figure out how much said assistant would cost.
—*Phoebe Eng, 44, New York, New York; director, Creative Counsel*

•

All in a Day's Work

7:00 a.m. Now I'm working on a book review. Don't ask. I've just had a potentially PMS-induced disagreement with some editors on the last review, which I'm hoping comes out okay. I don't have much to say about this new book except that I liked it, it's fun, read it. I'm afraid seven words does not a book review make.

—*Nancy Fontaine, 45, West Lebanon, New Hampshire; librarian*

8:00 a.m. I try on the two sleeveless blouses. Both look bad. I look bad. What can I say? I'm in my fifties and my looks are shot. I gave myself a year to get over this two years ago. I used to go into shock when I looked in the mirror. I'd call my friends. "Emergency! Emergency! I look hideous." Now I've moved on. Also, I'm having some success in NYC playing a sad quirky mother of a soldier missing in Iraq. It's a new play in development. We've done it in a couple different venues, and people love my performance. I think it's partly because I don't try to look good. I just put it out and the character slowly unravels like a Greek protagonist, with all the accompanying horror and pathos.

—*Faith Catlin, 57, Lyme, New Hampshire; actor, theatrical director*

I just responded to an e-mail about rabies. A woman thought that a relative might have rabies because of a dog bite five years ago, because the person now refused to bathe. Supposedly, his doctor did a test and diagnosed rabies and then put him on some type of pill. This poor woman was thinking that the relative needed to be confined and was obviously very concerned about his health. This woman had more misinformation about a disease than I have seen in a long time. She had stated

fashion designer

that she had gotten much of it off the Web. Amazing how much crap there is out there in cyberspace.

—Patricia Quinlisk, 52, Des Moines, Iowa;
epidemiologist/medical director, Iowa Department of Public Health

2:45 p.m. Back from store. I have two copies of a woman's magazine under my arm. There's a full-page article on my book. My kids and husband give me high fives. They've been very supportive of the book, cheering me on the whole way. However, my oldest son and husband seem equally entranced by J.Lo on the cover in a skimpy pink dress cut down to there. My eleven-year-old only wants to know if I remembered the Pop-Tarts.

—Anita Bruzzese, 48, Columbia, Missouri; author, 45 Things You Do
That Drive Your Boss Crazy . . . and How to Avoid Them

6:00 p.m. Eat dinner from the Crock-Pot while I feed my mother, who has advanced Alzheimer's. One small bite at a time, I have to feed her and she eats very slowly. She has to drink through a straw, and sometimes has difficulty figuring out how to do that. She can only eat soft foods. My sister escapes to a used bookstore to get a break. She has been with my mom all day while I am at work. We have a caregiver who comes in three afternoons a week, but other than that my sister and I trade off doing all the chores. The work is too intimate and disgusting to ask my teenage boys to do much to help. During dinner my mom asks me, "Who are you?" Most of the time she knows I'm family, but couldn't tell you my name or our relationship. Tonight she doesn't even know that.

—Karen Grove, 57, University Place, Washington; foster care social worker

Used Bookstore Owner

VALERIE STADICK, 47, MINOT, NORTH DAKOTA

A year ago, she left her $27,000-a-year job at a local nonprofit to open up her own bookstore. For a former food stamp recipient and a recent "older-than-average" college graduate, taking this risk was huge. Now, no more full-time benefits and comp time, and plenty of financial worries. "Sometimes the reasons for having my own store get muddled with the overdue invoices and small bank deposits." On the other hand, her degree is in English and she fits the cliché—a lover of books. "So can people ever be a failure if they are doing what they love?"

8:00 a.m. I drop my thirteen-year-old son, Brian, off at school, then my daughter, Jessi, granddaughter, Emma, and I go to Wal-Mart to buy supplies for my bookstore's one-year anniversary. Should I admit to shopping at this evil store? I bought cups, plates, and forks for this afternoon. At least I bought my cake local—a full sheet with coconut frosting and real coconut cream in the batter. I'm excited about this cake.

I also dropped off three business deposits at the bank. I wasn't too embarrassed this time. It's the deposits for my twenty-dollar days that make me want to take the drive-through at the bank late at night with my lights off. Do the tellers share this information with the world? At least those kinds of deposits are getting fewer and farther between. They still hurt, though.

9:30 a.m. My store is in downtown Minot. Whenever I walk down this street lined with historic brick buildings, I get that at-home feeling. Some say that the downtowns are dying, but I can't see the demise of this one. I see new building. Renovations. I see artists in basements and children on bicycles and families out for strolls. I don't see the empty store fronts with "For rent" signs and vacancies. Or maybe I see them as an opportunity for change, to meet a new neighbor or business owner. Maybe I have to think this way some days to keep me going.

My key sticks in the old, glass door when I unlock it. After I vacuumed (still the same borrowed vacuum; I was hoping to afford an Oreck by now), I went to open the store at ten. Just like any other day, I suppose. But I could feel it coming. I don't cry easily, but it just kind of gushed out of me. I went in the back room for a second and composed myself. One year ago today I also felt that gush, holding back tears as the Chamber of Commerce cut the ribbon and took a picture. My first-day sales were $172.98. I felt pretty good about it, too. The next-day sales were $68.

I am thinking about my daughter, Jessi, who has a doctor's appointment today at ten thirty for her seven-month pregnancy check. She has bipolar disorder and has been averaging four hours of sleep a night for the last two weeks. She wakes up at one in the morning soaked in sweat. Is this normal? We all live together and I can't pretend that the stress of a new baby girl in the house won't cause problems. What I worry about most though are her moods and her ability (or inability) to handle them. Some days the lines I have to throw her when she needs them aren't very long.

I busy myself straightening up stuffed animals, wiping down the cash drawer area, and making the pot of coffee. I take a quick look at myself in the mirror hanging next to my New Age book section, and fix a few stray hairs that were clipped back hastily. I think briefly, again, about going all gray, as the roots seem to be winning the war with the blond.

11:30 a.m. I sent out 750 postcards to my three-day anniversary sale. Yesterday, I had a full house of used-book shoppers. Today, the sale is on new books, but the till has been silent all morning. I don't freak out like I did a year ago. I used to check the blinking "open" sign when business was slow, to make sure I had turned it on. Sometimes I would go as far as to check the doors to make sure that they were unlocked. I lost six thousand dollars the first year. Well, if you count the salary I didn't make, and the bills owed after I ordered books on credit that I was sure would sell and didn't, and the toys that I am paying for in monthly installments.

I can see my "Open" sign flashing in the store windows across the street. Today there are a dozen beautiful red roses on my table, draped and ready for the arrival of the sheet cake. My mother sent me the roses from California. Actually, she paid for them and my wonderful, supportive husband, Terry, hand delivered them. The smell mixes with that of the jute rugs and real wood floor, and old and new books. It smells like a Midwest spring—musty, a mix of the snow melting and mud, and the faint scent of rose.

12:36 p.m. I have customers now, and there are books on the counter creating small piles. *A Catcher in the Rye* sits atop *A Dakota Cowboy*, which sits on top of *History's Great Untold Stories*. A child, standing on tiptoes, lays *Go Dog Go* on another small pile. Several groups of people are mingling now. Springsteen is on the stereo singing, "I came for you, for you. I came for you." Certainly, I will have my first sale by 1:00 p.m.

1:26 p.m. An elderly lady (like I am young, or what?) is sitting on the couch perusing the health books. She has decided on one title already, a paperback copy of *Healthy Aging*, which she has left on a corner of the counter. It sits next to a copy of the book *I Hate Ann Coulter*. Another woman walks by and comments, "I just don't know why everyone hates Ann Coulter." I smile and say nothing. This is a lesson I learned from marrying a Conservative—never discuss politics with people who disagree with you.

I offer a young man who is new to the store a mini tour:
"Here are the best sellers.
"Here are the local authors.
"Here is the free coffee.
"Here is the big red leather couch.
"Here are the new fantasy books.
"Here are the used fantasy books.

used bookstore owner...

"What author? Oh, maybe one or two. Not that title though. How about this one?"

After an hour, the young man leaves with two used books and one new book tucked under his arm.

"I could spend all day in here," he tells me. I'm glad.

2:31 p.m. My till is now sixty dollars over what I sold a year ago today. Sometimes you hear about people killing themselves over failed businesses. I never used to understand that sort of thinking. It's just money. There are messages you send yourself when bills are stacking up, though. Cash doesn't come in. People walk through your store and look briefly, not touching, judging you, your decor, your selection, your empty smile behind the counter. And then they walk out empty-handed.

It is a very personal thing. Some days you are loved and some days you are rejected. There were times throughout that first year that I understood the shotgun-in-the-mouth mentality. Almost. You really put yourself out there when you open a business. It's not just a bookstore. This is me! Look! Love me! Please!

My daughter will be bringing the cake by in about an hour. Will there be enough? Too much? Which scenario is worse?

3:19 p.m. I talk to the father of my daughter's baby. He is concerned about some tests Jessi is having. Something to do with blood sugar levels. Her last pregnancy, there were many tests for Down syndrome that scared me. I try not to feed the worry. I tell him, "I'm sure everything will be fine."

4:00 p.m. Daughter arrived at 3:45 with no cake. "Chill out," she told me. "It's not like there's anyone in here. I need money for the cake."

"It's already paid for," I remind her. After she left, her doctor called the store. She left a number for Jessi to call her back.

4:30 p.m. I now have the cake, and a little activity going on. People mingling, laughing, eating, spilling coffee. My daughter returned her doctor's call. Possible gestational diabetes. I looked it up on the Internet and it sounds like the doctor might be telling her to do all the things I have been telling her to do for the last five years (watch her diet, exercise, get fresh air . . .).

There is a young man here who comes in twice a month. He buys children's books. I think he lives around the corner.

There are a lot of older people who live downtown.

There are a lot of people who live in the assisted living facilities and the housing for low-income people, and people with disabilities who can't work. They like coming here. They like having a place to sit when they can't stand for very long. They like that sometimes I see them coming and hold the door for them, and bring them coffee. Maybe it is just the simple process of placing a book in someone's hand that connects me to this community.

The cake is delicious. Light and white and coconut. It looks angelic and pure next to the red roses. Like love. Like Valentine's Day, only better.

6:00 p.m. Partial customer list: I had a small child who threw a temper tantrum; a man dressed quite nicely who dropped a piece of coconut cake on the floor in front of the register; and a favorite woman friend from my book club that I host. When I mentioned that I'm thinking of disbanding the club due to lack of interest, she exclaimed, "You can't possibly do that." There was also a gifted poet from my writing group who bought two books of poetry. And another regular, a local businessman who spends well and reads even better.

I think that the bills are covered for the month, except for my book wholesaler. But, hey, who needs books when you have a bookstore. The other bills are older—bills with promises to pay by such-and-such a date on them. I will pay the bills first that have the collectors calling, threatening to cut off my legs.

7:00 p.m. I think about my wonderful husband and the hot pizza waiting for me at home. Lock the doors. Turn off the blinking "Open" sign. Turn off Clapton. March in North Dakota smells like spring but looks like snow. Forecast says above-average temps.

The last hour was quite slow. "Layla" on the stereo with no one to hear. I have one-third of a cake left. I should make a sweep for cups and plates. It was a good day. Lots of smiles. Puppets on hands. Grown daughters trying to bite their mothers with dinosaur puppets. My last big sale was $77.77. I think that this is a good sign. I think that I can do this for at least one more year. I don't think, though, that coconut was the best choice for cakes— too messy.

On March 27, 2007 . . .

52 percent of day diarists worried about money.

●

Race Car Driver

SARAH FISHER, 26, INDIANAPOLIS, INDIANA

She's competed in six Indy 500s (the first at age nineteen), and been voted Most Popular Driver four times in two separate series (IndyCar and NASCAR). Her records still hold: the fastest woman ever to qualify for the Indy 500 with a speed of 229.439 miles per hour; and the best IndyCar finish by a woman (second). But success comes and goes. "In 2006, I was working for a marketing company and trying to find a way back to open-wheel racing after nearly two years away. I didn't have a job opportunity waiting on me, but I said I'd find one and I did."

7:30 a.m. I wake up in my motor coach, parked just steps away from the pit lane at the Sebring International Raceway in Florida. It's my second home during the racing season, homey and with all the necessities—microwave, stove, washer and dryer. With three slide-outs, the living area turns into a big enough room for Wrigley, my hundred-pound chocolate Lab, to play fetch. Andy, my fiancé (and crew chief) stays with me. He has already walked over to the hauler to start working. Now it's just me, Wrigs, and my dad, who is sleeping in the queen-size pullout in the front of the bus.

Waking up at seven thirty is like sleeping in for me. I'm used to meeting with my personal trainer at 7:00 a.m. back home in Indianapolis. We do cardio, and interval training to simulate yellows and stop-and-gos, plus mental preparation using flash cards during sprints, and working with reaction-timing balls. In races, I'm going 220 miles per hour for two and a half hours, so I need to be able to keep my heart rate up to compete and win. My attention to detail means my life, and my hand-eye coordination must be perfect.

7:35 a.m. If there was a Starbucks nearby, I'd be their first customer (I sure wish they were one of our sponsors). I need to wake Dad up for the day. He seems tired. My crew guys worked so late last night. I think everyone on the team is just about out of fuel. We've been on the road for almost a week and have another week to go before we jet back to Indy. Then we'll be home for a week and a half, and then it's off to Japan for the only IndyCar race out of the country. And the season has just begun.

Being on the road is a lifestyle for sure, but I like being mobile. And being busy is much better than being bored. I would rather be pulling my hair out wondering how I am going to make the next appointment than wondering if I actually have one.

7:40 a.m. I take Wrigs for a walk. Sebring has lots of grass, so he loves it. Dad will tidy up the coach. He's been really helpful this weekend with keeping it clean for us. One of the reasons I chose this particular model was for the two bathrooms. This way, my parents have their own space when they come. I drove for my dad in our own race cars until I was eighteen. We prepared them ourselves and traveled to an average of sixty races a year, just the two of us, which is why we're so close.

7:50 a.m. Got changed into a pair of jeans, at least for now. As soon as we start running on track, I'll have to put on my firesuit, which is really hot, especially with these temperatures. Coffee is ready (with creamer) and I'm out the door to pit lane.

Sebring Raceway is a 3.7-mile, paved road course. My team, Dreyer & Reinbold Racing, is here because I've never competed on a road course professionally. For the past couple of years, I've been trying my hand at NASCAR, but for 2007 I have returned to open-wheel racing. The last time I raced IndyCars, it was an all-oval schedule. Now those same cars race on road courses, and I will have a whole new technique of driving to study. Basically I'm a rookie again, no matter my background on ovals.

8:00 a.m. Reconnaissance laps around the track in a mid-size rental car. I'm with my teammate, 2004 Indianapolis 500 winner, Buddy Rice, and our team owners, Dennis Reinbold and Robbie Buhl. Today is only my second day on a road course in an IndyCar. I'm learning about the different corner entries, depending on the crown. Buddy really helps with this! Sebring is an especially challenging course because there are ten turns here, all different, so, accordingly, you approach each one with a different technique and racing line. Buddy has tested here several times, so he is very familiar with the surface and the different racing lines to try.

8:40 a.m. Head back out on the track in the rental car again, but this time Robbie is driving. He used to be a driving coach back in the day, and was even my teammate in 2002–2003 at Dreyer & Reinbold. Now he is one of the team owners. Both Dennis and Robbie have been very good to me, and believed in my ability to drive enough to put me in their race car.

9:00 a.m. Track goes green. I'm behind the wheel, all strapped in this little cockpit. We're waiting on the final setup before we can get my car (no more rental) out on the track. I race an open-wheel, single-seat, open-cockpit car that features a 3.5-liter, 32-valve dual overhead cam, normally aspirated V-8 engine optimized to run at 10,300 RPM, with an estimated 670 horsepower. We painted the outside red, white, and blue with an edgy design, and "AAMCO" splashed across the side pod. AAMCO is one of my sponsors, and I'm the new spokesperson in their "I Got a Guy" ad campaign. It was really fun shooting the commercials because it added a bit of sparkle to my girl-next-door image.

My teammate, Buddy, is testing here today, too. His car is ready and out he goes. Later on, other teams—Vision Racing, Rahal Letterman Racing, and A. J. Foyt Racing—will be joining us on the track.

9:30 a.m. Finally my car is ready. Green, green, green. I'm out of the pits and on track. We are running rain tires to start. The car feels really squirmy but this experience needs to happen. The goal right now isn't speed or to set new track records. It's a serious test environment to help me learn as much about the car as possible, and to gain technical skills. I'm anxious to get in these first laps.

I've never had that much fun in an IndyCar! It's amazing how nimble these cars are. The track was a lot flatter than I had expected. Now Andy's on my left with his hand out where he wants me to stop my left front tire. My engineer, Chris, is right in front of me, reviewing my lap times. Klint, my PR guy, is holding an umbrella to keep the sun from my face. Nick, on the right tire, is waiting for the car to go up on its air jacks so he can check for any cuts on the tire.

Gary, Ivan, Joe, Ron, and Kyle round out the rest of my pit crew, a team of athletes who must get me in and out of the pits in less than eight seconds during a race. They need to change four tires, put twenty-two gallons of ethanol in the car, and make whatever adjustments are necessary to help me move to the front of the field. It's all about speed and accuracy.

I forgot. Before I came into the pits, I was supposed to radio to the crew, "Pit in." There are so many new bits of information that I am trying to cram into my head, the small stuff doesn't seem as important. What I really feel after this run is exhilaration.

10:07 a.m. More laps. The focus is on my braking zones and how their improvement will dictate future car handling and speed. It takes confidence, as well as experience, to know a car's limits—how far you can get down the straightaway before braking into the corner.

"Pit this lap."

"Okay pit, pit." Robbie is on the radio telling me about the different corners, and what lines I could maybe take to put more power down—more speed—out of the corners over the bumps. If I follow the right line through the corners, meaning I'm in the right location on the track through the corner, I'll be able to accelerate faster coming out of it. We don't have traction control, so it's a challenge to just flat-foot these cars over the bumps.

10:15 a.m. Now the Vision Team's two cars are testing with us on the track. It's a beautiful day. The sun is out, the scenery around the course is all green. My future in-laws are with us for this

Florida racing swing, staying at the hotel that overlooks the race course. It must be nice to watch us run laps from the pool! I guess normal people would be in the water on a hot day like today.

10:18 a.m. I'm off track in turn five. When I was turning, I hit a bump and was still on the throttle at the same time, and spun around. It was just a rookie mistake on cold tires, a learning spin that will teach me more about the car. That's why I'm here, to learn about these issues before the race this weekend in St. Petersburg. Thankfully, nothing is damaged.

My crew is radioing to me but it's all static. "Radio check . . . Radio check . . . " Nothing. What is wrong with this stupid radio? Delphi Safety crew comes to tow me into the pits. Thank God, a new radio!

11:00 a.m. Pit in. Time to get out of the car for a bit. It helps to take a break. When you are competing on a road course, your body shifts an average of thirty times per lap, and endures g-forces up to three times the weight of gravity under braking. My elbows feel a bit bruised.

11:50 a.m. Back in the car. Pit out. Back on track. Seven, eight laps. I am gaining seconds on the lap. The break really helped me figure out some areas where I could do better. My tires are shot. They have too many laps on them and don't have as good a grip anymore. "Pit in."

12:00 p.m. Barbecue for lunch. It isn't my favorite food for training, but I can't eat a lot anyway. Nerves can't stand intake!

Back in the rental car for more laps with Robbie. I tell him where I'm at on the track on entry and exit, and when I'm putting power down and how. Andy's little brother, Kyle, is in the backseat. He's into karting at home, so it's great experience for him to know how we go over these tracks in the big cars. It's neat having him ride along.

I also meet with my engineer, Chris. We talk about what improvements I can make in the car. Mostly just the braking zones and the center roll speeds, adjustments that will come with time and more experience on a road course. Sebring is just a one-day test, so I won't be able to digest this info over night, then come back and apply it here. There just isn't time.

1:00 p.m. I'm waiting on car changes to be finished. New tires, gearbox, etc. All the teams in the IndyCar Series run a Honda engine. The Honda guy (we all get assigned a Honda engineer to work with us each weekend and during tests) mentions how well I'm doing, and to keep my head up. I must be doing okay if Honda thinks so. Little bits = big bits = more speed. Less time. I am learning at a good rate. We are getting faster, which will be a good springboard going into this weekend's race.

1:43 p.m. I am all belted in, helmet on, ready to go. Another radio check. The car is not accepting the setup so we can get back on track. It's an electronic problem that takes about a half hour to solve. I wish I had a Starbucks. I am so comfortable I fall in and out of sleep while waiting in the car.

2:06 p.m. Finally back on the track. I feel better getting to power. Car is the same though, handling wise. This road course stuff is challenging for the first time, but I have some really good coaches. Wallah! Seconds are coming off my times!

2:16 p.m. Pit lane. I'm continuing to work down the line, trying to perfect the improvements Robbie and I talked about over lunch. The tires are wishy-washy. I don't feel stuck anywhere on the track. Minor changes. Back on track.

2:27 p.m. Pit lane. Where's my water bottle? Red Gatorade keeps me hydrated while on track. In races, I lose four to seven pounds, and need to rehydrate to do it again by the next weekend. Still just logging laps. Back on track.

3:11 p.m. My engineer says, "Pit this lap." I need some time to sit and think. I am trying really hard, but it's hard to think in the car going two hundred miles per hour. At this point, I think I've learned almost as much as my brain can capture for the day. Everyone knows you learn more if you don't try to learn it all at once.

"Kinko, pit in," I say.

3:30 p.m. Back on track for a while. Long, long day. My neck is the only muscle that is achy. It takes getting into the car to really tell what muscles you need to train. I didn't know that road courses took this much muscle effort from the neck!

6:00 p.m. I am hanging out with the team while they load up the car and all our equipment onto the transporter. It ends up weighing about seventy-nine thousand pounds (legal limit is eighty thousand pounds). Everyone is really happy with my performance. For our second day in one of these cars, on one of the tougher road courses, they all agree that we had a successful day because we learned a lot.

Wrigley and I go for a walk. The guys really like Wrigs. It's amazing what dogs do for your mental health.

7:00 p.m. Andy is done loading with the team. He's tired and wants to just hang at the bus and make sandwiches. He always wants to do that. I love to go out to dinner and leave the track behind for a bit. Dad and I talk him into grilling out, if we cook. We are all by ourselves in the bus in the middle of the track, but it is nice and peaceful.

8:00 p.m. Dinner is over. They had steak and I had chicken with some mac and cheese and veggies. Clean-up looks like a chore, but I am lucky tonight. Normally I race all day, then cook, then clean, but right now Dad is doing it all. He sees how much Andy and I are doing and wants to help out. Life on the road looks glamorous, but it is really a lot of work.

9:30 p.m. We all watch TV and let the day go by. It's like ripping a tear off my helmet. Then to bed. Andy and I are so tired. It looks like tomorrow will be a day off for us, but with racing you never know. I don't expect anything, that way my feelings don't get hurt if plans change. I put a *Friends* episode in our DVD player. It's our favorite show and we watch it every night.

There is a ringing noise outside from some factory that is next to the track, but in a few minutes we won't even know it.

Doggone It

5:02 p.m. Someone brought their two young kids into the building and they follow Dave's dog, Dally, into my office. Dally hides under my desk, which is fine. I don't mind the dog, but I shoo the kids out and shut my door. We can bring dogs to the office, but this isn't a children's daycare.

—*Debra Nickelson, 49, Phoenix, Arizona;*
marketing manager and veterinarian

•

175 Table Games, 2,600 Slots, and 22 Poker Tables

11:00 a.m. Time for the weekly meeting with the executive director of surveillance, Ron Buono. We hold these meetings in my office, located just off the casino floor, to discuss any procedural issues that surveillance has observed regarding both players and dealers.

There are 1,200 surveillance cameras for a gaming floor the size of MGM Grand's, and every gaming table has camera coverage on it twenty-four hours a day. Any time a dealer makes a mistake, the surveillance operators write a report that goes to the appropriate vice president, general counsel, and/or chief operating officer. After twenty-nine years in the casino business, I still take this much too personally, and have the urge to defend my staff whenever these reports are sent.

Today we discuss Bob, a dealer who has been making several careless errors. The surveillance tapes show Bob's shuffle times are three times longer than the standard dealer's, and he is not following the procedure for the six-deck shuffle. All dealers are expected to shuffle six decks in about ninety seconds, and deal about four hundred hands per hour. The fact that Bob's shuffles take as long as three minutes, and he is dealing less than half the standard amount of hands per hour, is completely unacceptable.

Because Bob is a seasoned professional with twenty-plus years' experience, Ron and I assume he is just getting too comfortable or lazy. We decide to develop a retraining program for him to reiterate our house shuffle procedure. I will meet with Bob and his shift manager, and show them the surveillance tapes and reports. I hope this makes it easier for Bob to accept he's not up to the same standards as the other dealers, but it's still going to be difficult. I'm sure he thinks he's doing a good job, and most dealers typically feel picked on when I show them the surveillance. This is not part of my job that I enjoy, but we have to comply with State Gaming Control Board regulations.

Ron gathers up his tapes and reports and leaves my office. I do see the benefit in these meetings, but I often wonder if any employee anywhere could tolerate being watched for the entire eight hours they are working without feeling targeted. It also bothers me that surveillance reports are never written when my staff members do something correctly; only when the rare mistake is made. I know surveillance is a fact of our job—I can watch any game on a monitor while sitting in my office—but I also know I couldn't tolerate a camera above my desk.

—*Debra Nutton, 50, Henderson, Nevada;*
senior vice president, casino operations, MGM Grand Hotel

Administrative Assistant, Del Monte Foods

CONNIE MCNALLY, 39, PITTSBURGH, PENNSYLVANIA

She's "connie.com" to her co-workers, and a "top-tier performer," according to her last four annual reviews. What makes her a good assistant? "You have to be a take-charge kind of person. My job is to make everything run smoothly internally. VPs shouldn't be involved in administrative duties." She's been offered plenty of promotions but this position, and near family, is where she wants to stay. (She married her high school sweetheart twice—the second time by Elvis in Vegas.) The best part of her job? "Everything."

7:55 a.m. The drive into work wasn't too bad this morning, but last night I woke with a toothache and now my tooth is killing me. I pull into the Del Monte parking lot at our old facilities on River Avenue (the old H.J. Heinz plant) and wait for the shuttle. Del Monte provides free shuttle service to our new facilities on the North Shore, which we moved into a year ago February. A very nice perk. (You can park in the public lot at the new facility, but it costs five dollars a day, so why incur the expense?)

7:58 a.m. On the shuttle I run into Troy from field customer marketing. He asks me how jury duty was yesterday. "It was an interesting experience," I give him the details. The defendant was on trial for armed robbery at a bank in downtown Pittsburgh. He was pleading innocent. All the people in the jury pool had to answer questions: where we lived, and if we or anyone in our family ever worked in a bank. I know you should consider someone innocent until proven guilty, but I kept thinking to myself, *Security cameras can't be wrong.* By the end of the day, I was not selected as a juror.

8:01 a.m. The shuttle arrives at the beautiful new Del Monte Center. Troy and I take the elevator to the fifth floor and walk together to our desks. "I have something to tell you," he says. The crowd from the elevator is now gone. He says he resigned yesterday. What!!! He accepted an opportunity with Heinz in town. Wow. I wasn't expecting that. I've worked with him for four years now and we kind of moved side-by-side during corporate restructures. I am sad to see him go, but this is a good opportunity. He has a wife and four kids. You can never get upset at someone for advancing in his career.

8:05 a.m. My open cubicle is perfect, with a riverside window where I can glance up from my monitor and see the three rivers and Point State Park, a swimmer's lap from our building. The morning sun is shimmering off the waters. I place my laptop in my docking station and turn it on. (My computer takes forever to power up!) Today Tim, my VP, and the directors, Craig and Josh, are traveling to Chicago for a meeting. This is good. I will be able to get caught up from being out yesterday.

I glance around my desk to see what was dropped off while I was out. So far, not too bad. I gather the loose receipts for Don's expense report (a third director), organize and paper-clip them, and set them aside to do later. There is also a customer event invitation for me to convert to a PDF, and another signed expense report that needs the receipts affixed to it and audited. They both go in my "Will Do Soon" pile. I am a very organized person so I always immediately do the quick items to get them out of the way, then I create piles—the "Must Do Now" pile; the "Will Do Later" pile; the "Do After Everything Else Is Done" pile . . .

Now it's time to open Outlook. As my inbox synchronizes, I decide I can quickly convert the customer invitation to PDF with a push of a button on the network printer, so I run over to do it. As I am there, a senior manager approaches me. He needed a FedEx package to go out yesterday. An admin who assisted my team yesterday with a webcast advised him she would be happy to do this. But, the package didn't go out! Our preferred vendor is UPS and they stop at our building two times a day, but if you have something that needs to be sent via FedEx or DHL, you must call them for pickup. Surely this admin knows this. I told him I would take care of it.

While we are on the topic of yesterday, I ask him how the webcast went. He says it went well, except for a slide or two of my VP's quarterly sales figures. The numbers were all over the place when the file was uploaded to MSLive. I thought to myself, *Why wasn't the presentation checked after it was uploaded?* It isn't the responsibility of the senior managers, directors, and VP, but a quick task for the admin who was helping me. I am a little disappointed, but there was no way to be here for a webcast when I was summoned for jury duty.

Back to my desk, my voice mail light is on. It was a message from Tim, my VP. The US Airways flight to Chicago that he and my directors were on was canceled due to mechanical problems! Knowing they need to be in Chicago before lunch, my panic button goes off. I immediately call Teri in our travel department. A handful of people are already calling her from the airport. They were all on the flight that was canceled.

Luckily, Teri is able to secure a United flight for Tim and one of my directors that departs at 9:30 a.m. She is able to secure another flight for my second director on American. While she is scrambling, I call Tim back, but it appears he may not be able to make that early a flight. Traffic is heavy. So I contact travel again and Teri secures a second flight that departs closer to eleven, and one that departs around one. At this point, I now have three flights secured for my VP.

My voice-mail light is on again. This time it is Jim, a director from San Francisco who is also going to Chicago for the meeting. He is making changes to some slides. Since Gail, his admin, won't arrive in his office for three more hours, I tell him I would be more than glad to help. I'm so glad to be back at work. I'm glad I am here for them, and they all know they can reach out to me when they need help.

9:05 a.m. Okay, now it's time to start my day again. I still need to get the morning sales numbers out, so I go to our corporate portal to

administrative assistant, del monte foods

see if the field updated their forecast numbers for Q4. Noticing there was a change, I download the file to incorporate the new numbers into my report, but when I open the live data pull for my report's first page, every cell of the Excel file has a page break in it. What in the world? I contact our help desk and place a ticket for this bizarre occurrence.

My VM light is on again. This time it is good news. Tim made it to the airport and was boarding the 9:30 a.m. United flight. He was back on track and that was a relief to me.

9:37 a.m. While going through my e-mails, I start to print some documents and notice something funny. The Excel files I open in Outlook look fine, yet the Excel files I open from my desktop have page breaks in every cell. I then discover that the default printer on my computer was set to my UPS Label Maker. How in the heck did that happen? I adjust my printer and voilà . . . I cancel the ticket at the help desk. Now I attempt to get my morning coffee and a couple more Tylenols. My tooth is hurting even worse.

9:47 a.m. Just as I am getting up to get my coffee, an e-mail comes through from our Delhaize Team office. They need help adjusting their daily report, a duplicate of my area report except it has customer volume. Trying to teach Karen, the Delhaize Team admin, to understand how it works, I e-mail her the directions step-by-step. You know the theory—Give a man a fish, he eats for the day. Teach a man to fish, he eats for a lifetime.

I finally get my coffee. Troy is starting to clean out his cube of product samples. He sings, "Connie.com la la la la," then asks if I want any canned StarKist. "Why sure," I say. I'm on a diet and I have been eating a lot of it lately. He has three cases in his cube! I surely don't need that much. Joelle sits diagonally from Troy, so I ask her if she wants some cans. We pick through the different flavors. Troy continues singing "Connie.com," as he cleans out more product samples—this time cat and dog snacks. I know why he is whistling, but no one else does. That stinks. I hate to see him go.

Back in my cube, the phone rings. It is one of the directors wanting to make sure I received his expense report (the one I needed to affix receipts to and audit). He asks that I get it processed quickly; payment is due on his corporate Amex card. I take the expense report from one of my piles and finish it up. Then I receive an e-mail request for a conference room tomorrow for a region manager. Our Pittsburgh broker is coming into the office for the entire day. Conference rooms are hot commodities, but luckily I am able to find a room on the sixth floor.

10:29 a.m. My co-worker and dear friend, Carol, calls. I take breaks with her, and we bounce our daily stresses off each other. We started working together at Heinz over seven years ago, and we were spun off into Del Monte Foods when they acquired the pet and tuna businesses. "Sure, I'll meet you in the lobby." I tell her. I know when she calls, it's time to reset.

I gather the outgoing mail and the expense report that I need to push through quickly. Off to accounts payable and then to our main mailroom on the second floor. I ask our mailroom supervisor about the FedEx package that never went out. He states that the admin who dropped it off yesterday picked it up about a half hour ago. Hmm. I'd better follow up with her later to make sure it goes out. I head to the lobby to meet Carol.

10:49 a.m. Back from my errands and break. I start working on my piles. My tooth really hurts, so I schedule an appointment with my dentist for tomorrow morning.

11:20 a.m. Time to prepare the interoffice envelopes and find out the status of the FedEx package that didn't go out yesterday. On the sixth floor, I first stop by Cass's cube to say hello. She always lightens up my day, and we crack a few good jokes. Then I approach the other admin, who says she called FedEx to pick up the package yesterday but they never showed. So she called them again and they stopped by this morning. I take it for what it was and thank her for helping me out yesterday. Sometimes, anyone you can find to help, you are grateful. We are all usually pretty busy within our departments.

11:35 a.m. My VP calls to obtain some numbers that were published on trade funds. He reminded me about his travel on April 11 to Cincinnati.

Wow. **12:20** already. I head to the fifth-floor satellite mailroom. Just as I suspected after being out yesterday, waiting for me is a ton of mail in four different department slots.

12:35 p.m. Carol calls; we are heading outside for a walk on the river walkway.

1:01 p.m. Time to sort and distribute that pile of mail.

1:10 p.m. I call Teri in travel to schedule the flights for Cincinnati. Every once in a while I can hear humming and singing as Troy walks by.

1:39 p.m. Thunder. You can't have spring without thunderstorms. I see thousands of raindrops hitting the river. Some folks wander over to the window to watch the storm, and to get some candy from my candy dish. A little treat is good throughout the day for everyone.

2:08 p.m. I finally finish auditing and putting together all the expense reports that were on my desk from this morning. I also complete coding and signing a stack of catering invoices. Over the past two weeks, we have had all-day meetings that required catering for breakfast, beverage refreshes, lunch, and afternoon snacks. Time to print Fiscal '08 planning materials and put them into binders for our East Area Field Customer Marketing team.

2:10 p.m. The rain has stopped and the sun is back out shining. I love spring!

3:05 p.m. Just finished printing the revised Fiscal '08 planning materials. Now to gather the team's spiral-bound booklets I put together a few months ago and insert the new materials.

3:47 p.m. All done. Now everyone on the team has an up-to-date folder. Just as I finish, Lisa, a co-worker and friend, stops by to see if I am heading to Curves after work. We joined together and are each other's support. "I sure am," I reply. Over the past three years, I've gained fifteen pounds. Wow. Fifteen pounds. So with summer, baseball, Disney World, and other activities coming up fast, I decided it was time to start dieting. I started a diet two weeks ago and joined Curves.

4:48 p.m. I continue reviewing e-mails and filling requests. My tooth is still hurting and I take a couple more Tylenols. I call home to have my twenty-year-old daughter, Ashley, wake up my husband, Tom. He has to leave for work by 6:15 p.m. Then I call an 800 number to see if I need to report to jury duty tomorrow (I have to call the courthouse every day for two weeks). Yes! I don't need to go. I'm relieved I can leave at five. I reorganize my work piles for tomorrow. Since everyone will still be in Chicago, I will have time to get some unfinished projects done. No sense in staying late. I don't mind but, when you can leave at five, you take advantage!

6:20 p.m. Just walked through the door and Ashley (who lives with us, along with her two-year-old son, Richard) greets me as I head toward the kitchen. She tells me Daddy had to go, then hands me a brochure from Eddie, Tom's partner from work, who has a relative with a catering business. Eddie dropped the brochure off with the possibility of my using them at Del Monte. I will keep them in mind, as I am definitely a catering type of girl. Plus, the party for my grandson's third birthday in May is just around the corner. With busy days and the weekends committed to spring cleaning, ball games, and special work events, there is no possible way I will have time to cook for fifty people.

As my daughter and I are talking, I get the coffee on and start my dinner. Did I say *my* dinner? I did. This is a great night! If Tom was home this evening, I would have to prepare two different meals—one for him and the gang, and one for me. I prepare tuna salad on rye for me, and leave it to Ashley to make what she wants for her and Richard.

6:43 p.m. Phone rings and my grandson wakes up from his nap. It's my father-in-law calling to see how Tom's appointment went with the surgeon. I explain that the appointment isn't until tomorrow. (My husband, who never goes to the doctor, finally went after I had noticed a bulge on his stomach. No, it wasn't a beer gut. It turns out he had a hernia. So I immediately made him an appointment with the surgeon for this Wednesday.) I then spoke with my mother-in-law to find out what time everyone was coming over to their house on Easter. I need to schedule our day of activities at church, my parents, and my in-laws. I actually look forward to holidays and seeing both sides of the family. Time for my second cup of coffee.

6:53 p.m. Wait. The phone rings again. It's Tom, letting me know he used the last of the lunchmeat. He wants me to go to the store. I tell him tonight is *American Idol*, and I am still in sweats from my workout. I wasn't planning on heading back out tonight. He then nicely says, that's okay, he will stop on his way back from the doctor's tomorrow. I must say I am shocked. Music to my ears.

Tom does ask that I print him directions to the surgeon's office tomorrow. I try to explain that it is at Saint Margaret's; he's been there before. He says, please, just print him the directions. I kind of spoiled him by printing directions for just about everywhere he goes that is out of his normal routine.

6:55 p.m. I'm making my second cup of coffee and decide to play Zelda on our new Nintendo Wii. This game is like a little side adventure for me.

8:00 p.m. Wow, that hour went fast. See there, those video games are definitely addictive. Time for *American Idol*. As I watch, I go through two days' worth of mail, placing the bills in my "bill-paying pile" in the inbox in my study. My adorable grandson comes over and wants to play "baseball." After fifteen minutes of my pitching to him in the family room, he scurries out. Five minutes later, he is back with a handful of fragrant candles from my collection. Two minutes later, he leaves. *American Idol* is almost over and I now have a bat, ten balls, and a bunch of candles scattered throughout the family room. Time to redd-up.

10:01 p.m. Better get a move on and look up Tom's directions, and maybe check my work e-mails for the evening. Oh wait, here comes my Ashley.

10:05 p.m. Ashley asks if I noticed she cleaned up the study/computer room. I tell her most definitely, and thank her. She proceeds to tell me about a movie she just watched and how it made her cry. I don't know what the movie was; I'll ask her tomorrow. If I ask tonight, this would lead into a fifteen-minute conversation. I love her, but at times she can really talk and I'm starting to get tired.

Noteworthy

10:30 a.m. One set of minutes down and now I can tackle transcription of the other set. I think about the many meetings (over the past twenty-five years) in which I've sat in on to document the happenings via my Gregg shorthand skills. I remind myself that this skill is a dying breed as time passes. I take so much pride in having acquired this skill and having had the good fortune to use it throughout my career each and every time I record and transcribe meeting minutes. I also am reminded of the many compliments on my minutes that I've received over the years.

—*Joyce Evans, 56, East Millstone, New Jersey;*
executive secretary to the president, Carrier Clinic

administrative assistant, del monte foods

Snake Babe, the World's Sexiest Magician

MARIA GARA, 39, LAS VEGAS, NEVADA

She's performed on *Animal Planet,* the *Jerry Springer Show,* and Las Vegas's Adult Entertainment Expo. Her magic act is called "Venom" and includes, among other things, fire eating and pulling a python out of a male audience member's pants. On any given day she may be booked at a corporate event, an animal show for kids, or a bachelor party. She's also got a girlie Web site. Married for ten years, she and her husband run a rescue operation for abandoned reptiles. Why snakes? "Maybe it's because I've been allergic to fur all my life."

7:15 p.m. I first go to Bambi's cage, a five-foot-long Asian water monitor. I drain her water bin and spray it with disinfectant. She comes over to say hi. Well, that's what I tell myself. She's really just checking to see if I brought food. I scratch her back, then start refilling her bin. As I'm refilling it, she crawls into the water. Please don't go potty, please don't go potty . . . She sticks her head under the running hose. It's halfway full and she goes potty in it, so I drain it and start over. She is so cute.

7:25 p.m. I give a peek into all the other cages to make sure everyone is doing okay. First the big boas and pythons, then all the little guys—corn and king snakes. The iguanas and bearded dragons are already in sleep position, legs all sprawled out. I check on our desert tortoise, who is doing very well. When we got him last fall he was too sickly to survive hibernation, so we kept him in a warm cage all winter.

Last, I check on Lord Nottingham of Turtleshire, our African Sulcata tortoise. He has his own pen outside and does not hibernate, so he has a custom-heated indoor pen in his outdoor enclosure. He is not in there, so he must be in the underground burrow that he dug. It's about six feet deep now. I'm just waiting for him to pop out in my neighbor's backyard someday.

I have to hurry now. I have a surprise bachelor party tonight at ten thirty, and I have to shower and wash my hair. The party is in a house, though I prefer working in casino suites. People tend to be crazier in a house. The best man called earlier, wanting to make sure I'm bringing my albino python. I told him I would, as long as she is not shedding, which she isn't. Everyone wants the giant albino snakes at their parties. They have no idea that albinism is a genetic defect that bad people breed purposely. I'm looking forward to explaining this at the party when I start getting questions.

7:30 p.m. I take off my clothes and only quickly glance in the mirror. I have got to get going to the gym again. Halfway through my shower my hubby, Steve, joins me and we soap each other up and kiss a little. We just had sex four nights in a row in L.A. (we got back late last night from an adult/porn star convention) so he's probably good for another twenty-four hours, although I'm sure if I instigated it he would not have said no. I plop into bed, just for a few minutes.

8:26 p.m. My birds are squawking in their room. I wake up to find myself snuggled up against Steve. He is sooo warm. I wake him and go feed the birds. We have three umbrella cockatoos that are very vocal. Seymour, our dove, is in the living room. She hears the commotion and starts cooing. Seymour was a TV star, but was abandoned in a shower stall in a show's green room. When we picked her up she was afraid of people, but now she wants attention 24/7.

8:30 p.m. I throw on a thong, turn on my hot curlers, and start drying my hair. This could take awhile. The joys of having long, thick Latin hair. I start wondering what kind of party this will be. When I started out sixteen years ago assisting Steve in his juggling act, people were pretty mellow. But when we moved to Las Vegas from Chicago thirteen years ago, I didn't just get a change of weather! Besides the typical come-ons—*accidentally* brushing against my butt and offering me hotel keys—there is nothing harder than trying to do a card trick when guests are grabbing at the cards like children.

8:55 p.m. My hair is still a little damp but dry enough to put in curlers. I hear Steve changing in the bedroom and I yell out, What does he think I should wear. He says my rhinestone pasties, but then tells me they didn't pay the rate for that. Steve manages my bookings and usually asks clients if they want G, PG, R, or X-rated costuming. If they want X, he gets them someone else, but I charge $300 extra for my sexier costuming.

I tell Steve I don't want to wear the pasties anyway because, last time, my skin had a reaction to the glue. He reminds me that I should not even ask him for his opinion because he'll always pick the skimpiest outfit.

He yells, "Love you," as he leaves the room. I make a kissy noise with my lips.

9:10 p.m. I'm walking around the house topless in my curlers and thong; Steve kisses one of my boobs as we pass in the hallway. I can't find my boots but then I remember I wore them in L.A., so I find them in my still-packed suitcases. They are platform black vinyl go-go styled boots and put me over six feet tall. It's fun to tower over most of the guests.

9:16 p.m. I hear Steve calling to me from the garage, asking me which snakes he should pack up. I tell him Sperm, Scooby, and Sharona. He yells back that he'll bring Hollywood, too, since Sperm is due to poop. I start putting on my makeup, outlining my eyes in heavy black eyeliner, then adding black eye shadow with light purple glitter on the outside. I have the tiniest eyes and really need to open them up, so I add fake eyelashes, but not too long. When I'm in a close-up environment, I tone it down a little.

9:41 p.m. I put on my fishnets, my orange booty shorts outfit, and slip into some slippers. I'll put on my boots when I get there. I check the mirror one last time. I like what I see but really miss the muscle tone I had when I worked out regularly. It may be arrogant, but I'm happy I'm able to compete in a market where most girls my age had their careers end ten years ago. Steve always jokes, I may be an oldie but I'm a goodie.

9:45 p.m. I help Steve load Sharona, our twelve-foot albino python, into our cargo van. She is so heavy, about seventy-five pounds now. Steve drives to the party so I can relax a bit. I ask him if there will be any other performers or strippers there, but he doesn't know. I'm hoping I am starting the bachelor party—I work best as what we call a "meet-and-greet the guests" performer. If I start after the strippers, the snakes are still a great attraction, but then the guys are always expecting me to get naked. I spend more time explaining that I don't do that, instead of entertaining the guests.

10:05 p.m. Wow, what a house. At least four million. Towering white columns and lush green landscaping with mature trees, and one of those arch driveway entrances, full to the hilt with cars. The party seems to be in full swing. I can hear the music blaring and see lights changing color in one of the windows. The street is full of cars for a couple of blocks so Steve double-parks to find out where we can store the snakes. I start putting on my boots.

10:10 p.m. Steve learns the four-car garage is being used by the caterers, so someone is going to move a car out of the driveway for us. Also, I can start early. Cool, that means I can finish early (thoughts of sleeping). Wake up, time to work . . .

10:15 p.m. I get Sperm, the corn snake, and head into the house. Strolling entertainment, as I'm doing tonight, is easy. Nothing says, "Hi, stop and talk to me," like a snake chick. People immediately surround me, asking questions about the "cute little guy" between giggles about Sperm's name. There are maybe eighty people here, including women, which is good for me. The guys don't seem to get as drunk, and most ladies just love snakes. Steve is always joking that more women hit on me than men. I don't notice any other performers here except a DJ and a bartender who does some flair/juggling with the bottles.

10:30 p.m. The crowd around me dies down so I start my way through the house, stopping to answer more questions and take photos. Since the guests have already been drinking for a couple of hours, I let them pet the snake; but if they want to hold it for a photo, I tell them they can hold me instead. I don't ever want to endanger the little guy. After posing for so many years, I think I look the same in every picture, head tilted to the right with a cheesy smile. The snakes are another story. They don't always sit still, and you can't force them to pose. I just hold them gently toward the camera.

10:35 p.m. I work my way to the outside patio/pool area. The pool has a stone bottom and a waterfall and slide. The yard is not very large, which is typical in Las Vegas, but has a lighted stone path with lots of palm trees and tropical-looking plants and shrubs. The landscape lighting is incredible. I love red lights and they're used a lot.

10:40 p.m. I make my way back to the garage to change out snakes. I like starting with the smallest and work my way up to the big girl. Dramatic build. Steve is reading a comic book in the van. He stops to help me, putting away Sperm and getting out Scooby. I tell him he should check out the backyard. Ours is still a dirt plot, so we are trying to decide what to do when we are ready to start landscaping.

10:45 p.m. This seems like a fun crowd so, when I am asked the snake's name I say, "Little Fellatio," which is actually the name of one of my other snakes. As people cautiously pet the snake I do my scripted joke, "There's no reason to be afraid because a little fellatio never hurt anyone." To one of the guys I say, "I like the way you're stroking the snake. You must have lots of practice. Are you married?" I walk away to the sound of laughter. I am enjoying myself.

11:05 pm. I finally meet the groom as I make my way through the pool table room. He is Italian, maybe, shorter than me with my heels on, and cute, but his hair is too short. I like long hair like my hubby's, which reaches the back of his knees. I can tell the groom's been drinking a lot by his speech, but he isn't obnoxious drunk.

He loves the snake and tells me he used to have one. I ask what happened to it, knowing it probably won't be the first sad snake story I'll hear tonight. It was still very young when he fed it a live rat, left the house, and came back to a chewed-up snake. I am furious but remain calm on the outside, as I explain about the frozen prekilled process. He says he couldn't get his snake to eat dead food, as almost everyone says. I mention that I have had hundreds of snakes come through my rescue, the majority from live-fed homes, and I easily converted each one.

He is pretty drunk and probably won't remember our conversation tomorrow. I casually say I'm going to go and share me and the snake with some of the other guests, which is what I say a lot when I feel it's time to move on.

11:10 p.m. The women are pretty tipsy and getting bold. The guys always give me lines like, "Want to hold *my* snake?" but this time a woman says, "You should see my boyfriend's snake." She points to his crotch and I say my standard comeback, "Only if it's bigger than mine . . . " She laughs as she pets the snake and retorts, "Nope, he's Jewish."

I'm offered a drink and food, but say, "Thank you, maybe later." As a professional courtesy I never eat or drink on the job. I'm paid very well to perform during my time here, not eat. I cringe when I see other talent on gigs helping themselves to the food.

11:15 p.m. The snakes are such a hit I don't even get time to do any of my naughty magic tricks. The best man keeps asking me which

snake babe, the world's sexiest magician

snake is coming out next so now it's time to get the big girl. I put Scooby away in the van and start changing costumes—a black velvet thong and semisheer black-and-purple robe. You can see my nipples under the colored material, but they look purple. I wear the same boots.

11:25 p.m. Steve and I make our way through the garage with Sharona, the albino Burmese python. A couple of the catering help scream and run outside. We situate Sharona on a lounge-style sofa in the formal living area. I lie next to her, holding her head up and letting her tail wrap around one of the couch feet. We leave room for anyone who may want to sit with us for a photo. About twenty people quickly surround me. I hold the part of the snake that bites; they can pet the part that poops.

Steve stands at the tail end, making sure everyone pets nicely. I get lots of compliments on my outfit from the guys and girls, and one woman mentions she saw me on *Ripley's Believe It or Not*, which is fun. I mention that was taped years ago, but they rerun that episode a lot, luckily for me. I feel good that someone recognized me, since I have hardly done any TV in the last year or so. Most of the new offers have been for reality-style shows, and I don't care for how people are treated on them. I also don't think a reality show would further my career.

11:40 p.m. I'm still hanging with my snake when I notice three women walk in—two blondes in super-skimpy bikinis and a brunette in a very tight tube dress. All three are wearing spiked heels and smell of too much perfume. They have got to be strippers.

Right away, the bachelor is brought into the living room and plopped into a chair. The DJ starts some music, and the three women do their thing. One starts massaging his neck. Another starts giving him a lap dance. The third is slinking around the room, probably looking for another guy to include in their show. This is my cue to leave. Some of the things I've seen, I just don't want to see again.

Steve helps me get Sharona off the couch and back into her carrier. I always prefer to leave at this stage of the party. The best man comes out to our van with us and gushes about how cool the snakes and I were. I like gushing. He tells Steve he was impressed that I actually knew what I was talking about with the snakes, and also how much he liked my boobs. He gives me a two-hundred-dollar tip and says he's sorry he can't chat; he wants to catch the show.

11:45 p.m. The adrenaline from the whole loud party atmosphere is wearing off. On the drive home, Steve tells me how hot I looked, and that if he wasn't so darn exhausted he would love to do me in this robe when we get home. I close my eyes. I love my hubby.

We are coming up on our ten-year anniversary on Halloween. I promised Steve we would renew our vows with a themed wedding, so I need to start making plans. We are either going to have Dracula marry us at a graveyard-themed chapel, or I may do a dark wedding with eerie music, lots of candles, and bloodred roses. A sideshow performer friend of mine is going to fly in from New York to eat glass and pounds nails into his nose, among other gory, fun things. Steve doesn't seem to want to be involved so much in the planning, which is okay with me since I am a control freak. As long as the wedding has a dark gothic theme, that's all that matters to him.

On March 27, 2007 . . .

17 percent of day diarists had sex.

•

All in a Day's Work

6:50 a.m. I'm at the river and it is howling. The flags are all straight out. I don't think my clients will want to fish today, but we'll see. If not, I need to go out by myself. I had such a rotten day yesterday. I just need to get out there and I don't know if anyone understands this. I don't know if my husband understands it to this day. If I don't get out at least once a week and fish, things just don't go right.

—*Marcia Lapham-Foosaner, 58, Palm City, Florida;*
saltwater fly-fishing guide

8:00 a.m. I wake to my nurse saying, "Good morning, Jane," as she sticks a thermometer in my mouth and an oximeter gadget on my finger to measure the oxygen in my blood. Even though I work at home, there is never a day of lazing around. I have amyotrophic lateral sclerosis, or Lou Gehrig's disease, a motor neuron disease that slowly paralyzes a person. I can no longer walk, have very limited use of my arms and hands, and use a ventilator to breathe, so I need 24-hour nursing care. For the next three hours, I will be bathed, suctioned, dressed, fed my breakfast and coffee, given medications, and overall preened by my nurse and an aide. Although my nurses and aides are lovely, caring people, it takes stamina and a lot of patience to give up control and the solitude of the morning routine.

—*Jane Babin, 51, Laconia, New Hampshire;*
retired university professor and poet

11:00 a.m. I've just finished a conversation with the ranking Republican (and former chair) of the finance committee. When I extended my invitation to have the Republicans participate in presenting the budget he politely refused, saying they were going to vote against the committee budget and prepare an alternative budget. "How do you know you are not going to support the committee budget when we haven't finished our work yet?" I asked. His answer, "If we agree, we won't have anything to use when we run against you." So much for my efforts at bipartisanship and inclusiveness.

—*Marjorie K. Smith, 66, Dunwoody, New Hampshire; representative, New Hampshire House of Representatives*

12:59 p.m. My four-year-old, Talia, had been so excited to play Moses' mother in the school performance. But as soon as she saw me, she started reaching out and crying the entire time. She didn't stop until I left, and that's only because by then she was screaming. Also, her teachers had forgotten to set her a plate at the lunch table, which set off a new round of hysterics. What happened to my confident, happy girl? She's been like this ever since her sister was born, so I suppose it isn't rocket science to figure out that she's jealous. I leave her screaming, "Don't go back to work, don't go back to work!"

—*Amy Gebler Ashkenazy, 35, Seattle, Washington; marketing manager*

7:15 p.m. At the JCC Café in D.C., gulping down some hummus and pita before the show. I look across and see Senator Joe Lieberman at another table. He smiles at me. I'm a familiar face, but I can tell he's not sure from where. I've only done his makeup about thirty times!

—*Cathy Kades, 48, Rockville, Maryland; freelance makeup artist*

snake babe, the world's sexiest magician

Chief Medical Examiner for Saint Louis County

MARY CASE, 64, ST. LOUIS, MISSOURI

Her job is to lead the investigation of individuals who die in homicides, suicides, accidents, or other unnatural or natural circumstances. Over the years, she's done about ten thousand autopsies; averaging three hundred a year. People often ask her, "How can you do what you do?" "It doesn't bother me at all. I don't go home and think about all this terrible tragedy. The work is very clinical, but it has made me cautious because I can see how easily life can be lost. And there is a whole lot you can do to keep bad things from happening to you."

4:50 a.m. My beeper begins playing a soft melody. I am always ready to start the day. My four dogs (all rescues) are also eager for me to start the day by feeding them. My home revolves around these little guys. As they run outside, I prepare the pills for my male, Dakota. He needs thyroid tablets, antihistamines, and prednisone, plus I give him an allergy shot weekly. Small trouble for the pleasure of his company.

Once the dogs are all taken care of, I make coffee and eat a bowl of oatmeal while I read part of the paper. I like to begin the day unrushed, so I purposely get up early. Back upstairs, I shower and get dressed. I am very particular about my appearance and makeup and I dress in a professional way. Yes, I could get away with wearing scrubs (except to court) but that is not my way. I enjoy nice clothes and I think it shows respect for those I work with, as well as the families who come to my office.

Before I leave, I wake up Max, the man I have lived with for the past nineteen years. My friends find it strange that we don't marry, and maybe someday we will, but this works for us. We've both been married and divorced before. Max works from home in entertainment management, which sounds much more fascinating than my work. I enjoy his stories of the famous and would-be famous recording artists. We speak briefly about when we might expect to see one another. We do not have large blocks of time together except on weekends.

By **7:00 a.m.** I am off to my office at Saint. Louis University, where I work one half-day a week to take care of the paperwork generated by the cases from St. Charles, Jefferson, and Franklin counties. My office here is very small, only a desk, since I spend the majority of my work days at my county office, where we actually do the work with bodies.

At the university, I work with a staff of three wonderful women. One of them, I have known since 1978, and she has worked with me in various capacities while her children were growing up. Another came to me at age twenty-one to work as a secretary, and has subsequently become the first child death specialist in the country, a position I created on the spur of the moment to entice her to stay in the office. I value the women I have worked with over the years and stay in touch with them.

8:00 a.m. Today, I do not have a directors' meeting with the other doctors who lead divisions within the pathology department. This means I can start early on my paperwork: reviewing autopsy reports; looking at microscopic sections taken from the autopsies; reviewing toxicology reports; and speaking to families, attorneys, and others who may have questions about the cases.

My first call is from the daughter of an elderly woman who had severe pulmonary disease and lung cancer, as well as back pain. While having a procedure done in the pain management physician's office, she developed respiratory failure and died. My office investigated her death and I have signed the death certificate. The daughter wants to know why her mother died. I tell her it was from the pulmonary disease. I found no evidence that her death was related to the procedure. She was not accusatory. People often need assistance in understanding what has happened when a family member has passed, and I am happy to be able to help.

My next call is from an investigator at the Division of Aging and Senior Services, asking about an elderly couple, both of whom died from carbon monoxide intoxication. An ice storm had knocked out their electric power and they were using a generator, which was in the garage where it could vent exhaust fumes into the house. The investigator needs to know if someone neglected them in some manner, or if their deaths could have been prevented. We have had several of these sad, needless deaths during the recent winter of power outages.

At **9:00 a.m.** I am steadily working my way through my stack of cases. So far I have signed out two suicides, the second most common type of death a medical examiner sees, after natural causes. I am still amazed at how readily some people can end their lives. One of the two today is a seventeen-year-old boy who sadly used Ecstasy, a dangerous recreational drug that can cause hallucinations, confusion, and sometimes such depression that users commit suicide.

The police report notes that he left a message for his girlfriend on Facebook, which expresses his disappointment in being imperfect, and a final "I love you." The world has new ways for leaving our final messages. The report also notes that the girlfriend is pregnant and wants to obtain a specimen for DNA studies to determine paternity. Social Security provides benefits to children whose parent has died. We receive frequent requests for this testing and comply without need for court orders or other legal maneuvering.

At **9:45 a.m.** I speak to a prosecuting attorney from an out of state county who wants me to testify in a trial. In 1993, I did an autopsy on a woman who was murdered there. I am intrigued to learn they now have a very likely suspect after all these years, and are going to trial in June. We speak about the case. The woman was beaten and stabbed thirty-two times—what the medical examiner refers to as a homicide and whose legal term is murder. A young man who was fifteen at the time of the crime is the defendant, and he has been living a very normal life since then.

By **9:50 a.m.** I am checking the neuropathology reports on brains that I examined last Friday. In addition to being a forensic pathologist, I am also a neuropathologist. Neuropathology is the study of disease and injury of the brain and spinal cord. Only about ten to fifteen people in the United States have these duel board certifications. This special expertise is very helpful because many unnatural deaths are head injuries. Many other forensic pathologists I work with and around the country call upon me to consult on cases involving such injuries.

10:00 a.m. I speak with an attorney who wants to engage my services for a private consultation involving medical malpractice in defense of a doctor. I do a fairly limited number of these cases at night and on weekends, due to time constraints. I'm also only willing to do so where I really have some expertise to offer.

11:00 a.m. I go to the Saint Louis County Medical Examiner's Office, about thirty minutes away. My office here is large and filled with my collections of child abuse cases and other cases that I have looked at over the years, which I am saving for teaching and writing. Today, I am on call for bodies for my three outside counties, but when I arrive, I only have one so far.

Before going to the morgue, I have lunch with two women with whom I usually eat. I always try to break for lunch, even if briefly. I believed that women should have connections with the other women they work with, and eating is a good time to make them. I do not eat at my desk. It is unsanitary because case files placed on the desk have papers that have been in the morgue. The morgue is very clean, but I am fastidious, so we eat in the lunch room.

While eating, I get a call from one of my investigators that I have another body coming in. A young man who has a history of heroin use has been found dead in his apartment. Unfortunately, we see lots of heroin deaths, and this is probably another one.

One of the pathology residents from the university stops by our table to ask if he can get a file on a case from some twelve years ago. This case involves a young man who was playing water polo on his high school team and died during the game. This may seem strange, but I remember the case, as I remember many of the cases I have seen over the years, although they now number in the tens of thousands. The resident was a member of the water polo team and was in the game when the young man died. He is now preparing to do chairman's rounds, where he will present a talk on athletic deaths, and he wants to include this case.

I happen to have a video that a parent took of the game. It shows the young man going under the water, then being pulled out and CPR carried out to no avail. The resident watches the video in the resident room and sees himself on that long-ago day. What a strange circumstance. I ask him, "Is this experience why you want to go into forensic pathology?" He is not certain, but he thinks it did have some influence.

I have a great curiosity about death, and I believe most forensic pathologists do. We accept it as a natural happenstance, but I think many of us do the work we do to learn something that will answer the eternal questions about fear of the unknown, of which death is certainly the most unknown. So I am interested in the effect on this resident of seeing a friend actually die at a young age. I do not think it has damaged this young doctor by any means. But it has given him a perspective few have.

1:00 p.m. Our morgue has been recently renovated and is now a beautiful modern facility. The walls are clean and white, the floors are deep blue and sparkling, and all the cabinetry is stainless steel. Bodies are placed onto carts that allow them to be x-rayed, autopsied, and later stored on the same cart. The cart attaches to a docking station, which has nearby water, suction, instruments, balances, and other equipment.

I have changed from my clothing into a scrub suit and comfortable shoes. In the morgue suite, I put on an operating gown, head cover, mask, glasses, shoe covers, plastic apron, and two pairs of gloves.

My first autopsy is on a forty-three-year-old woman who had some minor medical concerns but no known serious problems. She was found dead in her bed. She did have lots of medications, including oxycodone, present in her home. Although none are missing beyond routine use, I suspect that medication may be the cause of her death. We have lots of people who take lots of medication and die of accidental overdoses.

The autopsy assistant has weighed and measured the body and done the X-rays. I begin the autopsy with an incision to open the chest and abdomen. I examine each organ in situ, then the assistant helps me in the physical labor of removing the organs individually to examine them further for any abnormality. Fluids and tissues are retained for toxicology testing.

Next, I open the head and examine the scalp and skull, then remove the brain and examine it. I then open the neck to look at the vessels and muscles, and remove the airway to examine it. In this autopsy, there are no findings in any of the organs that provide a disease or abnormality to explain why this woman has died. As I work, I make detailed, handwritten notes.

By the time I finish this woman's autopsy, the young man I suspect may be a heroin overdose has come in, and I autopsy him also. Again, the organs of the body do not demonstrate any abnormality. I take blood, urine, vitreous humor from the eyes and liver for the toxicology laboratory. In both cases, we will wait for the results of toxicology. Testing of these specimens will take eight to ten weeks and includes identification and quantification of substances such as alcohol, drugs, medications, poisons, and inhalants.

The autopsy assistant sews up the body and cleans the fluids from the body and table. The body is stored in a cooler inside a body bag, and can now be picked up by a funeral home to be taken for embalming and, later, whatever disposition will take place based upon the family's wishes. I do the paperwork, consisting of forms for toxicology and histology when microscopic sections are needed, and then I dictate my findings.

3:00 p.m. Back to my office to catch up. I have a manuscript to review for the *Journal of Forensic Sciences*, which I am able to do rather quickly. This manuscript is from a foreign country and has serious language issues, as well as extensive problems with the reference section. It will not be accepted for publication unless it can be revised in significant manner.

4:00 p.m. I am going home to change clothes to go to my health club. I do this twice a week—one hour of step aerobics and one hour of weight training on each of those days. People ask me how I find the time to do this. I reply that I do not "find the time," but that I do make it. I am fortunate to have very good health and do all that I can to maintain it.

4:35 p.m. I arrive home and let the dogs out. Max, of course, could do this and would, but I like to spend this time with them. After I change into my workout clothes, I feed the dogs and give Dakota his pills.

5:00 p.m. I love Juanita's class, which I have been going to for five years. We are all fiercely loyal to Juanita. She has been in treatment for ovarian cancer for the past ten years and is now is her sixth round of chemotherapy. When I arrive, I learn she will not be here tonight. She was diagnosed just after our last class with blood clots in the veins of her legs. The class is very concerned. She has been an example to all of us of courage and brave spirits.

7:45 p.m. Back at home, I eat a frozen meal. I decided years ago that my schedule could not accommodate cooking during the week. On Saturdays, Max and I go out to wonderful restaurants, and on Sundays I cook. I recognize that my life is not typical, but it works very well for me. During dinner, I read the paper. Again, this is a brief period of time I give myself.

8:00 p.m. I'm preparing for a trial that I will testify in on Friday in Illinois, a case in which a physician is being sued for wrongly prescribing the medications that caused the patient's death. I am testifying for the attorney who is defending the physician. My role is to assist the jury in understanding the forensic issues of why the patient died and what the toxicology means. Fortunately, it is not to say whether the physician was right or wrong in his practice. In this case, the preparation involves some thirty hours of reviewing material.

When I am not working on legal cases, I read fiction. I do not watch television. I do not clean the house, although others do this for me twice a week. I work very hard, and what little time I have left over, I spend on myself. I am very selfish and I have always recognized that about myself. It is why I never had children. I do not make excuses for this attitude. I am the happiest and best-adjusted person I know.

10:00 p.m. I let the dogs out for their evening run. When they return, I go to bed. Max is a night person and will not go to bed for a few more hours. I usually fall asleep almost immediately, but before I do I give thanks for my good health and many blessings, and for being able to do work that I love. I have more than I need and I never forget that.

Crank It Up

12:30 p.m. I grab my clipboard and nursing bag, hop into the car, and head onto the highway and out to rural Ohio. I record the time I am leaving my house and reset the odometer. I'll need that information for billing. I so enjoy these solitary car trips, often into unfamiliar areas. This is when I recharge. There is nothing so therapeutic as breaking out of the city, opening the sunroof, turning the radio up, and singing my lungs out. As I speed along, I notice I forgot to repair my nail polish. Oh well. "Sky rockets in flight! Afternoon Delight. Aaaaaafternoon delight!"

—*Rebecca Stanton, 52, Columbus, Ohio; home health nurse*

Television News Cameraperson and Editor, KNBC

SUSAN MONROE, 44, SAUGUS, CALIFORNIA

Depending on the day, she's either editing or shooting footage for Southern California's number one morning news program, *Today in L.A.* The key to good editing—"Even if the sound is off, the pictures should tell the story." The show covers the gamut—from the Paris Hilton circus, to the governor's press conference, to the war in Iraq. "I'm a nosey person, I like knowing what's going on where I live and around the world, and I have it pretty much at my fingertips." Two thing she doesn't like about the job: the hours, and people jumping in front of the camera yelling, "Hi, Mom."

1:15 a.m. I'm running late. Bear, the dog, doesn't want to go outside 'cause it's raining. I'm happy I'll be inside editing today instead of out in the field, shooting with the reporter. I hate doing rain liveshots/stories. I think it's crazy that we're standing out in the pouring rain telling people it's raining. Look out the window!

2:05 a.m. I exit off the 134 freeway (where Nicole Richie was arrested for driving drunk and going the wrong way) onto Buena Vista/Bob Hope Drive, and arrive at the NBC/Universal lot. I enter through one of the side gates to a "card access only" parking lot. Since NBC bought Universal and merged resources, security has increased, which is good, because coming in at two in the morning I've encountered some nuts hanging around.

The lot is pretty empty, and I make the trek past the Ellen DeGeneres and Carson Daly studios, through the field shop area where all the microwave news trucks are parked, across the

water cooler diaries

midway to the main building, past the *Tonight Show* studio, and up the stairs to the KNBC/Telemundo newsroom and editing area. Sometimes I'm amazed at how lucky I am to be at the center of all this television activity. Other times, I wonder what the hell I'm doing awake at two in the morning.

2:10 a.m. Picture a small train car with eight edit bays, four on each side, and no windows. That's the editing room. Calendars, lava lamps, and postcards liven up our otherwise dull gray fabric cubicle walls. There is no privacy, plus it's always freezing in here!

I sit in the first editing bay (EJ-12) on the left because it's the only one with a TV hooked up to the cable/antennaplex that lets me watch the show and feeds from my desk instead of the monitors on the wall. I'm the Group 7 (the union and NBC classify our jobs in groups or pay scales), which means I'm in charge. I facilitate the editing assignments, address any problems with feeds, and coordinate with the producer to make sure the video she wants to show gets edited correctly. For this tiny bit of power and authority, I get a little extra money, and also the blame if an edited story is wrong or doesn't make air—even if I'm not the one who edited the story. People tend to pass the buck around here. Job security, or lack of it, I suppose.

Cleaning up my edit desk area with Lysol wipes. I swear the night-shift editors must not be able to see the crumbs and grime they leave behind, along with the scripts, soda bottles, and food wrappers. I guess they think the janitors clean up after them. Nah, they just don't care.

2:20 a.m. Finally, I can start editing stories for the two-hour newscast that runs from 5:00 to 7:00 a.m. and airs before the national *Today* show. I sort the scripts from the printer in the order that they will appear on the show. First, the major local stories, starting with a fatal traffic accident in Orange County. Then the major national stories—at the top of the pile, U.S. Attorney General Gonzales is under fire because of the eight U.S. attorneys who were fired.

Everything we need to edit is either on tape or already in the computer's editing system. We can call up video from NBC's on-demand network, which includes all of its affiliates around the world. The challenge is finding the correct video to pull so we can chop it up to match the current script. We also get self-contained stories ("packages") from Washington. Those we just edit out the countdown with color bars and the reporter signoff.

I boot up the two computers on my desk, one for editing and the other to log on to the newsroom communication system. This second computer has the rundowns/scripts for the show in real time, so we can see what has aired, what needs to be edited, or what has been killed. We can also topline (instant message) anyone who is logged on to the system.

I start in on the pile of scripts. My first story—a North Hollywood BB gun attack. The police captured a guy who was shooting car windows and threatening civilians. This story was shot by one of our stringers, people who have video cameras, police/fire scanners, and a very basic knowledge of how to shoot and edit. They fill in after our evening crews are done, but before the early crew shift comes in from midnight to 4:00 a.m. With stringers, it's usually slim pickin's because they make their money ($150 to $200 a story aired) with quantity, not quality, of stories.

I quickly scan the video: close-up shots of two shattered car windows, followed by a wide-shot of the same two cars from across the street; a medium-wide shot of five cops around the suspect sitting on the street behind a pickup truck; and a close-up of the suspect being walked to a police car and put inside.

I only have about twenty-two seconds to tell the story, even though we lay down forty seconds. So I start with five seconds of the close-ups of the shattered windows to show the damage. I cut to the wide shot of the cars for four seconds to give a sense of where it happened—on the street, as opposed to a parking lot or carport. Then I dissolve to the suspect on the ground for five seconds, and then dissolve to the close-up of the suspect being taken to the police car until forty seconds. This shows that the jerk was caught and is going to jail.

This process takes me about seven minutes from reading through the script, importing the video to the editing timeline, cutting (editing) the video, and sending it to the play-out server.

Some stories can be done in as little as two minutes or take as long as forty minutes, depending on the script, complexity, and editing effects likes wipes and dissolves.

3:00 a.m. Three more editors come in for this shift: Andrea, Tony, and Gary. Andrea is usually quiet, but we're so on the same page we don't have to talk. A look, a nod says it all—female connection. She grabs a few scripts from "the chair" on the way to her edit bay. I've designated this chair for scripts ready to be edited, otherwise writers have been known to leave them on bookshelves, or the front desk, or the basket marked "field tapes."

Tony asks, "Are these the scripts?" I don't want to dump on him because he's sick today, but he asks that question every time. I also don't want to catch his cooties.

Gary gets his coffee and sits directly behind me. He always asks, "Have I done Lew's list?" Lew is a writer who puts all of his stories with source info and editing instructions on one piece of paper. I made him start doing this to stop him from calling us every twenty minutes, or sitting with us to edit while he took over our newsroom computers. I hand Lew's list to Gary. That way I know he's working or, in theory, earning his paycheck.

Meanwhile, I can't stop thinking about my now former car insurance company's fucking me over! All they have to do is forward my claim documents to the insurance company of the drunk idiot that hit me six months ago. Because my now *former* insurance company is so lame, the at-fault driver's insurance will only pay for a portion of my car rental. Stupid asses!

3:30 a.m. Stories are trickling in to be edited. King Drew Medical Center is on the verge of being shut down . . . Mayor Villaraigosa went to Washington, D.C . . . Pretty mellow stuff so far. That means the shit will probably hit the fan later. The work often comes in bursts, or at the last minute. Sometimes we get only four minutes before it airs.

4:00 a.m. I watch the New York feed of the *Today* show. They're talking about the pet food recall. My roommate Cobie's cat,

Tess, got sick from her Iams wet food. Her kidneys were damaged and she lost so much weight. It didn't look like she was going to make it. I took her to the vet yesterday because I didn't feel comfortable trying to give her an IV two times a day.

4:30 a.m. This room is so cold and breezy. That's why I dress like the Unabomber and am wearing my New York Giants throw blanket over my head and shoulders. I need another one to keep my feet warm. At least I'm not stuck out in the field doing a story about a Peeping Tom on the USC campus. (They couldn't find anything else to cover?) Amazing they're not doing a rain story! How will the people know it's raining outside?!

Half hour until airtime. We have two reporters, Robert and Natasha, who go live during the two-hour broadcast, with stories that hit every thirty minutes. I assign Andrea to work with Robert, and Tony to work with Natasha on the USC peeper story. Sometimes, if things are slow, I'll take a reporter, too, and jump in to help if there's a time crunch to make sure the videos/story make air. But I always have to keep my eye on the show and the real-time rundown on the computer. The rundown indicates the finished stories online in yellow or cued; other stories offline in purple; and killed stories in blue.

5:00 a.m. Four hours of sleep is not enough. I have to go to bed earlier but I'm hooked on the TV show *Prison Break,* even though I TiVo it.

I check the rundown to make sure the producer didn't add a story without telling anyone, including the writer. No problems today, but, yes, it happens. I'll be scrolling through the rundown and see a story as an orphan—no writer initials assigned to it, no placeholder. So I'll have to topline a writer who I think is in a good mood, to see if the story belongs to him. Of course, he'll have no idea what I'm talking about, so he'll call back two minutes later in a panic—Can I help him find the specific video?! Later, the producer usually gives a lame, "Oh, sorry."

5:15 a.m. Am I the only one who can hear the printer? Gary needs to stop looking at photos of property in Bulgaria that he hopes to buy (he already owns two apartments there), and pay attention to the fact that the machine is whining and spitting out scripts sent directly to us from the writers' computers. He has already walked by the printer two or three times to get his coffee and morning snacks, usually apples that he eats louder than normal and in about twenty seconds. Sometimes I purposefully leave scripts on the printer to see if he'll grab them. About 30 percent of the time he'll pick one up, but then hand it to me so I can ask him to edit it. Nice!

6:00 a.m. One more story—Northern California snow. They had a nice storm up in the Sierras. Now the only jobs left are some ten-second previews of upcoming stories—teasers. The 6:00 a.m. show is a repeat of the 5:00 a.m. show.

7:00 a.m. I have to make a copy of my green card/physical certificate in order to continue my training to be a satellite truck operator. Right now, I drive the microwave truck, but there are some areas, like the canyons, where we can only broadcast live by satellite transmission. This training is a great opportunity to become more useful to the company, and to keep myself employed!

On the TV in my edit bay, I just saw a commercial for British Columbia. Not my first choice, but I'm ready for a four-day weekend. I need a break. Even though my shooting days are usually more action packed, it feels like the same-shit-different-day syndrome. Sad when covering a murder is routine.

7:30 a.m. Time for breakfast/lunch. I'm off to the commissary. Down the stairs past the *Access Hollywood* and *Tonight Show* studios. Whenever I see Jay Leno drive up in one of his million classic cars, he's always good for a quick hi and good morning. Today, Jay's musical guests have their instruments assembled in the hall, waiting for the set to be lit and decorated before they rehearse.

I run into a lot of celebrities in this area, usually after breakfast, or on my way out at **11:00 a.m.** One time I was walking toward the *Tonight Show* studio during one of their outdoor concerts, and a man in a huge cowboy hat came toward me. When I realized it was Garth Brooks, I told him I loved his song "The Dance." I'm sure he didn't count on having a five foot three black woman from California as a fan. We had a great little chat.

7:45 a.m. In the commissary Marianna, the cashier, showed me her cell phone with a picture of Buckwheat on it. It yells out like a present-day hood rat—"You got a damn message!" I thought it was funny. Talked to Jen, our morning coanchor. She had video on her cell phone of her puppy on a raft in her pool. Makes me miss my dog, Tyler, who died of bone cancer two years ago. Great companion. He was with me fourteen years, and the only male I loved other than my father.

I get blueberry pancakes to take back upstairs and eat. A lot of the actors from *Days of Our Lives* are getting a quick breakfast before returning to the set. The rain has stopped and it's cool and crisp outside. I feel refreshed and ready for the rest of my shift.

9:00 a.m. Chris, the other morning coanchor, comes into the editing area. He does the walk/talk like that character Ron Burgundy in *Anchorman*, but not as obnoxious. I had the New York Giants Web page up so we had to talk about football. How many months until the 2007 season starts? Chris is wondering if anyone could record his track (narration) for the LAX runway incursions package. Everyone says no, just to mess with him, then I do it anyway.

10:00 a.m. Things are slow. I'm waiting for my "relief" to come in, the next Group 7. I'm officially done at ten, but I always stay longer to help during the crunch between ten thirty and eleven. I check to make sure that the stories for the *Midday Report* newscast are dubbed and dragged over from *Today in LA.* I also help make sure that reporters and writers for *Midday* have editors assigned to them.

11:00 a.m. Time to go home. As I'm leaving, I hear the familiar shrieks of panic at the assignment desk down the hall. The assignment editor is yelling to a reporter on the phone, and at the producer who is sitting only ten feet away. An LAX spokesperson is running late so the story might be compromised.

"I don't know!"

"No one told me!"

"When did they feed it to editing?"

How can the assignment desk, producer, writer, and reporter out in the field *not* know to talk to each other so that everyone is on the same page? One person knew file tape was needed, another knew the crew was waiting to speak to an official, and the last person thought everything was shot and the piece was finished. We're in the communications business, but the lack of communication in this company is astounding.

I hightail it out of there before they can blame it on the editors.

On March 27, 2007 . . .

37 percent of day diarists reported that their co-workers got on their nerves.

•

$138,095 . . .

. . . the salary a stay-at-home mom would earn if she were
compensated for all the elements of her job
—*Salary.com, 2007*

10:45 a.m. To be able to write this, I had to give two of my children spoonfuls of Cool Whip and put them in front of the television. The baby, thank heavens, is napping. Another one's due to get off the kindergarten bus in twenty minutes, and the teenager is probably at this very moment debating some teacher about something. I couldn't tell you what his schedule is. My god . . . I just realized I don't even know my oldest child's school schedule. Hmm. Guess I'll file that little fact under "Reason Not to Have Any More Kids #86."

So this is me, mother of five, wife of one psychiatrist, owner of one obnoxious dog that treats me like a waitress. (Trust me, you don't want to know what he leaves as a tip on the floor sometimes.) My husband and I had a fight last week. I was tired. Hell, I was exhausted. I said stuff that I shouldn't. At some point during the fight, my husband put on his shrink's hat and started analyzing me. I stood in our tiny kitchen—did I mention he's still just a resident?—and my eyes locked on the knife drawer. Seriously. One more word about my "projection" or "transmission" or whatever and I think I could have done him harm.

I am buried in this thing called motherhood and wifehood. Did I start out on this road thinking it was going to be all good all the time? Honestly, I couldn't tell you. Do you know how long it takes to load and unload four little children from a mini-van? My life is laundry and meals and baths and doctor visits and carpools and sex. Sex. I just lumped sex into the chore category. Ugh. I could go on, pages and pages. But the bus will be here soon and I've got peanut butter sandwiches to make.

—*Kelli Carpenter, 35, Norwich, Vermont; mom to five*

High School Math Teacher

LINDA HAYEK, 55, PLATTSMOUTH, NEBRASKA

When a student asks, "When are we ever going to use calculus?" she tells them that they may need it to make dog food. Or mugs. Or music. "It's like asking people, What are you going to do with the letter *A*? Being fluent in mathematics makes you marketable in almost anything—even if it doesn't seem 'mathy.'" She likes teaching adolescents, seeing them take off in life. "You can watch them become who they're going to become and think, in a way, that you're a part of it." She also appreciates their humor. "My students have carried me through a lot of hard times, even when my husband was dying, they could make me laugh."

5:00 a.m. The alarm rings. My Pomeranian, Palmer, eases over to my side of the bed to snuggle up and wait for the second alarm to ring at five seventeen. Then he jumps to the floor, as I make my way toward the door for the daily puddle ritual. I don't make any sudden motions like my dog does.

Some people think early risers are born to be morning people. In my case, the morning routine is a simple act of faith. That is to say, I believe that my joints will loosen, my mind will clear, and I will eventually feel good and the sun will rise. I believe this even though I see and feel nothing to support that idea at 5:00 a.m. My flat feet hurt from too many miles of jogging over the years, my muscles are stiff from riding my bicycle in the March wind last night, my brain is fuzzy, and it is very dark.

5:50 a.m. Showered and dressed in teacher-type clothing for the school day. Today, I settle for a neutral skirt that flows loosely and a cotton sweater. Flat shoes, of course, and a big bag to carry all my stuff. I've noticed for years that teachers have a certain style, and I gave up trying to avoid the look. The color varies, but the style could be described as sensible. Except on spirit days when I would call it festive or fun. I push the button on the coffeemaker and pour a bowl of my usual: Frosted Mini-Wheats. I pack a lunch of carrot sticks, a banana, and two slices of seven-grain bread. I will add the peanut butter later. Boring, but balanced. I steal the first drippings of the coffee and pretend that it is espresso. It's my favorite part of the pot.

6:05 a.m. The sunroom is still dark, so I light a candle next to a vase of daffodils. It's warm enough to open the window this morning and hear the birds singing before the sunrise and the chimes playing in the breeze. I can smell the lake down the hill and see a few lights reflecting on the water. Now I remember why I'm a morning person. This quiet space is reason enough to awaken early. I set the timer for thirty minutes, knowing I might not leave without a reminder.

6:15 a.m. I put my cup and bowl in the dishwasher and read the psalm for the day. *Hide not your face from me in the day of my distress.* I sit with the words, painfully aware of the date. Eight months ago yesterday, my husband, Dave, gave up the long fight with cancer. Tomorrow would have been our twentieth wedding anniversary. The ache is threatening, so I get busy rearranging my bag, walking out onto the deck for a different view. I will not invite the ache to sit with me this morning. Later maybe. Or maybe not.

6:44 a.m. Palmer and I are packed with our stuff into the car for the thirty-minute drive into town. There is a pond on the way where a couple of blue herons sometimes fish in the spring. Dave and I named them Phil and Flossie Flamingo. But the birds are gone today. Dave isn't here, either.

6:52 a.m. I cross the Platte River into Sarpy County. I enjoy this view, especially when the sunrise is brilliant. It is cloudy this morning and a van blocked my view to the east, but even so, "I believe in the sun, even when it is not shining." There's song like that.

I am listening to NPR on the way. Someone is making paper out of panda bear dung. I guess it has an exceptional amount of fiber. Wow. Who would have thunk it?? It's also the week of the local fund drive for public radio. I'm a dollar-a-day donor, or $365 a year, but I started wondering if I should double my contribution. I mean, think about it. Where else would I get feature stories about panda poop-pyrus. I sat with the thought for a little while, but I didn't reach for my cell phone. Then the urge passed.

7:15 a.m. A sure sign of spring—the street sweeper kicking up a cloud of dust in the parking lot at the Wal-Mart.

7:20 a.m. My daily stop at my parents' house. We share custody of my dog now that Dave is gone. It's a super-good deal for Palmer, who leads a very privileged life. They wait at the door to greet me. This morning, Mom gives me an article she has clipped from the paper. Did I know that one of students on the high school track team is close to setting a national record in high jump? "Have a nice day at school. Love you!"

Here I am, fifty-five-years old, lovingly sent off to school each morning by my parents. Just lucky, I guess. One of these days, it might be my turn to take care of them.

7:30 a.m. I arrive at Papillion-LaVista High School and park in spot #56. Tom is there, recently retired but serving as a substitute this year. He's suffering from a spring cold and (from his appearance) about thirty additional pounds. I wonder if things slow down after retirement. Things like metabolism and thinking. I hope not, but time will tell. I'm calling it a career this spring after thirty-four years.

7:32 a.m. Classroom morning routine. Lunch and purse go in the lower left desk drawer. My grandson's picture on the desktop is so cute I'm distracted. Assignments and reminders on the board.

Two columns: one for calculus and one for precalculus. A challenge problem of the day. This is a puzzler from an arbitrary area of math that many students look for each day. If I forget to write a new one on the board, I hear about it all day long. I start sorting the endless stack of papers.

7:52 a.m. James arrives. He's a good teacher's aide; I love his gentle style and sense of humor. I give him a set of tests to sort, staple, and tally points. "No problem," he tells me.

Stephanie stops in. She is a math teacher here, too, as well as one of my students a decade ago. As I retire this year, I am proud to be able to "pass the baton" to her. She has talent and enthusiasm to go with her youth. Right now we are planning some new strategies for a course designed for not-so-successful algebra students, and she has some details to run by me, the math department chair. She plans to team with another strong teacher to keep the students involved in math with a variety of strategies such as games and hands-on models. It will be a double-block class with intense assistance for the students with a past record of struggles. She understands the importance of listening to each student and communicating with parents and has the makings of a strong teacher. What a blessing to work with her.

8:02 a.m. My teacher pace has kicked in by now. Trip to the office for coffee and mail pickup. Talk to the assistant principal about Stephanie's ideas. Another teacher, Laura, catches me in the hall to coordinate on precalc plans. She will take my calculus classes next year. Again, good hands.

8:21 a.m. Back to room 318. I pick up the pace a little more to prepare my examples on the SmartBoard. Speaking of which, this is the best development in education since the Ditto Master. (Not that I could improve on the smell of those purple-blue Ditto copies fresh off the machine.) But seriously, I can do so many interactive, memorable things with my SmartBoard. It brings my entire computer to life on a touch-sensitive screen for the class to use. Students love to change the colors and write on the screen, so I don't have to beg anyone to participate at the board. Or I can show a clip of a movie to demonstrate a concept very spontaneously. Today, we're studying area between curves. It takes half the time to teach and makes for twice the fun, with student involvement. I wonder if I can take this with me next year when I retire.

8:48 a.m. Just in the nick of time . . . again. Lessons are ready for the day. What would I do without first-hour plan?

8:50 a.m. Calculus begins. It's a good attendance day. For seniors in the spring, full attendance is the exception rather than the rule. It's a welcome change after last week with the school musical, debate tournaments, all-school blood drive, college visits, whatever. I'm worn out from the individual tutoring sessions and makeup paperwork. Speaking of which, Steve stays for the next period to make up a test from last week, when he was gone for a college visit.

9:45 a.m. Next class is precalculus. Cary stops at my desk to let me know that he will be gone on Thursday and Friday to go fishing with his dad. This is an annual event for him, he tells me. Will he miss anything? I point to the assignment sheet to let him know how far the class will be. Perhaps he can multitask, I suggest. He smiles. I have this dream that, one day, all of the students will agree on the same days to be absent. Probably not.

9:55 a.m. Trade and grade. "Um, Mrs. Hayek. Did we have to do those last three?"

"Yes."

"But they were hard, and I didn't get them."

"The answer is, yes. You will not get credit for problems you did not try. And, no, leaving a space for the problem does not count as trying it. Nice idea. But no go."

10:35 a.m. My desk is piling up now. Tyler wants extra help. He sang the lead in the school musical last week. And he was sick, but just during the daytime. He was able to sing during performances in the evenings, largely because he was a hero. Now, then. Could I catch him up on conic sections? And then he would be able to take the test. And then I could grade it separately from all the rest. Sigh. Of course. I do like him so much. And he did an outstanding job in the musical. Kids are amazing.

10:40 a.m. The line for extra math help continues to form even as the bell rings for homeroom. Mixed into the line are early-arriving homeroom students who would like to buy Pop-Tarts from me. It's a fund-raiser idea of mine. I buy the food. The students pay a dollar per item. The entire amount is donated to the senior project for the big, new marquis to show off the school and for special announcements. Sometimes I can't remember why I thought the fund-raiser was a good idea. "Don't you have any S'Mores flavor?" "Do you have change for a twenty?" "You don't?"

10:47 a.m. E-mail from a fellow math teacher, looking to save some planning time. I have to admit he has a style about asking for favors. He writes:

> Dear Master Teacher of Pre-Calc,
>   What is your schedule for chapter 10? One day on each section? Are you skipping any? Thanks.
>   Sincerely,
>   Tremendous Slouch

It's hard to turn him down. I write:

> Jake,
>   Laura and I have left no child behind in Chapter 10. All of our students have mastered all the sections. We are simply putting a little polish on the concepts. For your students, however, I would recommend reviewing 10.1 (from Alg 2) and then doing sections 10.6, 10.7, 10.8. Emphasize multiple representations—graph, solve algebraically, and show your work numerically. Finish by Easter break.
>   Linda

Jake decided to leave some students behind.

10:57 a.m. More e-mail messages:

- Special invitation to teachers to attend prom. (*No date this year. Not in the mood.*)
- See the principal when you have time about something that needs discussion. (*Now what?*)
- Budget is due on Friday. (*Oooh . . . where am I going to get the time?*)
- AP audit is due. (*Oops, forgot the deadline is coming up.*)
- A parent wants a grade update. (*She's not going to be happy about this one.*)
- Reminder from my choir director about the extra rehearsals for Holy Week. (*Long day.*)

11:01 a.m. Lots of movement in homeroom. What's up? I suggest they all take a seat and enjoy a conversation without moving around. It's not a gymnasium.

11:10 a.m. Loud screaming in the freshman locker area outside my room. I thought I would find a fourteen-year-old girl in trouble. It was Kenny . . . an honors student of mine. He was just *pretending* to be a freshman girl. He needs a lot of attention. But here's the truth. He cracks me up! It takes a couple of minutes to calm the group. It's hard to compete with stuff like this. Kenny gets the crowd going and then I have to follow with "solving systems of equations." Life is not fair.

11:55 a.m. I call Celeste up to my desk at the end of class. Her last test was unfinished and she left with tears in her eyes. The note on the test stated that she might have to drop the class, but she appreciated all I had done and that I was a good teacher. Okay, Celeste, talk to me. Insomnia for a variety of reasons. Long story short, we agreed that she should stay in the class and we would try to come up with a plan to make up/catch up/ something. But don't just walk away. Okay? Hugs. Thank you.

12:02 p.m. Time for the peanut butter sandwich. Guess what? Kay and Brian have peanut butter, too. Cool! Doesn't take much to entertain ourselves. Stephanie has ham, though.

12:10 p.m. Students stop in the classroom to practice for the upcoming Knowledge Masters Open competition. They work at the SmartBoard on trivia questions.

1:30 p.m. Calculus again. The after-lunch group is drowsy. I hate to stoop to bribery, but I do. I pose a problem and offer the "pick a number" method. The person whose lucky number is chosen gets to answer the question in return for a bonus point. Sometimes I give a choice between earning the point and receiving chocolate. Same result. Instant participation. I check to see if they are salivating. I feel a connection with Pavlov.

2:15 p.m. Erin works on a makeup test. Her father had a heart attack last week and she looks pretty tired. She turns in the test later, and I ask if she is okay. I don't believe her when she says yes.

2:35 p.m. Jami comes in to ask a few questions, and her work looked good. She has been gone for several days for a college visit. She wanted to drop calculus until she found out that it would mean taking an F. I hope this means she has decided to give the class her best again! It's hard to know when to push and when to back off. I really do want what's best for the kids. And I know I will miss them next year.

2:45 p.m. Sara comes for a note to verify her absence from study hall yesterday when she made up a test in my room. She didn't know that the Study Hall Gestapo would be checking up on the student tutors.

2:55 p.m. Mr. Cudly stops to verify Sara's note from me. Wonder what's up? I think seniors must be pushing the limits these days. I understand, though. It wears us all down to the point where you don't know what excuse to believe.

3:25 p.m. Kenny, Jake, and Tyler come to make up the test. That makes the last of the list of fifteen make-ups from last week. What a relief to put the list in the trash.

3:50 p.m. My daughter, Kristen, calls my cell phone to let me know that their house in Florida just sold. Good news for their move to Colorado in June! I don't stay on the phone because students are taking tests, but I enjoy thinking about being chief "grandma" next summer to help Kristen and Eric transition in their postresidency careers in medicine.

3:52 p.m. E-mail from Sharyl, my stepdaughter, about having lunch. I have two grown daughters and two stepdaughters, but I like to think of them as four daughters. Daughters are good friends.

4:35 p.m. The last of the students is done with the makeup tests. I pack my book bag for home and meet a fellow teacher in the hall. Janie is retiring, too, and a replacement teacher was hired today. We chat a minute or two, and I mention that tomorrow would have been my twentieth wedding anniversary. My eyes well up, and I know that I need to go home and tend to the grief. I won't shut it out tonight. I will stay home from choir and allow the ache to stay this time.

4:45 p.m. I stop for my dog and sit for a minute with Dad. I am so lucky to have friends and family and faith. I don't forget that. Still, I hurt. It doesn't have to make sense.

5:30 p.m. Dinner at home. I find a container of chili in the freezer. How old? I don't think about it that long, just heat it up. And a bowl of cottage cheese and pineapple. Dessert is chocolate chips with walnuts. I decide to call it trail mix.

6:18 p.m. It's raining hard. I love a good storm. The smell. The thunder. The sound on the roof. It's so beautiful on the lake with the lightning. I love this house that Dave and I built together shortly before he died. I sit with my thoughts about two decades with Dave . . . angry, grateful, sad, loving, funny, hurt, lonely, passionate, and wonderful thoughts. I just let it all wad up together in the rain.

I let the ache sit with me tonight. I miss Dave and feel close to him at the same time. I think of last year's anniversary celebration. We hired a limousine to take us to our favorite restaurant in the Old Market. It was hard for Dave to walk because the brain cancer had advanced, but maybe that made it all the more special. We snuggled into the back seat of the limo, listening to fifties music, knowing that life is very, very precious and good. I might buy myself some flowers tomorrow to celebrate our years together. I think Dave would like that. I think I would like that.

10:00 p.m. Time to take Palmer for a puddle again. Life has a tendency to go in circles.

Teach Your Children Well

7:45 a.m. Fire up the computer. Just an e-mail from my son, Klint. He always astounds me when I think of the quiet little boy he was, and now he has turned into this driven publicist for a race team. I am really proud of him. As a mother, I can't think of anything more rewarding than to see your children be successful and happy. I think of that often when I interact with the students in the Academic Success Center, and the ones I teach in my Introductory Sociology course. I always say to myself, that is someone's son or daughter. I think it makes me a better educator to think of students in those terms.

—Jennifer Buller-Briney, 46, Browning, Illinois;
Title III activity director/transition specialist, Spoon River College

●

Life Coach

LISA DALTON, 46, NORTHLAKE, ILLINOIS

She's reinvented herself professionally more than once. First, fifteen years in the entertainment industry, including production management on a world tour with Janet Jackson. Next, a marketing career that went bust after 9/11. Now, a life coach and speaker. As a single mom with no financial net, she made this last leap under protest. "There were a thousand no's in my face but I knew it was what I was supposed to do. I love what I do. Oh my god, I can't even tell you." Her pitch for working with a life coach? "It puts people in action toward the life they want."

6:30 a.m. Stumble into the bathroom, blinking hard against the lights Steve has turned on to get in the shower. It is still an adjustment to have someone living with me these past six months. I think about it at weird times like this, when it feels a little in-my-face. Then I think about waking up to his snuggle, and I get over it.

6:49 a.m. I come in to my home office to check e-mail. There's my client Pam's to-do list that she sends me to keep her accountable. She's a virtual assistant in Indiana, and does more in a day than I do in a week! Shit. I forgot to reply to a woman who had sent possible times for her trial coaching session. I send her the times I have today and Thursday. I have two complimentary trial sessions today already, which is cool. My trials go sixty minutes plus, but I can't help it. I love hearing people's stories. I can usually tell in ten minutes if I can help them.

Yesterday I had a young woman who found me on the Internet after Googling, "How to be complete without a man." Bless her heart, she actually Googled that. It sent her to the workshop on my Web site, "You (Don't) Complete Me . . . Dispelling the *Jerry Maguire* Myth." We talked for ninety minutes, then she hired me for a twelve-week program. The woman who just e-mailed me about a trial coaching session also contacted me about this topic.

I used to be the poster child for feeling incomplete without a man. I spent eleven years as a single mom—dating, struggling, dragging myself and my son through the middle-aged/divorced-with-kids labyrinth, thinking the Right Guy must be out there. I worked years with my own coach until I finally *got it*. And when I let go of all the wrong guys and the excuses why it was okay to date them, the Right Guy came along. And now I am getting married in September.

8:00 a.m. Today is my mom's sixty-seventh birthday. She lives in her own apartment in the back half of our house. I carry my coffee over to wish her happy birthday. She is annoyed that Steve parked at the end of the driveway and her newspaper was thrown under his truck. She is annoyed that it is warm again today and will be hot at the firehouse office where she works two days a week. She is annoyed by the little things a lot. I think it gives her something to talk about, though the big things she handles with grace and strength.

I love her so much and know that she has lived for my sister and me in so many ways. I don't think I live the same way for my son, and feel guilty that I don't feel guilty about this. I have always continued to pursue my own life, my dreams (and all those wrong guys), along with my role as Mom. Zac is fourteen now and a fantastic kid. He knows that he can do and be what he wants to in this world—the advantage of a Life Coach Mom. He could list many disadvantages to that, I'm sure.

I give Mom a kiss and tell her to have a wonderful day.

8:20 a.m. Grab another cup of coffee and try to ignore the skillet in the sink caked with the egg remains of Steve's breakfast. I think of the snuggle instead. I don't have time for a shower before my eight thirty in-person client. Good, I can get on the treadmill later and then shower. I really will do it today and not get caught up in surfing the Net for wedding dresses that won't look good with this extra twenty pounds on me.

8:45 a.m. Client is running late. That's okay. I am free until my ten o'clock. Another regular client calls to set up a four thirty today. She has struggled with the ongoing issue of leaving a man who is basically a jerk and won't commit after three years of dating. She remains entangled but seems *so close* to really letting him go. He treats her like a Barbie doll and she has let him. She deserves so much more than scraps of love. Last summer, I had her buy a Barbie, strip the doll down, and write on her all the bad things she felt about herself: insecure, stupid, weak, slut . . . Then we gave the doll lots of love and buried her behind my house by the creek. It was so emotional.

8:52 a.m. I leave a voice mail for my best friend, Karen, to send her love and prayers before the breast biopsy she has to undergo today. I wish I could be with her but she lives five hundred miles away.

10:00 a.m. Rush up from my session to find an e-mail that my ten o'clock trial has to reschedule. But the session I just finished was awesome. This client was so excited about last week's assignment to write twenty-five things that make her smart. My god, what a list. She rattled off raising two sons, creating a thriving business, battling addiction successfully, the courage to fight breast cancer, leaving a terrible marriage after twenty-five years, and being a good driver, to name just a few. Not on the list was the fact that she is also a world-class cake designer who has made cakes for the likes of Oprah and Elton John. She sees these great things yet doesn't *feel* them.

I assigned her homework to go through her list and imagine having lunch with this woman she described, as if she is meeting her for the first time. What do you want to know about her? About her triumphs and challenges? I tell her to take herself and her journal to lunch and answer these questions. This excites and scares her.

She also listed the ways she supports feeling stupid, and sees that this is an old story told to her long ago that she believed but is not true. She is willing to believe something different now; believe in herself. She tells me that in sixty years she has struggled to find the truth and now feels whole. She thanks me for asking the "good questions," and I am moved to tears. This is the most amazing job on earth, and I have toured the world with rock stars.

10:40 a.m. Taking deep breaths while arguing with my teenage son. Attitude flows from his pores like sweat and I can't stand it. He is on spring break and is on a campaign for the new basketball hoop he wants *now*. I tell him to go to the park (which will get me some peace). He ignores me with his head buried in his laptop.

I reach Karen. Her doctor's appointment is at three o'clock. She sounds fine and we discuss my benign biopsy six years ago and how they did it (lumpectomy). She is having a needle aspiration, she thinks. We agree that she will be fine, and I say a silent prayer that this be true.

11:30 a.m. On a high from a great trial session. As predicted, the call went over an hour. This woman has a self-defense studio in Knoxville for women and kids and was close to closing it for lack of enrollment. We shifted her message from self-defense to the empowerment of personal safety, came up with intro presentations she can do for schools and businesses, and a plan for follow-up. She is so excited! She is already talking about continuing as a client, and I would love to work with her.

1:15 p.m. Going to the treadmill. I know that I need to walk my talk in my own life. Literally.

2:15 p.m. Two-point-six miles and ab work. I feel great! I always do afterward. It's getting down there or to the gym that is the hard part. Not hard, just not what I choose in that moment. "Every single choice we make truly matters," I tell my clients. I will memorize this feeling for the next time I want to blow off exercise.

Zac has gone to a friend's and the house is quiet. Glancing around, I see the basket of clothes on the stairway, papers all over my desk, dishes on the counter, and an assortment of things Steve and the boys (we have his thirteen-year-old son, Alex, on weekends) have left lying around. I make a mental note to straighten up before the cleaning lady comes tomorrow. This is my greatest monthly indulgence, when I can afford it. People always asked me how I did it as a single mom. I look around and think being the mom in a family of four is much more work.

When I got out of the shower, I saw that Steve had come home early to work on our foyer. The joy of having a remodeling contractor mate. He has also just started night school to gain home inspection licensure, giving him more income options. I am proud of him. Money is tight with plans for our wedding. I worry about it more than I want to. But my practice is thriving and we are rich in love and trust and respect.

Steve catches me in the bedroom after my shower and we have an unexpected romp. I make my next call in my robe with wet hair, smiling. Working from home has its benefits.

3:00 p.m. The trial session is uplifting. This woman is an artist who works as a mortgage broker in San Francisco. We work on carving out time for her to paint between work, motherhood, and marriage. She is committed to making art dates with herself and wants to have a show next year so she feels like she hasn't totally sold out. We do real coaching and it is great.

4:25 p.m. My four thirty calls to cancel and it annoys me. This is not unusual for her and I don't charge her, as she is tied up at work. I feel like I have been busy all day, yet I realize I have only done three sessions. Having two cancellations is unusual.

4:50 p.m. My girlfriend calls with the latest installment of her romantic drama. My heart aches for her and her partner, who is also my friend. They are recording artists together and deeply love each other, yet he is a somewhat tortured artist and it exhausts her to be on that ride with him. I tell her to focus on herself, finish the paintings she is contracted to do, and get clear about what she really wants, regardless of whether she thinks she will get it with him.

5:20 p.m. Steve is making dinner for Mom's birthday. Michael Bublé is playing and I ask him to dance. He spins me around the living room to "That's All" and I imagine our wedding day. God, I love this man.

6:14 p.m. I call Karen again. It turns out her appointment was only a consult; the biopsy is scheduled for Friday. She sounds good.

Three clients have e-mailed me graphics they would like me to proof for upcoming events. I am happy to do this. My marketing background is a plus for them, and I love to see their work between sessions. One is a speaker who has booked two national engagements since we started working together. I am a speaker, too, just not on that level yet. I am surprisingly not jealous. I love that she is successful, and my hand in it as her coach feels like enough. I am happy to be focusing my energy on my family life right now and not beating down doors to get *out there*. That day will come later.

7:30 p.m. We have Mom over for a wonderful dinner. My sister stops by, too. Zac is outside now and Steve is studying. I'm watching a little *American Idol*, checking e-mail. Got assignments in for tomorrow's clients. One is a eulogy I assigned to a client who has dreams to live a big life reaching the world. She is a healer/therapist whose programs teach others to live authentically. "Take the LEAP and know the net will appear," is her motto. I love that. I *do* that. The eulogy was a way for her to write about her life and legacy without feeling self-conscious. I absolutely love so many of my clients, and most I have never met in person. How cool is that?

I need to go finish the dishes.

8:55 p.m. Spent most of the evening on the couch reading *What Remains* by Carole Radziwill. It's her story of joining the Kennedy family. Poignant. My ankle hurts from twisting it on the treadmill.

I am hoping this will not turn into an excuse. Zac calls to stay out later. It's easier to say yes than argue. I tell him, "Nine thirty, and please don't call again for more time."

10:02 p.m. I half watch *Frasier* while Steve takes a school quiz online. I check e-mail and book a couple of sessions for next week. Zac returns home on time. All is winding down for the night. It has been a great day. Many of them are. I am blessed to be doing the work I do with such amazing people. And I know that as I am changing their lives, they are changing mine.

Kiss Clutter Good-bye

Today I received a testimonial from Sherry, a young woman who received a favorable job review. Her impediment to advancement was her lack of organization. She and I worked to overcome this. I had to laugh when she wrote that her supervisor picked up my book from Sherry's desk and kissed it! It feels good to make a positive difference in people's lives!
—*Mary Pankiewicz, 60, Whitesburg, Tennessee;
professional organizer, author of* Clutter-Free & Organized

●

All in a Day's Work

7:47 a.m. Train pulls up. Why is that girl looking at me so nastily? Do I know her? I've caught her three times now, and I don't understand why some people are so bitchy for no reason. Clearly, something about me bothers her. So I decide to plop myself down in the empty seat directly in front of her. A little exposure therapy never hurt anyone.

—*Elena Padua, 28, Silver Spring, Maryland;*
pediatric oncology social worker

11:00 a.m. *The Drowsy Chaperone* calls. They have a put-in and the new actor likes a particular bra. *Sweet Charity* is out on tour and they need more tights and, let's not forget, the orange fishnets. *The Pirate Queen* is in tech and getting close to opening night. They need help. The little girls in *Grey Gardens* need new panties. Kilt socks? No, not in stock, but I will find them for you! And so I do, for *Mary Poppins*. Wherever they initially purchased them, these socks are no longer available. I am tenacious in my attempt to find them and after an hour of searching, success! Brown kilt socks. Will they meet the costume designers' demands? Remains to be seen, but I can rest knowing that I did my best.

—*Lori Kaplan, 51, New York, New York;*
bra fit specialist/theatrical wardrobe consultant

Noon Eat salad and my NutriSystem soup "bucket." Me and Mom have been on NutriSystem since the end of January 2006. I went from weighing 311 pounds to being 226 pounds this morning—an 85-pound loss! Mom has lost just about the same. The combination of NutriSystem and Curves is what we did. And that's why when the Curves location down the street went up for sale—I bought it.

—*Lisa M. Wilber, 44, Weare, New Hampshire, business owner,*
The Winner in You

2:40 p.m. The media session. This guy is talking smoke. I really disagree with the disingenuous media messages that use true but poorly relevant data facts to create excitement or buzz about the cervical cancer vaccine. The message should be that all women need the vaccine, and women as young as twelve will eventually benefit. It isn't an ethical practice to take science and mince it up to your own needs, ignoring all other facts. Oh, my.

—*Diane Harper, 48, Hanover, New Hampshire; physician,*
lead investigator, cervical cancer vaccine

6:23 p.m. The kids and I stop at a park to play in the good weather and soak up the last of the day's sun. I try to type on this laptop while pretending to spend quality time with my daughters. I remember that a partner at a law firm where I once worked told me that just being in the room with your children justifies quality time. I think he was confusing his kids with billable hours, which probably explains why he was twice divorced.

—*Shawn Little Dickerson, 40, Columbus, Ohio; lawyer*

life coach

Archivist and Reference Librarian

TONIA N. SUTHERLAND, 31, SOUTH HADLEY, MASSACHUSETTS

She splits her time between two positions at the library, plus she's got a young family, and is earning a second master's degree. "I'm thriving on this kind of frenetic energy, but there are definitely 'those' days—and they are not few and far between." As an archivist, she fell in love with the field when she was putting together an exhibit on W.E.B. Du Bois. "I realized you could actually be a part of history. Part of the process is knowing what records to keep. Fifty years from now, what I decide to put in a collection is what people are going to remember."

6:22 a.m. I'm awake, despite the fact that I didn't go to sleep until nearly 2:00 a.m. Last night's glass of red wine didn't do the trick. I take a deep breath. My four-year-old, Asa, is crying, and it doesn't sound like a nightmare. It sounds like the cry of a sick child, and I have four meetings today, including the one I set up with my supervisors to talk about my future at the university. My husband, Kevin, is stirring next to me (he once slept through the roof's falling in during a storm at his mother's house in South Carolina) and mumbling something about one more snooze. If I wasn't so tired, I might laugh out loud.

By 6:40 a.m. I've checked in on my son, taken his temperature (103.4 degrees), and called and left a message at work that "I might be in late." It's ludicrous, I know, because I'm going to be out for the whole day, and perhaps even the next two or three days, but somehow I want to assure them that I'm reliable, that I'll make every effort to be there.

My husband is half in and half out of his scrubs, running late as usual for his 7:00 to 3:00 p.m. shift as a nurse's aide. The job pays ten dollars an hour (half my salary) and comes with no sick days, personal days, or vacation. Even as I kiss him good-bye, I'm wondering when he's going to send in the application to nursing school.

7:58 a.m. I've called the library and told them I'll need to take family sick time. I heard the usual sigh on the other end of the line, and I'm already fighting anxiety. I know that dwelling on work will be a distraction from taking care of Asa. And I know that taking care of Asa will be a distraction from the upcoming changes at work.

I've put just over one year into a two-year research library residency that requires me to split my time between two departments: Special Collections and University Archives, which I love; and Reference Services, which I don't. The split duties are taking a toll on my sanity, reminding me of my years of working two part-time jobs.

The worry about work is compounded by uncertainty about what will happen to my job (and income!) when the residency ends. My bosses have alluded to the university's desire to keep me on staff, but nothing has been said about what a permanent position might entail. (What department? What rank? What duties?) I've been fighting for months to arrange for one work space (instead of two), one set of responsibilities (instead of two), and one supervisor (instead of two).

The associate director, who is the end of the road when it comes to making these decisions, has a reference background, and—not surprisingly—my battle to be a pure archivist has been uphill. Adding insult to injury, the culture of the research library is not, by nature, child friendly. It isn't going to help my case to be out with a sick child today of all days. I am constantly reminded by seasoned librarians at the university that the administrators think children make employees unreliable.

Immediately after this phone call, I fleetingly try to remember where I've saved the most recent version of my résumé and wonder (again) if I've made the right choice, to work at the university. I feel lucky to be there—library schools are putting out more archivists than academic libraries can hire—but I think about when I worked in the public library part time and stayed home with my son, and how less anxious I was then.

8:03 a.m. I'm covered in sick and the cat has peed on my bedroom floor. Part of me is cursing Kevin, resenting his nonchalance as he walked out the door and told me, "Have a good day." This is a point of contention in our marriage. Kevin's job doesn't offer sick days, so unless he calls two hours before his shift, he'll be written up. As usual, there was no discussion—just the assumption that I'd be the one taking the day off.

I quickly set Asa up in my bed with a movie and a bucket (the biggest pot I can find in my kitchen), then I strip out of my pajamas for a fast and lukewarm shower. As the water hits my shoulders, I remember that it's Sara's birthday (my bridesmaid, Asa's godmother, lifelong friend). I make a mental note to call her.

10:26 a.m. and my cell phone is ringing. It's Kimberly, a senior whom I supervise at the university. She broke up with her boyfriend a month ago, and I'm fielding calls because she's so heartbroken she can't sleep. Because she can't sleep, she can't work. *Who am I to judge?* I think. I'm not at work today either. She's saying something about her doctor's suspicion that she's OCD. I don't doubt it. I'm in the middle of telling her I'm sorry she's so upset and I have to go, when Asa gets sick again. Ginger ale and toast, and I'm covered again.

The thought crosses my mind that I might just rather be at work, and then I quickly berate myself because only a terrible mother would think such a heartless thing.

10:52 a.m. Before I strip down for shower number two, I remember to clean up the cat pee. I remember because I've just stepped in it.

Post-pee cleanup, I steal a moment to sit down and check e-mail. My mailbox is at 98 percent capacity and I spend twenty minutes just clearing out the overnight spam. There's a message from one co-worker and an e-card from another, both wishing Asa a speedy recovery. I'm grateful for these two colleagues, also parents, who sympathize. There is also a message from my history professor reminding me about our meeting this afternoon. I send the dreaded e-mail and am relieved to receive an immediate (and mostly compassionate) response.

12:49 p.m. Asa has fallen asleep watching *Ice Age* in his room, and I'm ready for a nap. The phone startles me awake. It's Kevin. "Were you sleeping?" Yes. And when I check the clock I realize I haven't even gotten a full thirty-minute power nap. The tears are starting to form. I'm irrationally angry and can't admit, even to myself, that I could have been resting instead of checking my e-mail. Not working at all for an entire day just doesn't seem like an option when you're trying to get ahead (or even remain employed). I tell Kevin I've got to go and barely hang up before I start to cry. I'm having a bad day.

2:30 p.m. Asa wakes up from his nap, rousing me from a fitful sleep. We've got matching marks on our faces from the blankets. He's soaking wet. I check his temp again and it's come down to 100.1 degrees. The fever seems to be breaking. I call the pediatrician to ask if there's something going around and the nurse practitioner laughs, "There's always something going around." I am not comforted.

As soon as I hang up, the phone rings again. It's my co-worker in reference who is known as the "Time Nazi." She's wondering whether I'll be in tomorrow. I'm impatient with this phone call because my work isn't brain surgery. In fact, tomorrow would have been the "better" day for Asa to be sick because I have no meetings, no reference desk shifts, no course work due. The library will not collapse because my child is sick.

I tell her I don't know if I will be in the office tomorrow and quickly get off the phone. For the hundredth time this week, and the second time today, I think of looking for another job. Then I remember the phone call to the pediatrician and the years without health insurance. I sigh. Asa, looking concerned, asks what is wrong; if *I* am okay. I pull him close to me, overcome with guilt, and tell him I love him and that Mommy's fine.

5:17 p.m. I managed to escape to the local college pool and swim laps when Kevin came home at three twenty. I'm feeling more optimistic. Asa seems to be feeling better and the fear that my job is in jeopardy begins to subside. I call my therapist's office and leave a message, asking if he can see me this week. I haven't gone for an appointment in almost six months. It feels like whining and I usually leave feeling deflated. I share this with Kevin, who says, "If it doesn't help you, don't go." I know he's right.

7:00 p.m. Asa has been put to bed after a dinner of water crackers and 7UP. Kevin took care of dinner for us (ordered Chinese) and I'm grateful. We sit down together on our bed, our safe place that we affectionately call "the raft," and relay how our days have gone. He's been applauded at work for his caring attitude toward the residents. I've been puked on, stepped in cat pee, and had a good swim. Finally, we laugh and he gets two beers from the fridge. This is why we're married.

9:10 p.m. Two hours of television and talk. I remember again it's my friend Sara's birthday. I'm feeling bad because Asa is sleeping and won't get to sing to her. I call anyway and am surprised when she answers, delighted to hear her voice.

We talk about the students in her high school writing class and the collection of faculty papers I just began processing, those of a recent widower. I tell Sara, who will understand, how it is breaking my heart to read the correspondence between him and his wife as I inventory the collection. We talk about our families. I tell her Asa has read his first book. She says that's the best birthday news she's had.

10:30 p.m. Kevin has fallen asleep, and it occurs to me that I still have work to do for tomorrow. I head to the office down the hall to work on a paper on sick-child care and family-friendly work practices that I'm writing for my women's history class. The irony is not lost on me (at all) when I finally go to bed at almost 2:00 a.m.

On March 27, 2007 . . .

19 percent of day diarists worried about job security.

•

Newspaper Carrier and Motel Desk Clerk

JOAN ZIESER, 63, VINTON, IOWA

She and her husband raised six kids and owned a tavern for twenty-two years, before selling it in 2002. About six months after retirement, a friend whose son wanted out of his paper route kept bugging her, "Joan, you ought to take it, it'll be good exercise." So she took the job. "A lot of people feel sorry for me, but I really enjoy it." She also works part-time as a motel desk clerk and candy-box stuffer. "I didn't want to work full-time after I retired, but now I'm up to over forty hours a week. I guess I went a little overboard."

3:30 a.m. Time to get ready to deliver the *Cedar Rapids Gazette*. My fourteen-year-old grandson, Alex, and I have a paper route. Must go come rain or shine, or hell and high water. I took on this paper route three years ago to force myself to get up early, and to get some exercise.

4:00 a.m. Drove six miles to my daughter Jenny's house where the papers are dropped off. I need to get Alex out of bed. We usually have only thirty-seven papers, but today we have ninety-four. Eddie, the carrier for the other side of town, has taken ill so we were asked to do his fifty-seven deliveries until he is better. (I wish him a speedy recovery.) I try to be quiet so as not to disturb the sensible people who are still sleeping at this hour.

This is a school day so I guess I will do our regular thirty-seven papers by myself so Alex can get another hour of sleep. I will come back and pick him up at 5:00 a.m. His parents are worried about his being tired in school.

There is something almost spiritual about being up at this early hour. I still get awestruck at Mother Nature when the sky is full of stars, or the moon is full, or it is pouring rain, or blowing snow. In Iowa, you get all kinds of weather. Today, it is cool but not cold, dark but not dreary.

This regular route is in the old part of Urbana, a small town of a thousand people, more or less. Some of these houses have been here for over one hundred years. In fact, I delivered to a couple of these same folks when I was a kid. My kids also delivered to most of them. And now my grandkids are newspaper carriers. We usually deliver by car during the winter months. In nice weather, we divide up the papers and either walk or ride bikes. Today, I'm taking the car.

5:00 a.m. Pick up Alex to go to the new part of town to deliver Eddie's route. This could be a foreign country for as much as I know about it. We are using a list of addresses given to us by the *Gazette*. Alex is a great help. He can spot those house numbers a lot faster than I can. I call him Eagle Eye. I must admit that this part of town is quite nice. The houses are all new. The lawns are dormant now, but I'm sure they will be beautiful in the spring.

6:00 a.m. We think we have gotten all the papers delivered to the right places. If not, Jenny will probably be getting a phone call at 6:01 a.m. I drop Alex off at his house and head for home. I would say two hours of this could be called exercise.

6:15 a.m. There is a message on the answering machine from the *Gazette*. "Eddie is not getting along as well as expected. Keep on doing Eddie's route until further notice. Could be permanent situation." I will have to give this some thought.

Usually at this time I read the paper, do the crossword, solve the sudoku, feed the dog, and eat breakfast. Today I decide to sit and ponder what to do about the paper route. It is one thing to help out for a few days, but to do that many papers every day could become more of a job than a little exercise. Alex's parents won't want him getting up that early during the school year. Must think.

Fall asleep in husband's favorite chair. There is something about this old recliner that puts a body down.

8:30 a.m. The phone rings. Wakes me up. A friend of mine calls to tell me she is selling her car, and is giving me first chance to buy it. Great news, since my faithful, old 1994 Buick has 202,000 miles on it and is moaning and groaning. My friend's 1998 Buick has only 100,000 miles. I tell her I will call her back as soon as the bank says they will give me a loan.

9:00 a.m. Call the banker. He says the loan will be no problem. (The problem is paying it back for the next three years.) I am working these part-time jobs to pay off some credit card debt. I have just put my husband, Keith, on a budget. He is not happy about it, but since retirement, things aren't going exactly the way we planned. We had a rental property we fixed up to sell, but our youngest son decided to move in there. I told my husband, if we could quit charging for a year and pay off all our loans, then we will have money to spend any way we want. I hope I'm right about that.

9:15 a.m. Call insurance company to get insurance on new used car. Call the vet. My little dog, Buddy (a Shih Tzu), needs a shave and a bath. He smells like a dog. He is a dog but don't tell him that. He goes on my paper route with me and keeps me company. (I tell my husband, he ought to treat me as good as that dog.) Call the eye doctor; I think I need new glasses. Discovered this today, trying to find house numbers on the paper route. Eagle Eye Alex kept saying, "Can't you see those numbers, Grandma?"

10:00 a.m. Usually at this time I would be at my candy-box-stuffing job, but we got all caught up yesterday. Good thing. I would have missed the call about the car. This job is three or four hours a day for a friend of mine, whose business is to put candy-for-sale boxes in workplaces. When the candy boxes come back to the warehouse, I remove any outdated or damaged product and replace the sold candy.

People pay for the candy on the honor system. I like the idea of people being honest. I told my friend, as long as the people of Iowa were honest with her, I would help out. There is not much exercise to this job, but there is a lot of chocolate around, which might explain why I need the exercise. I am always trying to find ways to go faster in filling the candy boxes. You know, idle hands are the devil's workshop, and you can't eat any chocolate while your hands are busy.

11:00 a.m. Order pizza for lunch. Don't know where my husband is. We live on a twenty-six-acre farm—a few cows and calves, a turkey, a couple of sheep and lambs. He does the chores, mows the lawn, rearranges snow (depending on the season), plants the garden, or just goes hunting and fishing. Plus, he works two days a week delivering auto parts for G & G Auto. I have given up trying to keep track of his comings and goings. As long as our yard keeps looking beautiful, I know he is around somewhere. I will eat half the pizza and leave half for him.

1:30 p.m. Ah! The best part of my day, a hot bubble bath. I use Dawn dish soap. It makes great bubbles and I soak away my aches, pains, and worries. (I am also one of those people who can't take a shower after seeing the movie *Psycho* back in 1960-something.)

2:30 p.m. Now that my troubles are all down the drain, I am getting ready to go to the Super 8 Motel in Urbana. I work as a desk clerk from 3:00 to 11:00 p.m., three or four nights a week. My job is to check guests in and out, get the money, take reservations, keep the bookwork straight, and keep an eye out for any problems. I started working at the motel as a housekeeper. I figured with that job, I would get paid for exercising. I worked as a maid for two years and really liked it, but then I was demoted to desk clerk. I had to find another form of physical activity so I joined a Granny Basketball team and signed up at Curves.

2:45 p.m. At the motel fifteen minutes early today. I was fifteen minutes late yesterday. That evens things up. The motel is really nice, and only five years old. Five of the rooms are theme rooms:

the Honeymoon Suite; the Roman Room; the Old West; the Oriental Room; and my favorite, the Jungle Room. My husband and I have stayed in the Roman Room and the Jungle Room. He is more of a Jungle Room–type guy.

We have a great staff of maids (I call them "maidens") who keep it very clean. All the maidens here lose weight. They literally work their butts off. Jan, our boss lady, is very good to all of us. She treats us like family. In fact, one of the compliments we get from our guests is the fact that the staff all seem to get along so well. One of our perks is the use of the swimming pool and hot tub. That's the reason I wanted this job in the first place. I asked the boss, if I worked here could I use the pool for nothing. When she said yes, I applied, and she put me to work that day.

4:00 p.m. I hate slow times at the motel. It won't be like this for long though. We have been taking lots of reservations for reunions, weddings, birthday parties. Earlier this year, we were full almost every night, with people working at the nearby nuclear plant during the outage. This is when the plant shuts down to refuel and do maintenance or updates. They hire hundreds of craftsmen from all over the United States (welders, boilermakers, pipe fitters, millwrights, divers, nuclear specialists, general laborers . . .). A lot of them stay at the motel anywhere from a few days to eight weeks. Some worked days and some nights, so we had services around the clock. It was a busy, fun time. I worked the last five outages as a general laborer but not this year because I didn't have the time.

8:00 p.m. Mary Jane called me at work. She's captain of our Granny Basketball team. She said practice would be Monday at 7:00 p.m. When Mary Jane asked me to play on her team about a year ago, I thought she was crazy. I still think she is crazy, but joined anyway. It's the most fun I have had in years. You must be at least fifty and still alive to qualify as a player. I qualify. We have about fourteen little old ladies on our team. The oldest one is eighty-one. What a gal. She is my idol. We practice once a week and have a league game once a month. Last Saturday, NBC was at our game shooting footage for the *Today* show. Mary Jane said the Harlem Globetrotters have invited us to play forty minutes before their game in Des Moines in April. I am so excited. My number is seventy-three and my playing name is Mama Zee.

9:00 p.m. Time to go around the motel and check on things. The pool and hot tub sure look inviting. Looks like everything is safe, sound, and secure.

10:00 p.m. Jan, our super boss lady, let me go home early, being as I have to get up earlier tomorrow to do the extra paper route. Husband and dog are sound asleep. Checking e-mail from all four of my sisters. I could write a book about my sisters. They are all characters of sorts. I tried to get them to write about a day in their life, too, but they just ignored me. They all said their lives were too boring. Like mine isn't?

My sisters and I try to vacation together somewhere once a year. I would like to go to a Minnesota lake for a week of fishing but will probably be voted down for something more exciting, like shopping. I hate shopping. Even on vacation I have a job—keeping my sisters on the straight and narrow. Now that's a job.

Between the Sheets

8:15 a.m. Five giant packs of clean sheets to make up into sets and distribute to the rooms for Sandy, our housecleaner, to make the beds. Laundry provides me with an odd kind of excitement. My husband, Bruce, can't really relate. It really does something for me. Pure unadulterated progress. He has figured out that when the dishes are done, it is the foreplay of foreplay. Productivity gets me all fired up.

—*Cindy Pierce, 41, Etna, New Hampshire; innkeeper, comic, and coauthor,* Finding the Doorbell: Sexual Satisfaction for the Long Haul

newspaper carrier and motel desk clerk

A Mission from God (on a Slow Workday)

1:45 p.m. I head to our rural ministry site in Vredenburgh to visit Patricia, a young mother we're helping with two little girls. The two-lane road gets rougher when I cross into Wilcox County, the poorest in the state. I cross creeks and pass meadows with cows and horses. There's a beautiful old home next to a tin-topped raggedy shack. Past Camden (at 2,300 people, it's the biggest town in the county), I continue another twenty miles to Vredenburgh, a community so obscure most natives of Alabama have never heard of it.

2:45 p.m. I drive into the poorest neighborhood, an area called "the quarters." This is a derogatory term referring to "slave quarters" that some white Southerners use to describe a poor neighborhood mostly populated by blacks. Lining the twisted, pitted roads are rusty trailers and old wood shacks. Some elders sit on their small porches and a few children ride bikes, since it's spring break. There are lots of dogs, a few yards with chickens and roosters, and some folks have filled old tires with flowers.

Patricia's single-wide trailer sits in a small yard near two other trailers and the two-room shack that she and her girls had been living in when I met them two years ago. Our ministry helped Patricia get her trailer, and we just got her sewer line hooked up. This is one of the reasons I'm here, to check on it, and to take photos for our donor who has "adopted" Patricia. Also, I just love Patricia and her girls and wanted to spend some time with them when things are a little slow at work (and the boss is out of town!).

The shared yard has several broken-down cars and an old stove, discarded pipes from some botched plumbing job, and some mutts tied to raggedy dog sheds. The front of Patricia's trailer is edged in with heavy undergrowth. It's common to find snakes on her front cement steps. (The first thing on Patricia's "wish list" for the donor was pest control!) As I walk up to the

water cooler diaries

door I hear, "Miss Tina is here!" The little girls' faces radiate happiness. You would think they lived in a castle.

I hug them and unload the "goodies." I never visit the poor empty-handed. Almost every delivery includes toilet paper, dish soap, cans of soup and stew. But the fun part is bringing special treats, like lotion for Patricia, and small presents for the girls—markers and posters, or jewelry.

Even though it's only March, it is *hot hot hot* in Patricia's trailer—far hotter than outside—but Patricia doesn't want to pay a huge electric bill for an air conditioner. We sit in her tiny living room, on old couches resting on cement blocks. Sweat trickles down my back. A Dora the Explorer blanket covers the window to block the sun. A rusty freezer taped with duct tape sits in the kitchen. Patricia has a pot of pinto beans boiling on the stove.

3:30 p.m. The girls tell me about kindergarten and preschool. On the wall, Patricia has taped a handwritten alphabet and numbers on typing paper. Chantess, four, recites the alphabet and counts to one hundred. Shada, five, spells simple words she has learned. Patricia is crazy about education. When I first met her, she had just graduated with honors from high school, tenth in her class, despite living in a shack with no running water.

The girls settle in to color their Dora posters. Patricia says she's glad I'm here. She's tired of not having any adults to talk to. She is taking classes online, studying criminal justice, and loves it. She wants to be a lawyer. "We just had to research a robbery case and write a police report ourselves."

4:15 p.m. The girls and I play Go Fish and make sticker books. Patricia shows me their new Easter dresses that one of our donors helped her buy. Later, the girls sing into my tape recorder— "Twinkle, Twinkle, Little Star" and "The Itsy-Bitsy Spider."

It would have been better if Patricia had not gotten pregnant at fourteen, but her childhood was so horrifying I can see wanting to leave it at any cost. This is not an easy place to visit,

newspaper carrier and motel desk clerk

even for a short time. But my work is about finding ways to make a difference. My faith is about showing a difference by "walking with love."

I admire Patricia's spirit and am richer for having her as a friend. To be stuck in this backwater community with no car and no money and no clear way out, I don't know what I would do, but I don't think I would press forward like she does, sure that the future holds possibilities.

—*Christine Weerts, 52, Selma, Alabama;*
information director, Edmundite Missions

Model Turned Actor

ANGIE EVERHART, 37, NEW YORK, NEW YORK

Career highlights and headlines: The first redhead on the cover of *Glamour* magazine; television ads for CoverGirl and Levi's (the "rear-end" girl); a brief engagement to Sylvester Stallone, posing for *Playboy* in 2000, and acting gigs including the big screen's *The Last Action Hero*, the made-for-TV movie *First to Die*, and the reality series *The Ex-Wives Club*. "I love my job! It's never boring. There is a whole lifetime of characters I can play, and I have a feeling it is only going to get better!"

8:30 a.m. Normally, I wake up to the sound of Jim Morrison of The Doors singing "People Are Strange" from my cell phone. Today, my mother popped her head in my room to wake me for the day. I'm in Phoenix, where my parents live, shooting a Universal picture called *Kids in America*. Topher Grace, one of the stars, is adorable, as nice as he is handsome. So far it's been a great experience, and, trust me, they aren't all fun and games. Doing a comedy for producer Brian Grazer makes me happy because I took two years off from acting, and the first thing I do after my time off is this movie. Go figure!

I have been here a week already and will be here one more before we wrap the whole movie and go back to L.A. This movie has been shot mostly at night, so we go to work at 4:00 p.m. until the sun comes up. After a while the system gets used to it, but the beginning of night shoots is always hard and I have been drinking a ton of Red Bull. Later this morning I have my fitting for my character, whom I call the modern-day Mrs. Robinson. The movie is a retro comedy that takes place in the eighties, so I'm sure there will be big shoulder pads and bad shoes.

Early riser I am not. Coffee is a must, but my parents don't drink it anymore so I will have to stop at Starbucks on the way to pick up my usual Van Halen (vanilla hazelnut) latte. Since today is my fitting, and not a shooting day, I have to do my own makeup and hair. Sometimes I can go a week without putting a brush through my long red locks. It sounds gross, but it looks good when it is all messy. In my opinion, anyway.

Makeup is just as easy; because I have worked with so many makeup artists who have taught me tricks over the years, I think I could do my makeup with my eyes closed! I am living out of a suitcase, which is the story of my life, so clothes are limited and the choice today is quick and easy. Jeans. I do have those days where I try on ten things before I like what I am wearing, and leave my room in a complete shambles. My cleaning lady just loves me.

10:00 a.m. I hop into my parents' silver minivan and head to the production office for my fitting. I've never met these people and want to do a good job, so I'm a bit anxious. My character has to take her top off in one of the scenes, and, let me tell you, I hate to do nudity more than anything else in a movie. Standing half naked in a room filled with men is awful. The set gets cleared and only those who need to be there are present, but I am not someone who is comfortable being nude in front of people. This scene is supposed to be funny so maybe it will take the pressure off, but I highly doubt it. I am hoping my costume will be easy so that I don't have to worry about that, as well.

It sounds so trivial to worry about my fitting and what I am going to be wearing in my scenes. But this is part of my job and I always like to do the best that I possibly can. I have learned through experience that if I am not comfortable, then I don't perform as well. Of course, if the scene required me to be a bit uneasy, then I might push to wear something tight to promote those feelings of physical unease.

10:30 a.m. George Michael and I are getting down in the minivan! I am always singing to myself in the car. Music takes me to another place, and head banging is one of my favorite things to do.

11:00 a.m. The production office is in a large warehouse, and the wardrobe department is located in the front of the building. I walk in and there is a rack to my right with my costume hanging on it. It's a black leather skirt and cream-colored silk blouse with—just as I thought—large shoulder pads! After the nice-to-meet-yous, the costume designer and her two assistants get the outfit prepared for me to try on.

Given the business I am in, I have to change in front of people all the time. Especially when I was modeling and doing fashion shows, I'd have to rush through four or five outfits a show with a dresser I'd just met to get back on the runway fast enough. Back stage at a runway show, there are dozens of people around, but today there are only three who will see me naked, and this is the only outfit I have in the movie.

Within five minutes I am completely topless. The scenes that I will be shooting call for no bra. Yikes. Now I'm standing in front of these people I've just met in a garter belt and stockings, with my hands over my boobs while they fix the shirt. They want the blouse to open easily and be very low cut, so it has to have no buttons, just a tie. The length of my arms are measured so that the sleeves will fit perfectly. The costume designer has the idea to put loads of pearls around my neck, and that is an understatement! Then the shoes with gold stiletto heels come out for me to try on, and I am an image of eighties movie magic.

As they pin and pull, I stand there feeling very self-conscious. Now that I'm thirty-seven years old, things just don't look the way they used to when I was in my twenties. There is nothing I can do but pretend everything is cool. I don't want people to know that I am uncomfortable. I had an acting teacher once tell me, "Fake it and you'll make it." When we finish up, I give them my phone number so they can schedule one more fitting. This way there won't be any scrambling around on my first day of shooting.

Noon Driving back to my parents' house, a car spins out on Highway 101 right in front of me! I could see the whites of the guy's eyes. Pins and needles shoot through my body. Thank God the man sails past me and off the road so no one else will hit him.

12:30 p.m. I stop at Starbucks for my usual latte. The girl behind the counter asks me if I am Angie. I nod yes and she screams, "Oh my god, that's so cool." I smile. It is always flattering when someone recognizes me. I am still shocked when people call out my name or ask me if I am me. I often get, "You look a lot like Angie Everhart." Usually my response is, "I get told that a lot."

When I was eighteen and living in France, I became friends with the tennis player Yannick Noah. He had won over Roland Garros (the French Open) and was one of the most famous people in that country. He always took time with his fans to shake their hands or give them an autograph. I think of him as a role model: in respect, to being kind and generous to fans.

I did have a famous boyfriend once who was not kind to his fans and never gave autographs and had his bodyguards keep people away. I never liked that because these are the people who spend their money to go see us work. They are the ones who appreciate us, and I appreciate the opportunity to give back smiles and handshakes. I think it is part of the job and, if you don't like it, then change jobs.

12:45 p.m. My parents are having lunch when I get home. They are so cute together. My father is an engineer, not retired yet, and my mother is a housewife, always busy doing something. They live in a retirement community and go out more than I do! They are avid golfers so when we get together, we play a lot of golf.

My dad notices my coffee and I tell them what happened at Starbucks. They are very proud of me, to put it mildly. They have always been so supportive of whatever I am doing. I did worry about what they would think about me posing for *Playboy* in 2000, so I called them up and told them I was thinking about doing it. My mother said, "If you can still look at yourself in the mirror, then do it." I posed for the magazine, but I kept my hand in front of my pubic hair region in every picture. Even when I do nude scenes in movies, I tape underwear over that area. It puts up a guard of protection. There are some things that are meant to be private.

12:55 p.m. My brother, Mike, text-messages me, telling me that I am number five on Yahoo!'s top twenty hits of the day. He wrote that I even beat *American Idol* and the IRS, and it's almost tax day. Wow! Then we looked at the Yahoo! Buzz Index and I was the number one top-moving search term. That means people are interested enough to take the time to look me up on the Internet more than any other actor that day. Pretty cool! I feel like I won a People's Choice Award.

My brother joked that he could be in the top five, too, but first he would have to kill some people to get there. He makes me laugh more than anyone I know. My brother and I grew up very close and I love him to death. He is married now so I don't get to see him as often as before, but we have had a bunch of fun together. One year I took him to the Cannes Film Festival in France, then we came home and I took him to the Oscars. Being famous definitely has its perks, and being able to take my family along for the ride is *fun*!

Back down to earth. After taking two years off to move to New York and *live*, I have a new perspective on my career. When I made the decision to go back to work, I was worried no one would want me. In this business you are only as good as your last movie or project, and an aging model is not going to get the kind of parts she used to get. That is so okay with me. Let some other girl take her clothes off. I want to do the mother roles, and the fabulous women that I have not yet played. Life does not only happen in your twenties.

1:00 p.m. My mother and I hop in the minivan to head over to get permanent makeup tattooed on my eyebrows. I have natural red hair, so my brows and lashes grow red. My mother had her brows done and I loved the way they looked, so I decided to do it, as well. It's awesome because you don't have to put on eye pencil anymore. We drive to this woman's house and she has a small studio next to her kitchen. I am feeling nervous because this is not a doctor's office, and because if she makes a mistake, it's on my face!

Ouch! It hurts. My mother drives us home as I apply ice to my

model turned actor

brows. They are red and scabbing up so they look really dark. If you could only see me now. But I don't have to worry about my eyebrows wiping off anymore. I love it!

I have always been one to try to look good every time I walk out the door. I don't feel good when I am in sweats and wearing clothes that are not flattering. I think if I am depressed, it helps me if I dress up and get out of the house. My mother always looks nice, and she taught me that appearance is important. It really is, especially in my line of work. I never know when someone is going to take my picture or notice me. Even when I have on a baseball cap and sunglasses, people have recognized me and said hi.

5:30 p.m. Off to dinner with my mom, dad, and their lovely friends Janell and Al. I order a beer and a salad. I'm trying to watch the weight, but my brows hurt and the beer is cold. Mother orders a salad as well. She just lost twelve pounds! Daddy, he is always eating healthy and looks terrific. The girls in my family have to watch what they eat, although I can't say no to cookies and chocolate. But if I allow myself too much, then I have to run my butt off. If I don't work out, I start to feel guilty.

8:30 p.m. I climb into bed. I am a night owl and usually don't hit the pillow until after midnight, but I am tired. My day has been wonderful! Being in Arizona with my parents while I am working on a movie is a treat. They are awesome parents, and the happiest couple I know. They have showed me that with a little hard work, a marriage can last and you can be happy! I dream of having that one day, of having children and the life that goes along with raising kids.

I have sacrificed that to build a career as a model and now an actress. I love to work, but I also would love to find Mr. Right and settle down and pop a few babies. I still have time, but that biological clock is ticking. I smile at this thought because I never imagined I would get old, and in my line of work thirty-seven is old. What a warped sense of reality this acting business puts on us. Anyway, I am sure Mr. Right is out there somewhere, but for now I will dream about him and my Oscar.

Ouch!

12:30 p.m. Had lunch with my dearest friend who also works at the same university as me. She had a wax appointment earlier in the day. All she ever has to say is, "wax appointment" and I'm done. Beyond eyebrows and upper lips, do I really need to know?

—*Georgeanne Hogan, 42, Rochester, New York; administrative assistant*

•

McDonald's Store Manager and Pro Football Player

JODI WIGGINS, 31, PENSACOLA, FLORIDA

At McDonald's, her goal is to make her fifty-five employees love their job, and serve every customer in three minutes and thirty seconds or less. "I want to be the best McDonald's in my city, so there's no compromise on customer service!" As a linebacker for the Pensacola Power (part of the National Women's Football Association), her goal is to hit hard and low. "I love to tackle, but there's an art to it. If you tackle the big girls correctly, they go down just as easy as the little girls. If you hit them wrong, you get your bell rung!"

6:00 a.m.! I grab my coffee and head for the computer room to look at my planner. I must mentally prepare for my day at McDonald's. Today is training day, when Victoria, our company training manager, spends the day in our store to see if our training program for the crew is on track. This ought to be a good day! I know I can relax because Victoria is fun, and our training is going well, so it makes me proud for her to check us out. I dress in my manager uniform, complete with tie and name tag; kiss my girlfriend, Andrea, good-bye; and I am gone.

8:30 a.m. I hook up the iPod and listen to Huey Lewis and Fergilicious (Fergie) to pump me up. This is how I make sure I have the right attitude for a leader. I am motivated and energetic. I like to have everyone around me happy. It makes for a more productive workday, and we serve our customers better.

8:45 a.m. The McDonald's parking lot is almost full. About ten cars are lined up in the drive-through lane, but it is moving steadily. Inside, I can see several people in line. My managers seem to have things under control by the way the customers are flowing. I love to see that! In the parking lot, I check for litter, picking up the big pieces of trash, but for smaller things I will send the maintenance man to sweep more thoroughly. Then I check the Dumpster area for any bad odors, and check the signs for cleanliness. Yes, we even clean the signs!

Inside, I look for smudges on the lobby windows and doors. At the drink bar, I wipe up some spills, remove trash, and check that the area is stocked. This drink bar is the most critical area to watch, next to the restrooms. The women's room is clean except for some towels on the floor that I pick up. The men's room needs the counter wiped and some toilet paper, so I tell the lobby person. I credit my mother for my alertness to restrooms. She always told me a person can tell a lot about a restaurant by the bathrooms!

I stop for a minute to chat with my "regulars," four retired guys who come in about five or six days a week. They always get coffee and usually the same sausage biscuit order, with one grape jelly. We talk about the upcoming football season and how our team is looking—*Is the quarterback any good? Is the running back faster than last year?* Do you ever notice that it is only retired *men* that hang out for coffee at McDonald's? Wonder why retired women never do that?

9:05 a.m. I finally head behind the counter, looking for those smiles! "Ericaaaaa," I say to the drive-through lady. "Whassup?" I say to Robert and Judi at the grill area. Everyone seems to be in good spirits, with easy smiles. (If they won't smile at me, they won't smile at my customers!)

At the back drive-through register, I say hello to "Z" (her real name is Izizi). Uh-oh. She doesn't seem her cheery self. After her customer leaves the window, I ask if she is okay. She says she needs to go to the restroom. Well, that's an easy fix. I offer to watch her register and she says, "Thank you, thank you, Ms. Jodi!"

I check in with the floor managers, Del and Sha, and Victoria, the company training manager. Any equipment issues, big orders, call-ins? Today we have one call-in for a 3:00 to 9:00 p.m. shift. No big deal. We call a few crew and it's filled.

One of the things I'm doing today is training Sha, who is in her early twenties. I hired her about a year and half ago, and since then she's moved up to crew trainer, then shift leader, and now has been newly promoted to shift manager. She is learning how to control a shift of fifteen employees, plus oversee cleaning, stocking, and of course, customers! Her motto is, *Destined to be great!* and I tell her she will be great! I am very pleased with her progress.

9:45 a.m. In the office I do my morning check of e-mails from the other managers on the shifts before me. We're required to leave each other notes about labor, wasted food, what areas were cleaned, employee issues, and any good things that happened. Right now my managers have their shift rocking up front, so I can get on with my agenda. I need to follow up on our crew people from Thailand, mostly university students who have been working here a week and will stay for three months. We have also worked with crew from Puerto Rico, Moldova, Chile, Turkey, Peru, and Brazil.

I used to be against outsourcing, thinking we were taking jobs away from Americans. Until, of course, I couldn't staff my restaurant with quality people. For every ten Americans I hire, only two or three actually work out. I just terminated one because she was late for work her whole first week. Even five minutes is *late*, but she didn't understand that. We suspended her and she came back to work four minutes late! I can't keep crew like that.

I begin training two of my Thai ladies on how to make sandwiches. First, the names of each product—pickles, onions, big lettuce, shredded lettuce, etc. One of the ladies speaks better English, so I teach her to read the screens so she can help the other young woman. Language is definitely a problem. You have to teach by showing, not telling, and most of them do not understand our slang, but they learn quickly. I demonstrate how to drop the bun in the toaster, and pull the wrap on the table. Soon they are working so fast I almost don't have time to correct them on something.

By **11:30 a.m.** we have about twenty people waiting to order, and a line at the drive-through. Erica is running the front drive-through booth, smiling with each order. Robert is putting meat on the grill as fast as he can on his one wooden leg. Ms. Carol is boxing the fries, but she isn't keeping up well today. Her gout is acting up but, bless her, she tries so hard! "T" is singing "My Girl" while making sandwiches. I finally have someone take Ms. Carol's spot, and let her go home. She understands she isn't as fast as most.

We stay busy pretty solid until about one fifteen. I help with cleanup and see how much money we did over lunch—$1,700 in two hours. Pretty good! Victoria and I get ready to eat lunch. Yes, we eat at McDonald's. Working nine- or ten-hour shifts, I eat McDonald's about two times a day, usually. Sometimes I even crave it when I am off. There is nothing like a Big Mac, extra sauce, and cheese!

4:00 p.m. Victoria and I have a meeting with our four crew trainers. Robert, in his forties, is my oldest trainer. In his younger, wilder days, he survived a train wreck, which is how he got his wooden leg. When I hired him, he was just a grill man at Hardee's and Popeye's, always working two jobs. Robert's teenage daughter, Kyrstin, is also a trainer. The other two are Tony, who is finishing his first year of college, and Laquisha, seventeen, who wears skirts all the time, and is one of the most sweet-spirited young ladies I know.

In the meeting, we talk about employee issues—someone not having the correct shoes; someone not wanting to train on a specific station. We praise them for their progress with the trainees, and I tell them we will be rewarding them with a party just for them. I have a $150 budget, and they need to have everything planned in two weeks. They shout out ideas like bowling and skating. We leave the meeting feeling uplifted.

mcdonald's store manager and pro football player

5:30 p.m. I look around the store once again for anything out of place. Then I go into my office and pay bills, and leave messages for the other managers. It's been a good day and I feel good about the direction we are moving as a team. It is a multimillion-dollar business, you know!

6:00 p.m. Driving home, I mentally switch gears. For seven years I've played pro football (my second job, but I don't get paid). Our first game this season is two weeks away, against the Nashville Dream. Last week's scrimmage was lackluster. No big hits, no sacks. We looked like the Bad News Bears. I know we will get better! I stop at Smoothie King and get a muscle-builder strawberry smoothie to prepare my body for practice. You learn in football that if you have practice at 7:30 p.m., you don't eat dinner after 5:30 p.m. or you will regret it!

6:30 p.m. I get home to my wonderful girlfriend, Andrea (who also works at McDonald's, as the director of operations), and her five-year-old niece, Kayla, whom she is babysitting. Kayla gives me hugs and kisses. She tells me how many "stars" she got at school that day. It's an awesome feeling to come home to people who love you. I really would have liked a nap before practice, but no time for that.

I get dressed in my football gear. First, I pull my way into the girdle, which is spandex and holds the thigh pads in place. Before putting on my pants, I put the knee pads on them, and the belt, so it is a little simpler to get them on. I feel constricted in my football pants, but also kind of invincible. Next I put on my socks, sports bra, and cut-off shirt. I grab my bag and a hat for later, when my hair will definitely need help.

6:45 p.m. I kiss my girls good-bye and I'm off to pick up my team-mate, Magz. She is a rookie this year, playing defensive tackle and doing pretty well. We head to the field, jamming to "Break Stuff" by Limp Bizkit, and Linkin Park. We need to get pumped up. We're going to be hitting people soon! We try to be at practice early because it takes a few minutes to finish putting on our gear—cleats, shoulder pads, and helmet.

7:25 p.m. It's humid tonight and would be so much cooler if it would rain. About twenty players are on the field, with a few stragglers in the parking lot. (Sometimes it's hard to get motivated to put on those extra ten pounds of pads and cleats, and run for two to three hours.) I go over and talk to the QB, who is also my best friend, Jamie. She is offensive captain and I am defensive captain. We holler for people to round it up for the big lap, which is about a half mile.

"Big girls in front," we say. We make the linemen lead because they usually run the slowest. This way, everyone has to stay behind them so we run as a unit. Your team is only as good as your slowest person. I am more in the middle so I can yell and motivate my teammates. "Good job, ladies!' "Keep pushing!" "What doesn't kill you makes you stronger!"

After the lap, we divide up into four lines. Jamie and I and the other two captains for the week lead the stretches. This makes for fewer pulled muscles and broken bones. Two years ago, I broke my humerus in two places and had to rehab for eight months. But you cannot think about these things or you will play scared and possibly hurt yourself again.

Time for ten-yard drills. Coach Will, our receiver coach, stands at the ten-yard line and we run to him and back—backward, side-steps, high knees, and about twenty sprints. I cheer on my teammates. They call me "Psycho" because no matter how much I run, I can always yell for someone. You always do better when someone is cheering you on. We finish the drill and huddle as a team for the chant, clapping and slapping our pads. Pat-pat-clap. Pat-pat-clap. "One. Two. Three. *Power!!!*"

7:45 p.m. Three minutes to get water, then I head to the defense huddle for drills with Coach Doug. Michelle and I are first up. We lie on our backs, head to head, with feet going in opposite directions. Michelle is holding the ball. Coach Doug blows the whistle. We jump up, I turn and lower my shoulder, and tackle Michelle with my arms around her waist and my head on the side she is holding the ball. I take her off her feet and down we go!

We do this drill about fifty times. The key is to hit low and drive with your legs until they go down, no matter how big or small the girl is. I am five foot five and weigh 165 pounds. There are lots of bigger girls, but you have to play tough, ten feet tall, and bulletproof! I think I did pretty well tonight, but I need to work on getting my head on the ball more so I can make my opponent drop it.

About **8:30 p.m.** or so, we line up in defensive formations of four linemen up front by the ball, and four linebackers (like me) behind them, in case anyone gets through. We run through more drills, then it's time for four sets of "gassers." Coach sets up five cones ten yards apart all the way to the fifty-yard line. On the whistle, we run to the first cone, turn and come back, turn and go to the second cone, etc. It ends up being the whole length of the field and then some!

I do pretty well for the first three sets, but it takes everything I have to do as well in the fourth set. I still keep yelling for my teammates because there are a lot of big girls out here running, and it's a lot harder for them because they aren't in shape. Whew! The balls of my feet are aching from stopping and going so much in these cleats! I can't wait for water. We finish practice by huddling around the head coach, Mike, and clapping until everyone is in the group. Then we yell, "One. Two. Three. *Hit!*"

Only five practices left until the first game. The butterflies are starting to flutter. I know this game will be a chance for some big plays, like maybe a sack on the quarterback. I always am hoping for that big tackle, the one where I just lay someone out and the crowd goes, "Oooh!"

9:55 p.m. I drop Magz off at her house and think about football the rest of the way home. As captain, I feel I have to work harder than the rest of my teammates. I want to be equal to a female Brian Urlacher, the Chicago Bears linebacker. I want the muscles, heart, and leadership that Urlacher has with his team. I want to be a hard hitter, intimidating to all running backs that come my way!

10:15 p.m. At home, Andrea is in bed watching *American Idol*. I give her a kiss and head for the shower. Whew! It is always nice to get clean after practice. I make two roast beef and Swiss sandwiches with a Mountain Dew, then go to the computer to get ready for tomorrow. I am training the new manager again and jot down a few notes on my to-do list about what I will show her.

Each day is different, yet the same at McDonald's. The only real variable is my people. Different day, different personalities, different motivators for fifty-five employees. My crew keeps me interested in coming back each day. Tomorrow, we serve Pensacola again.

Good Call

Morning Talked with my staff and all feel we should not do the deal with the investors from New York. It wouldn't be the first time that a group of men have tried to take over my women's football league. Heck, I've even battled the NFL.
—*Catherine Masters, 62, Madison, Tennessee; founder and chief executive officer, the National Women's Football Association*

•

mcdonald's store manager and pro football player

All in a Day's Work

10:30 a.m. Quick stop at the fabric store for a few things I need to finish today's project. I wish money wasn't an issue; they are having a sale and I would stock up on a few extra things if I could. The cashier asks me what the fabric I'm buying is for. I tell her a hat. She smiles and says, "Oh, isn't that *nice*! I mean, do people still wear hats?" I smile and hold back a smart-ass remark. Off to the studio.

—*Laura Hubka, 36, Chicago, Illinois; milliner*

Mid-morning My food delivery route takes me at least two hours and covers about sixteen households and thirty housebound people. The next stop—Willie's house—has a large X through it on the delivery list, so I don't stop. I suspect that when most people come to the door after I knock, it is the first time that morning they have looked outside. "It is a glorious day," I tell them. "Just look at your garden, the daffodils. Crocuses are poking up all over, and even the forsythia are out now!"

—*Myrina McCullough, 59, Washington, D.C.; volunteer*

1:00 p.m. Just got out of the mother of all meetings. My stomach is growling and there's no more bottled water in the fridge. Will have to go downstairs and buy a diet soda from the creepy store owner. He calls me "good mother." Whatever happened to the days of being called "Bay-bee?"

—*Marisa Treviño, 49, Rowlett, Texas; publisher/editor, Latina Lista*

Mid-afternoon The surgeon in the operating room sends a lymph node from a woman recently diagnosed with breast cancer. He wants to know if there is any cancer in this lymph node (called a sentinel node) because it is the first in the chain that breast cancer could spread to from the tumor in the breast. If

I see cancer there, he will take out all the lymph nodes in the axilla (that's armpit, to the rest of us). If I don't see cancer in the sentinel node, the patient won't have to have this done, which would be very good.

I take the lymph node, which looks like a small, pale, lavender-pink to yellowish kidney bean, cut it in half with a scalpel, and touch the cut surface of the tissue to a glass slide. The cells from the surface of the cut lymph node almost magically stick to the slide. I then stain them and look at the slide under the microscope.

What I hope to see is just the normal lymph node cells, cleverly called lymphocytes. But if there is cancer there, I will see the cancer cells mixed in with the lymphocytes. In this case, I see only lymphocytes. I call my result in over the intercom to the surgeon waiting in the OR, and the patient is spared the removal of all her axillary lymph nodes.

—Robin Eckert 45, Ashland, Oregon; pathologist

6:25 p.m. Arrive at Times Square. I dislike all the pushing and shoving of humanity as everyone getting on and off the train try to move at the same time. The long walk between Seventh and Eighth avenues seems endless, as it does each night. The proselytizers are out in full force. One man tries to hand out cards. Another man screams as people pass, "Accept Jesus Christ into your life!" He adds all sorts of admonishments of what will happen if we don't. It is fine if people want to celebrate their own spiritual life, but it gets tedious being screamed at every night.

—Margaret Morrison, 41, Mount Holly, New Jersey;
assistant principal, P.S. 199Q in New York City

mcdonald's store manager and pro football player

Consultant Dietitian

MARY SHEA ROSEN, 53, BRATTLEBORO, VERMONT

She's a caretaker on the job and off. At work, she completes nutritional assessments and dietary care plans, mostly for geriatric patients. At home, she cares for her husband, a gifted musician in the last stages of Lou Gehrig's disease. "I promised to keep him at home, but I had no idea." A broad circle of friends, family members, neighbors, and acquaintances make it possible. "They visit with Gary, provide hands-on care, play music, read to him, watch the Red Sox together. It's awful, this situation, but there is also a lot of joy to balance the fear."

12:48 a.m. I wake up at the kitchen table with my head on my laptop, eyeglasses in hand.

My husband, Gary, in the adjacent room is coughing. I go to him, wipe his lips and beard, and suction the secretions from his mouth. Then I reassure him that I will be right back. He blinks once, indicating that it is okay.

1:00 a.m. I walk upstairs to collect my favorite fuzzy brown pajamas and see that Penn, my seventeen-year-old son, still has his light on. "You'd better get to bed. Good night." I check the thermostat, turn off the hall lights, and go back downstairs.

1:20 a.m. I go to my air mattress that I inflate nightly, setting up my bed next to my husband's hospital bed so that I can reach over and hold his hand at night. Sometimes I get wedged between the two beds.

1:30 a.m. Not to sleep yet, as Gary continues to cough and moan over the sound of the BiPAP machine (a breathing machine that blows air through his nostrils, then helps him exhale) and the tube feeding pump. His nose is stuffy, so I search the dark room for some Vicks and rub it on his chest.

1:45 a.m. I suction Gary again and put Ativan (for anxiety) in the feeding tube. First crush the meds with the mortar and pestle, mix with water, draw it up in a 10 cc syringe, put meds into the feeding tube, then flush with another 10 cc of water. Now I can't sleep, so I reply to e-mails.

3:58 a.m. Awakened again by Gary's moaning. More suctioning.

6:30 a.m. Alarm off, turn coffee on, go to get milk on ice on the porch, go to basement refrigerator to not so easily find breakfast sausage, eggs, and Cheddar cheese to make the kids' breakfast. My two-year-old refrigerator died on Sunday. I make Penn and Eliza, fifteen, "Mommy McMuffins" to go. After much prompting, they are off to school and I give a sigh of relief. Hopefully they won't be late, as they have been on several occasions, often for valid reasons such as helping to transfer Gary out of bed.

7:45 a.m. I grab a quick shower while our live-in Polish caregiver, Barbara, watches Gary.

8:00 a.m. A hospice volunteer and friend arrives and starts range-of-motion exercises with Gary.

8:15 a.m. Male nurse arrives. I explained that Gary is now unable to comfortably stay off the BiPAP machine. Gary does not wish to "toilet" as he is too tired. It takes four of us to transfer him to his shower chair. The nurse and I give him a very quick shower, resume the BiPAP (breathing assist), and dress him. We then transfer him to the recliner.

9:30 a.m. Two friends who volunteer weekly arrive. I update them on college admissions for our son, refrigerator repair, and Gary's health status. They bring information regarding legal assistance for estate planning for my mother, who has been in and out of nursing homes recently, but is back at her home now.

10:00 a.m. To town to the bank to get a rush debit card for my youngest daughter who is going to England on a school trip in early April. We misplaced the first card in that very special spot too special to find.

10:50 a.m. Stop by the gas station store to buy milk. I run into a friend and we discuss Passover plans at our house. Although Gary no longer takes food by mouth, he has always led the music and we feel that the spiritual connection is important to him this year. We talk about Gary's health and thoughts of the future, and we both become teary-eyed.

11:15 a.m. Back home to find that the respiratory therapist has arrived. Gary is asleep so we go to another room to talk. The therapist feels that we need a plan, as Gary clearly is declining. He brings us a different mask for the BiPAP, adjusts the mask, and increases the setting on the BiPAP giving more pressure to facilitate each breath. He suggests that I speak with Gary's doctor about morphine.

12:45 p.m. I call our tax preparer/lawyer about a letter of special circumstances to be sent to college financial aid departments.

1:00 p.m. I kiss Gary good-bye several times on his forehead as he is sleeping, then head to my job in Bennington, Vermont, which is forty-five miles over four mountains. It is becoming harder every day to leave. Today was a very late start to work. Once en route, I call Gary's doctor to set up a plan on end-of-life issues, only to discover that he is in Brazil and will not be back in the office until May. How did I miss this? But one of the very nice nurses in his office said that they will be there for us, and she orders morphine.

1:50 p.m. First stop is at my mother's home in Bennington to deliver a pie and say hi. Like us, she also has a Polish caregiver, and a humorous moment happened the day before, when I had brought a quiche. My mother, who is almost eighty-seven, can't see well and Ula's English is a bit of a challenge. Mom thought that I had brought her a pie instead of a quiche, and Ula told her that she was saving it. So Mom thought that she was being denied the pie. Later that evening I figured out the communication lapse and we all got a chuckle out of it.

2:15 p.m. Finally I arrive at my first account—a long-term-care and rehab center.

I go into the kitchen and speak with the assistant food service director, who presented a resident complaint about dietary, which the resident had shared with her lawyer. I visit with the resident and we come up with a plan of correction. She is on a very restrictive diet and simply wanted more control over her menu selections. She apologized profusely for writing the letter to her lawyer. I document our plan in her medical record and notify the nursing and dietary departments.

Next, I review the status of several patients with the nursing unit coordinator and go on to visit each one. A ninety-one-year-old palliative care patient with skin breakdown, poor intake, and swallowing difficulty at high nutritional risk . . . A fifty-seven-year-old with diabetes, cardiac disease, depression, dementia . . .

When I complete a nutritional assessment, I review weight status, intake, medications, relevant conditions and diagnoses, physical and mental functioning, lab values, and skin condition. Then I calculate nutritional needs in terms of calories, protein, fluids, special diet, and supplements, and develop a plan of care, reviewing it regularly, or if the patient's medical condition changes.

4:00 p.m. Go to the locked dementia unit and complete six more nutrition assessments and care plans. I spoke with nursing about a new resident who has a failure to thrive with a diagnosis of Alzheimer's dementia with agitation. The psych nurse has been in with med changes, and I complete a nutrition assessment and recommend a mechanically altered diet and health shakes between meals because this patient's tooth loss makes chewing difficult.

Shirley, a resident, wanders into the nursing station where I am charting and says that she would be "so grateful for an ice cream." So I go to the nourishment kitchen on the unit and give her one, knowing that with all her wandering she is losing weight.

5:15 p.m. Off to another health and rehab facility. En route, I call home to see how Gary is doing, and talk with the hospice volunteer, kids, and our friend Skip, who had arrived from NYC. Gary seems okay, although his nose is quite stuffy. He and Skip have watched a couple of slide shows Skip has brought with him of trips they had taken in the seventies. Skip was the best man at our wedding.

5:25 p.m. Since it is mealtime when I arrived at the facility, I visit the dining areas and interact with several residents. I look at how they are handling the texture of the food, and for any indication of swallowing difficulty, such as coughing after drinking, a runny nose, pocketing food in their cheeks, or spitting out food. I also check for the percentage and types of foods eaten.

6:30 p.m. I stop by my mother's home on the way out of town to help get her ready for bed. It is becoming increasingly difficult for her caregiver to transfer her to bed alone. I help with washing her, changing her into her nightgown and putting on her CPAP machine.

7:00 p.m. Start the drive over the mountains, calling home to say that I am en route.

8:00 p.m. Arrive home, thank the hospice volunteer who is just leaving, kiss Gary, and give a hug to Skip. Touch base with our two teenagers and congratulate Penn on another college acceptance!

8:15 p.m. Visit with Gary and Skip, viewing a slide show on DVD that Skip brought of his and Gary's trip to Morocco in 1974. Gary looks so young in the photos! It was before we had even met.

9:00 p.m. Put together some dinner for Skip and me—squash soup and a vegetarian casserole. Skip is mostly vegetarian and he had throat surgery because of cancer several years ago, so he needs soft and moist foods. We eat at the kitchen table and talk. Gary has fallen asleep in his recliner.

9:30 p.m. Barbara, Penn, and I start to put Gary into bed. Since he is totally immobile, cannot communicate with words, and is now dependent on the breathing apparatus, it takes about forty-five minutes to transfer, wash and change; do mouth care; set up the tube feeding and BiPAP; give medicine; set up pillows just so; and then blow up my air mattress. The kids, caregiver, and I have the routine down by now. When Gary was first diagnosed in July 2004, I thought back then that I didn't want the kids to have to be so involved in his hands-on care, but it just happened over time. It seems so natural, very loving. The kids have been incredible in caring for their father.

10:15 p.m. Skip and I sit down to have a cup of tea and dessert. We discuss Gary's health status, fully aware that we are facing his final stage of life. At some point in our conversation, I nod off.

11:00 p.m. Skip says goodnight and goes three houses up the road to our good friends, who often put him up for the night when he visits.

11:15 p.m. I respond to a few e-mails, then start to work on a foot-high stack of financial aid applications for our two kids going to college. As the new day begins, I listen to the sound of Gary breathing on the BiPAP.

On March 27, 2007 . . .

24 percent of day diarists commuted more than a half hour to their job.

●

Doll Sculptor

ANGELA DUGAN, 38, BAKERSFIELD, CALIFORNIA

Winner of an Industry's Choice Doll of the Year Award 2007, she specializes in mini to life-size portrait dolls. Whether she's sculpting Elvis and Priscilla, a newborn baby, or a cake-top bride and groom, her goal is "to capture a moment in time in 3-D." A Jehovah's Witness, and mom to a three-year-old son with autism, she weaves work into her everyday life. "I have an awesome studio in my home, but half the time I sculpt standing up at my breakfast bar. My workspace is wherever my toddler wants to be at that moment."

12:00 a.m. I'm working on a baby doll at my dining room table, one that I hope to sell to the Middleton Doll Company, the largest collectible doll maker in America. This is my favorite part, putting the finishing touches together by painting and assembling the doll. I can still hear my three-and-a-half year-old, Manny, awake in our bedroom. He sleeps with us, and I'm wondering if Sam, my hubby, is awake, too.

I really try not to work at night, but I'm making up for lost time due to a big blunder a couple of days ago. I was curing the head of this doll in my oven and accidentally set the temperature one hundred degrees hotter than I should have. In ten minutes, I burnt the nose, cheeks, lips, chin, earlobes, and neck. I then had to carve off the charred features and worked an all-nighter to catch up. Thankfully, I sculpt with ProSculpt polymer clay, which cures seamlessly, so this disaster was fixable.

12:30 a.m. Now very lightly buffing out imperfections on the face, hands, and feet. Next I'll apply eyelashes and paint the eyebrows.

It's raining outside, which means it's probably going to be a beautiful clear day tomorrow and I'll be able to see the mountains.

1:22 a.m. Still hear my little boy, singing. I'm jealous of my hubby, who is definitely snoring. I have to get some sleep soon because one of Manny's therapists comes at 8:30 a.m. I need to have Manny up and fed by then. Fat chance, but I'm gonna try!

2:00 a.m. Stuffed the body with poly-fill and attached the limbs using my hot glue gun and large plastic ties. Everything lines up when I lay the doll down against my draft of measurements. I feel my second wind coming on. I'm excited to dress him! The outfit is so important to the artistic impression I'm trying to convey. Baby Ethan (named for his real-life inspiration) is wearing light blue, soft linen pants, a blue-and-yellow plaid shirt with a puppy dog vest, a sun hat, and cloth shoes lined with the same plaid to complete the ensemble.

I think Manny just now went to sleep.

2:20 a.m. I love it! Little Baby Ethan is finished. I try out a few different poses, including a little peek-a-boo pose with a blanket that makes him absolutely come to life! Now to clean up. I can't put it off because I work with scalpels, acetone, and other things that I don't want to end up in my little boy's mouth. Finally, time for some precious sleep.

8:00 a.m. One of Manny's therapists, Ramone, calls to cancel due to stomach flu. Hope my son didn't give it to him. Manny just got better two weeks ago. I'm sorry Ramone's sick but I'm going to take advantage of this opportunity to sleep in a little.

9:15 a.m. Woken up by a call from Kathy at the Head Start program, reminding me that I need to get a TB test done for myself and my son. I know if I don't get this done soon, Manny will be dropped from the program. We've scheduled it twice but they couldn't do it when he was sick, and to be honest, I hate taking him for shots. He gets so upset. Once, he even kicked the glasses off the doctor's face. I admit, I haven't made this a priority.

9:40 a.m. Since I'm up now, I may as well photograph Baby Ethan. I want to capture that look of excited anticipation on a baby's face when you do or say something silly. I hope I can convey this in the photo shoot.

10:55 a.m. My back is killing me. I have to hold these awkward, yoga-type poses to get the shots I need with a heavy 9 mega-pixel camera. My hubby is offering assistance but the trouble is, he can't get into my head to see what I need to see in the photo. I love him for trying, but am kind of impatient and driven, which he translates to his trusty catch-all, PMS. My heavy sigh told him to give me space.

Taking a break. My hubby is loading the photos on the computer. He is my in-home computer genius.

11:11 a.m. I'm viewing over fifty images to pick just the right ones to submit. If the doll looks stiff or posed, I delete the image. My husband is rushing me so we can go out to IHOP for breakfast, so I have to switch to love-it-or-hate-it mode.

12:45 p.m. Sam decided to just go get fast food for us. I gave my little boy a shower and a deep massage. Manny's clinging to me, so I take some time to love him and play with him in his jump house, which is currently inside the house. Yes, we have a ten-foot by fifteen-foot inflatable jump house with a climbing wall inside our living room. My husband found a great deal on eBay, and since my son couldn't be out in the sun due to an allergic reaction to some medicine a few days ago, we brought it inside. Honestly, I don't think it will make it outside all summer.

12:55 p.m. Sam came home with a McDonald's one-third-pound Angus Deluxe. Mmm. These burgers are going to be the death of me.

1:55 p.m. Just sent the e-mail to the Middleton Doll Company with image attachments. Call my contact there on her cell phone. She says, "Aw, Angela, I just left the office. I'll take a look at them in the morning." She also has the numbers and release dates for my last doll. Argh! I was so mad at myself for not getting it to her sooner. Oh, well, now I'll just have to make the best of my day.

2:00 p.m. I let my little boy get into his jump house again while I get his snack ready.

2:27 p.m. Need to tidy up, start a load, and look presentable before my son's new therapist comes at three thirty. I was in some old PJs, but now I put on a bra, sweats, and makeup. I rarely allow myself to be seen without a little makeup. Give Sam a grocery list.

2:42 p.m. Send an e-mail to a small group of professional doll artist friends. I start letting my insecurities get the better of me, wondering if the doll company will like Baby Ethan. It always helps to have other skilled artists critique my sculpts. I make lunch for my son, before his therapy session. Manny is so precious. He wants to help, so he is opening and closing drawers in the kitchen.

3:30 p.m. Meet Sarah, the new therapist. She's about twenty-two, beautiful, and I am glad to see she is dark-skinned and a brunette. My son's favorite, just like his cousins that he adores. Sarah shares with me that she has a relative who has autism and knows what it's like for us as a family. This touched me. I told her that I thank God every day that our little guy blessed me with the gift of motherhood. We had tried for eleven years.

My son is (I think) on the mild side of the spectrum. It has affected his ability to communicate and understand language. I told Sarah about a recent experience, taking Manny to a toddler gym class. It was the first time I had clearly seen the developmental gap between him and typically developing children. Manny was smiling much of the time, totally oblivious to some of the other

doll sculptor

children giving him looks like, *What's wrong with you? Why don't you understand what they're asking you?* That day, I took a deep breath and decided to join my son in his happy little world, and ignore mine.

I found myself holding back tears as I was telling this to Sarah, but I told her I didn't want any pity. On tough days, I remind myself how hard we fought the school district to get Manny one-on-one intensive applied behavior analysis in our home. Now we see small positive changes in him every day, thanks to this therapy. His eye contact has greatly improved, as has his vocabulary. I've even heard a couple of *I love yous*!

4:00 p.m. Get a wonderfully supportive e-mail from renowned baby doll artist, Jen Printy. She says that Ethan was a real cutie, and that he looks like he just got a new toy, the kind with lights and sound.

5:05 p.m. Get an e-mail from fellow sculptor Barry Cathers, regarding the IDEX Las Vegas industry trade show at the end of June. He and his wife want to know if my hubby and I would like to join them for dinner or a show there. I tell him we'd love to, and send him images of Baby Ethan for feedback.

5:11 p.m. Prepare dinner. Also receive an encouraging e-mail from another sculpting friend, Lynn Cartwright. This was important feedback because Lynn had previously beat me out for Best of Show at the Kern County Fair. The judges had thought I needed to do a better job on sculpting hands. Ouch! I have worked really hard at improving this, and Lynn writes that Ethan's hands are exceptional. Woo-hoo! I write back, joking that this year she has to bring it! 'Cause it's on!

Talked a little with my hubby about Manny's new therapist, Sarah. Then he starts teasing me, trying to have a pretend argument and get a little loving. "Babe," I told him, "I don't like to have a real fight with you! Do you really think I want to pretend to have one?"

6:01 p.m. Send photos to the real Ethan's mom to get her reaction. I've known Lindsay since we helped build our Kingdom Hall of Jehovah's Witnesses several years ago. When I saw her son, Ethan, with his dimples, great tan, and lush long eyelashes, I knew I had to make a doll of him. Lindsay's feedback: "Yeah, it does look like him. That is really weird." I love that response! I invite her over after our meeting tonight.

7:00–9:00 p.m. Get to the Theocratic School and Kingdom Ministry meeting a little late. Unfortunately, I didn't get to study beforehand, but I follow along in my Bible the best I can. We are able to associate afterward, which is so good for Manny. Everyone knows he has autism and treats him normally. They run their fingers through his hair and work to get his attention. We really enjoy going to a place where we feel accepted and loved.

9:15 p.m. After the meeting, Ethan and his parents come over to our house. I do this immature thing and had them close their eyes, then I bring out the doll. Lindsay says she gets a chill seeing it, and keeps saying over and over that the doll freaks her out because it is so realistic looking. She keeps expecting it to blink. I really do love, love, love that response!

The real Ethan's dad, Eric, said he likes the doll but wants me to fix the "dent" on top of its head. Lindsay chimes in that their Ethan has one, and she places Eric's fingers on top of his son's head to feel it. Eric says, "Okay, but it isn't that big."

Lindsay says, "But it was when he was that little."

Of course, I am giggling the whole time. I try to make my dolls as realistic as possible. I sculpt the inside of the mouths and noses and ears. I give them small fontanels. Maybe it will eventually be what I'm known for.

10:15 p.m. I read e-mail feedback from Barry Cathers. He gives me one point of constructive criticism I agree with, but I disagree on another. Barry cautions me against making dolls that look that real, and says I need to check with the company. His company wants him to make dolls that look really dolly, but I know for a fact the Middleton Doll Company is aiming to give collectors the option of dolls with stark realism. I feel it's because of the fast-growing "Reborn Doll" industry.

doll sculptor

Barry also says that I overpainted my doll. He is right on target. I used too much china and pigment paints for photography reasons, but decided at the last minute to use natural light as opposed to artificial light, which has a tendency to wash away color. Thus, the overpainted look.

I send Barry an e-mail thanking him for his keen eye. There was a time when all I wanted to hear was praise about my sculpts. I would feel hurt when someone didn't just love all my hard work. But I have matured over the years and welcome sincere constructive criticism, especially from those who know what they are talking about. My circle of sculpting friends and I call it "socking it to each other."

10:45 p.m. Now I'm going to love on my hubby who has been asking for it all day. Men. I don't think they ever grow up or get enough attention. I'm also going to play with my little boy before hitting the sack. I think Sam is getting Manny ready for a bath. I'm so tired.

Nearly 17 Million . . .

. . . home-based businesses are run by women.
—*National Center for Policy Analysis*

•

Dance Lessons

4:00 p.m. A young couple shows up for their appointment to learn a special slow dance for their wedding. Darling couple. I always let new students know that there are rules that help when anyone is learning to dance:

1. The only thing you can tell a partner is that they are wonderful. (Let the teacher do the teaching.)
2. A "lead" is an indication of direction. (Treat her gently and she'll follow you anywhere.)
3. A lady needs to keep up her end of the dance, the same as she would if it were a conversation. Times change and the lady needs to know more today than just "how to follow." She needs to be able to add something to the partnership. (Nobody wants to play tennis with someone who can't hit the ball!)
4. Never criticize a partner. If someone can't dance with you through a three-minute song without criticism, chances are they won't do much better when the music stops.
5. The *best* partner anyone could wish for is someone who understands that the ideal partner is one who wants *both* partners to look good. (They should not be in competition with each other.)

> —*Skippy Blair, 83, Downey, California;*
> *national dance director for the World Swing Dance Council*
> *(the "first lady of West Coast Swing")*

doll sculptor

Boutique Owner

STEVIE BINGHAM-DOUGHERTY, 29, HOUSTON, TEXAS

She was just twenty-four when she opened her glamorous clothing boutique, a one-stop shop that's first with the new designs. "My clients come back because they know they're going to find something fabulous that will get them noticed." Her job is to encourage women to celebrate their personal style; to help them look and feel their best. "Naysayers may view me as superficial for selling expensive clothing, but I see myself as a self-esteem builder, a retail therapist. Seeing a client leave my store feeling more confident, that's why I come to work every day."

8:26 a.m. Finally, I'm out of bed, exhausted. Arrived back from L.A. last night around 12:30 a.m., after a five-day buying trip for fall merchandise. These market days are nonstop, going to appointments, lugging around a huge bag, and running up and down the stairs in heels because of the slow elevators. I am literally fueled by Diet Cokes and Red Bulls, and end up eating candy that the showrooms have sitting on their tables. It was nice to visit with one of my friends during the trip, designer Rachel Pally. After much harassment from me, I convinced her to make her famous jersey trousers longer in length. Yay!

8:37 a.m. I stumble over to the computer; check e-mails, bank account balances, the dreaded American Express statement, and review online orders (our online store has been open for one year).

8:45 a.m. Off to the shower to rid myself of airplane filth. Then I rummage through my suitcase and partially unpack. People are always shocked that I can use a carry-on for five days and still appear fashionable—always something from Rachel Pally (her jersey clothing is comfortable and chic without looking sloppy); something silk and printed from Alice & Trixie (because it's stylish and folds into almost nothing); a Serfontaine denim jacket for the California chilly evenings; and my Louis Vuitton jewelry case (my birthday gift to myself), full of jewelry from Citrine by the Stones and Joei, just to add some spice to my outfits. Continental Airlines even featured me in a "Fashion Minutes" segment on how to pack for a long weekend with nothing but a carry-on. Some of my clients ask me to pack their bags for them!

9:40 a.m. Ah, deciding what to wear. After stuffing my face in L.A., squeezing myself into tight jeans will not work today. So, I decide on a one-of-a-kind strapless, smocked dress with colored thread by Alice & Trixie, which I pair with brown espadrilles. The shoes give me about five inches in height, and make me look like I've lost five pounds. God, I really need to go on a diet. None of my clothes fit. Ugh!

9:47 a.m. Kiss my husband, Shawn, good-bye and I'm off to work. Notice that I need to get gas. Another thing I didn't do before my trip.

9:55 a.m. Pump my gas and get a *big* Red Bull, (my version of coffee). It is definitely going to be a twelve-ounce day. My drive to work is one of my favorite parts of my day. I drive a gorgeous Jaguar Convertible XK-8 that I love, bought myself, and worked my butt off for. This is my time to think and get ready for my day.

10:34 a.m. At Bella, I wind through the maze of colorful clothing fixtures by our signature lavender walls, and head to my wrap desk and our office in the back. We've received a shipment from UPS—a replenishment of Trina Turk swimsuits and our best-selling DIMR'S (reusable silicone nipple covers). They are *absolutely amazing*! We check the merchandise on the invoices against our order forms, enter everything into our computer, and tag and sensor each item with antitheft devices. Then we hang the clothes on wooden hangers and sort out one of each style to be shot for our online store.

Say hi to my mom, Maureen, who has helped me out at the store from the beginning and has a vested interest in my business. She is great with clients and always keeps us laughing. Scuffle around my cluttered desk. Pleasantly surprised to see a card and a bottle of wine, a gift from one of the writers at *Lucky* magazine. The card reads, *I love everything that I've picked up at Bella. Your eye is so spot on! Keep doing what your doing . . .* I really respect this woman, so her words mean a lot to me.

10:45 a.m. Playing major catch-up. Packages are all over the floor in my back room, and fourteen orders came in from our online store while I was gone in L.A. My mom and I have to process and pack them, and print shipping labels. A Nanette Lepore blouse going to New York; a Milly eyelet dress going to Burlingame, California; an Ella Moss top going to Doylestown, Pennsylvania . . .

11:00 a.m. Open the doors for business. Clients start trickling in after twenty or thirty minutes.

11:50 a.m. Finally finish shipping the online orders. Christina, a Bella Boutique die-hard, calls ahead so I can start brainstorming gift ideas for her friend's birthday. She decides on our must-have travel companion, the "Wash Me–Wear Me" lingerie bag ($28), and an Artecnica bottle stopper (on Oprah's "favorites" list for $16), and has them gift-wrapped ahead because she is in a hurry. She also purchases a fabulous chocolate/green retro printed Milly halter top (featured numerous times in magazines) and a mint-colored Splendid cap-sleeve T-shirt that she can't resist while I am checking her out.

12:28 p.m. Pay my dreaded American Express bill online. I try to put everything possible on Amex—most of my inventory, bills, gas, and other expenses. I *love, love, love* my points!

12:46 p.m. Able to quickly grab a bag of Goldfish and a Diet Coke, my usual meal, while checking and responding to e-mails.

1:15 p.m. A client comes in and tries on tops to wear to her son's bar mitzvah. She is in a hurry to pick up her kids so she scurries out without buying anything. I hang up the garments correctly, and put them back on the sales floor.

1:38 p.m. My mail lady, Ruby, just delivers four days' worth of mail. Bills, junk, and more bills! I also receive a couple of magazines. Reading them is one of my favorite pastimes.

2:00 p.m. A client, Christin, comes in looking for clothes for her birthday trip to Las Vegas. We found her a great Trina Turk top. While I'm helping her, my 2:00 p.m. appointment comes in, a merchant services account rep for Wells Fargo. He wants me to change my service and offers lower processing fees. I ask him to do better on the rates, so he says he would try and leaves.

2:10 p.m. Seven people all over the store. My husband, Shawn, comes in briefly to pick up all of the orders that have to be shipped today. I can barely say hi, we're so busy.

3:04 p.m. Finally, going over all of the orders that I wrote for fall at L.A. market. Yes, fall. Typically, I buy four to six months in advance, assessing what trends I want to adopt and what trends I want to pass on. This trip I picked up Shoshanna clothing/swimwear and T-Bags, which are fun printed jersey dresses. Celebs like Jessica Simpson, Denise Richards, and Carmen Electra are all fans of Shoshanna. She's the trendsetter in the swimsuit industry.

3:24 p.m. Call Kasey, my sales representative at Shoshanna, and ask her to expedite the swimsuits I ordered in L.A. When I want something, I want it now. This sounds like something straight out of a six-year-old's mouth, but this is the first year that I've carried swimsuits and I want the line in my boutique ASAP. This will

boutique owner

give my clients more selection and make us a swimsuit destination. Kasey agrees to ship out my order overnight, which makes me happy, especially because I am a new account and have no established buying power with them. Usually, it take days for designers to go through the steps on their end.

3:33 p.m. I get a call from my client Lane (who works for Christin, who came in earlier). She wants to know if I have anything great for her to take to Las Vegas, too. So I make a call to my vendor Mikael at Alice & Trixie, known for their "get-you-noticed" prints and sexy styles. I ask Mikael if any of my March 30 delivery was ready, and to ship it to me overnight because my clients have an early flight.

The shipment will get to my store by 8:00 a.m. and cost me $117, but we'll be the first store in the country to receive these goods. This is Bella's trademark. I know that I must be at the top of my game because the competition is fierce. Houston has had six clothing stores close in a five-month period. This worries me.

3:47 p.m. Mikael calls me back to give me the tracking number on my overnight package, and some *great* news. She tells me to grab the new *InStyle* magazine and turn to page 254. There is a white pair of Alice & Trixie pants featured in *my* store! So exciting! More press! Call Shawn to let him know the good news.

4:30 p.m. The merchant services rep from Wells Fargo comes back with good news—lower rates! I sign the contract.

5:20 p.m. Call Lane to let her know that we had the Alice & Trixie merchandise shipped overnight for them at no charge, and that we will open the store early (8:30 a.m.) so that she and Christin can come by before they leave for Las Vegas. Lane is thrilled to know that she will be wearing clothes that no else has yet, which is important when frolicking around Vegas.

5:34 p.m. Preparing for tomorrow's shipment to save time in the morning. We know what Alice & Trixie merchandise is being sent overnight, so we check the items into the computer and print out tags.

6:30 p.m. I put the garments that came in from UPS this morning in my car. Shawn will shoot them tomorrow at our other office and photo studio, where we run the online store. He's a jack-of-all-trades when it comes to my business. His company, SDI Studios, does the photography, my print media, the Web site, my press kits, etc.

6:45 p.m. Closing duties. I turn off the lights, stereo, flat-screen TV. Straighten the store. Print out sales journals, send out credit card batch reports. Lock all of the doors and turn on the alarm.

7:00 p.m. Driving home in the daylight is so nice. No traffic!

7:16 p.m. A client calls me while I'm on the road. Many of my clients have my cell phone number, so I get calls and text messages all the time. This client moved to New York seven months ago and is having a really hard time. She is successful at her corporate job, but has an *awful* boss. We talk clothing a little, and I give her the "retail therapy" that I'm known for, joking around and telling her to come back home to Texas. This seems to lift her spirits.

7:48 p.m. Finally, I make it home. Kiss Shawn and pet my hyper but adorable dogs, Nikki and Toby. My husband has started a wonderful meal. He really has a knack for cooking and enjoys it. I like not having to worry about dinner, especially after my Goldfish lunch.

8:32 p.m. I am starving. New York strip with garlic butter and roasted red potatoes. It is a great meal, (as usual) paired with our favorite "house" red wine. This is why some of my clothes don't fit.

9:08 p.m. I start to do dishes and am really tired. I am off schedule because of the L.A. trip.

9:45 p.m. In bed, curled up with my favorite Barefoot Dreams blanket, a Christmas gift from Tawnia, a very special client. I bring Nikki with me, a big fan of the blanket, too.

9:48 p.m. Turn on the flat-screen TV, which is a somewhat new purchase that brings me much joy after a long day on my feet. I watch reruns of my favorite shows (*Sex and the City* and *Seinfeld*) that I have seen a hundred times. Flip through my favorite gossip magazines, only to realize that I read them on the plane a couple days ago.

10:52 p.m. Still watching TV. Shawn comes into bed after the basketball game. I know that I must get a good night's sleep because tomorrow I have to pick up my mom, drive in the unpredictable Houston morning traffic, and be back at Bella by 8:00 a.m.

Fowl Fashion

6:45 a.m. I'm desperately trying to pick out my wardrobe for the day. I need to dress nice, since I have to attend a Ducks Unlimited banquet this evening. What does a woman who is trying to sell hunting and fishing trips wear to a banquet full of men looking to drink scotch and win a shotgun in a raffle?

—*Paula Elert, 36, Luck, Wisconsin; outdoor travel specialist*

Boxing Promoter and Matchmaker

WANDA "FIGHTLADY" BRUCE, 47, WALDORF, MARYLAND

A hair stylist and a lifelong boxing fan, she went from being an inspector for the Washington, D.C., Boxing Commission to promoting the first all-female show, to managing her own women fighters and arranging matches for other trainers. "I want to see competitive, challenging matches, not catfights." She's got a rep for going the distance for her fighters. "If it means braiding their hair, or taking them for pregnancy tests, or helping them go pee after they have their gloves on, I'm there. It's all part of the game."

6:45 a.m. Get up and shower, put on something cool—my red shirt, red shoes, and tight blue jeans, not a lot of layers. These dang hot flashes are killing me. Heading for the airport, a big day. Signing another fighter in Raleigh-Durham, heavyweight Yolanda Fagan. Her fight name is Baby Tank. She's forty with ten kids and six grandkids. When her trainer calls me for assistance I tell him I'll help, but I don't work for free. These are my terms—I need to be the manager, which means I get 33 percent of the purse, make all the decisions on the contracts, and basically run the show. You can either agree or see you later. They think about it and call me back.

Before I leave for the airport, I wake up my twelve-year-old daughter, Ralphfelle. I need to tell her how much I love her before each trip. I prepare something quick for her to eat before school. Love you, Mommy is on her way.

7:30 a.m. The Maryland 210 highway is a wreck so I make an illegal turn to beat the beltway traffic. Luckily, I don't get a ticket. I fly standby on my ex-husband's flight benefits, which saves a bundle of money, but every minute counts. Parked in C-12; got to remember that or else. Wish I had got someone to drop me off. It's hot, seventy-two degrees.

Phone rings. It's Terrell, the man in the mirror, flirting as usual. He just wants to get some information about a fighter, and lots of small talk. Talking with Terrell is a job. He works for a major network and has a head as big as a workout ball. He also lives with someone but flirts all the time. I'm considering looking for a new man in my life, but Terrell could never be the man. My friend Nevelion and I have dated for four years but we don't always see eye to eye. I'd like to find someone I really connect with and love with all my heart. I want to feel unconditional love.

Wishing I had worn a suit and brought my briefcase. Knowing that the news cameras are going to be at the signing, I would feel a little more business. Oh, what the heck. It's in the gym.

8:15 a.m. Go through security, get a veggie panini and hot chocolate. I wanted a doughnut or two. I'm struggling with this diet, but trying to do the right thing. I call Nevelion to tell him I am safe and will be boarding soon. Nevelion does so much for me. He loves my kids and is a great guy.

8:45 a.m. Board the plane, instructions as usual. I fly a lot. I like to be at every boxing match and always be seen in the audience. I need to network and get to know everyone in the game. Say my prayers and we are on our way. I need a nap now.

9:10 a.m. Wake up having a damn hot flash. I need to see a doctor. Guess I better not take off my clothes. Thinking now—I need to pay my car note, and find a fighter for another manager for an April 6 card. I am looking for a girl who doesn't have many fights. A powder puff girl, someone his fighter can beat without any problem. This manager is trying to build up his fighter's record.

I'm also hoping Yolanda is a good fighter, with all the things that go with it. This means she trains every day or at least five days a week. She is willing to take a fight at the last minute because she has confidence that her skills are the best. She listens to her manager and trainer. And she takes pride in her looks, not looking like a man. She needs to be a real lady. I am strong on appearance.

Yolanda has a record of 2–0, both wins by knockouts. I don't know a lot more about her but this trip will tell everything. I will see her workout and train and see how good she is in the ring. If she has a little something, she will be okay. We can mold her if she is good. I need a heavyweight girl.

10:30 a.m. Get picked up at the Raleigh-Durham airport by Yolanda and her niece Fatima. They are a piece of work; what I consider country. Wow, country. They don't cut any corners of how they talk. Yolanda did not have any teeth in the front of her mouth. I told her the newspaper is going to be taking pictures. She laughed, "Oh, by the way, I have a set of teeth." Thank God. What have I got myself into?

11:00 a.m. Arrive at Yolanda's house in Wilson. It looks like a Section 8 property. I am thinking, *Are they on welfare?* One of her sons is lying on the sofa. Another is playing video games. Two of her daughters are there, too. Does anyone go to work or school? We're waiting to go to the gym to see Yolanda train.

11:14 a.m. Receive a call from another manager. He needs an opponent for one of his fighters for a card he is working on. He wants this girl to fight but is scared and so is she. Every name I give them, they say no. I hate it when these people act as if they know what they are doing and don't. They need to step up to the plate and fight someone who is credible.

11:30 a.m. Lost my earrings and want to buy a new pair. Can't take pictures without my earrings. Fatima says to me, "Girl, I know how you feel." She has on these huge earrings. That's not what I am looking for. The main mall was one hour away so we go to the beauty supply store. I find some cute sterling silver hoops.

Noon Yolanda, Fatima, and I go to the gym. It is very small and the smell is clean. I meet Marcel, Skip, and Cornelius, all boxing trainers. They could not be nicer. There are about twenty people there. A cameramen from the *Wilson Times* arrives to witness the signing—Yolanda and her trainer had contacted them. They are so excited about this big event, which I hope carries through the whole contract. With this kind of excitement, we could go a long way. I feel they will put their heart and soul into this venture. The town people love the signing process.

1:00 p.m. Watch Yolanda in the ring with her trainer, Cornelius. He is strong but she looks stronger, hitting him really hard. I am impressed. Yolanda moves great to be so big, over two hundred pounds but very light on her feet. I am amazed at how fast she is and how hard she hits. I feel sorry for the other women. Cornelius is a good-looking guy. He calls me Ms. Wanda. How country.

2:30 p.m. I told Yolanda and Fatima I am hungry. We go to the Mayflower and I eat tuna steak and a baked potato. I did not pick up the tab. If you start paying with these fighters, they will ask you to pay for everything in the future.

3:00 p.m. We have been using Yolanda's girlfriend's car because she doesn't have one. (Yes, I said Yolanda's girlfriend.) So now we have to pick up Yolanda's girlfriend's son from school. Didn't know I would have to do all of this stuff. Boring. Until I can get to the airport, I am stuck. I have had enough.

3:30 p.m. Yolanda says she has to find me a way back to the airport because her girlfriend needs the car to take her son to the doctor. What?! This is bull. Now I am worried.

4:00 p.m. Go to visit Yolanda's mother who lives down the street. Nice lady. They want to show me off. They make me feel at home. We borrow Yolanda's daughter's car. Now get me a ride to the airport. I am ready to go home.

4:30 p.m. Call Diane, another matchmaker, and have to curse her out for disrespecting one of my fighters. She had called one of the girls I manage directly and offered her a fight. You never call a fighter if she has a manager, and Diane knew that was me. The fighter called me and said I needed to call Diane because she was talking crazy. Diane calls me a black bi***. I cannot believe it. Once she calls me the name I lose it. Very angry and worried all at the same time.

Still at Yolanda's mother's house, I step outside to act ugly. Just get me to the airport.

4:45 p.m. We're heading for the airport. Hurray. Talked to Ralph-felle, making sure she is okay at home. Fell asleep on the way.

5:00 p.m. Arrive at the airport, say my good-byes, and thank you.

5:10 p.m. Call my oldest daughter who also works for the airlines, confirming my flight on standby again. Talk to Terrell. His father passed. I did not know his father, but I knew he was sick. I feel for him, knowing how it is to lose a loved one.

6:00 p.m. Receive a call from the accountant about bills. I don't want to hear about any bills. I need money. I am getting ready for a divorce and doing everything on my own. It is hard. Pay the bills, need an attorney—that's three thousand dollars I don't have. My hair-stylist job, along with the boxing work, is just making ends meet. Every time I think I'm ahead, it's three steps back.

7:30 p.m. Arrived in Washington, D.C. Put the top down on my car and enjoy the weather. Talk to my sister all the way home. Tell her about the whole fiasco of the day. Tell her about Terrell and his father. She catches me up on her day.

8:30 p.m. Arrive home. Glad to see Ralphfelle. No matter how long or short the trip, I miss my children.

9:00 p.m. Watch a little of *American Idol*.

boxing promoter and matchmaker

9:15 p.m. On the phone. Have to set my fighter who called earlier straight about respect. The situation with Diane could have been settled without an argument if she had just not talked to her at all. She gave more information than needed. All she had to do is say, *Call my manager.* This girl is young, twenty, so sometimes I have to treat her like a child.

9:30 p.m. Talk to my accountant again about the bills. She says I need more money. When I was married I had more. I need to get another part-time job. I'm doing the best with what I have.

9:30 p.m. Talk to Jackie Kallen (the "First Lady of Boxing"), who is a good friend. Also talk to Junebug, a female fighter, and Chris Mittendorf, a great matchmaker. I am looking for some fights for Junebug, and Chris called because he needs a girl fighter.

9:50 p.m. Called Rock Newman, the manager of world champion Riddick Bowe, to talk about a fighter in Bermuda. Rock is working with a female fighter named Teresa Perrozi who is looking for some fights in the states.

10:00 p.m. Get in bed, eat some chocolate and nuts. Even though I have ups and downs, most of all I love my people. I get a lot of calls because I find fighters for promoters all over the world. Today another person has entered into my world of boxing. I have a new fighter. This is one of many to come.

On March 27, 2007 . . .

31 percent of day diarists worked more than one job.

•

Public Relations Director, Canyon Ranch Spa and Health Resort

ERINN FIGG, 35, TUCSON, ARIZONA

She works at the ultimate wellness retreat—fitness experts, doctor, and nutritionists, energy healers; plus a globally acclaimed spa with everything from herbal wraps to stone massages to Ayurvedic treatments. "It's my dream job, but there are some days when life gets so crazy, I just want to throw my cats in the car and drive, drive, drive." She's had other PR jobs (strip malls, a fast-food chain, an automotive technician school), but this one really resonates. "I hate it when people think we're just a spa for the rich and the famous; it's a transformative experience that changes your life."

6:56 a.m. Ever since I turned thirty, it seems like my life has revolved around creams—body-firming cream, wrinkle cream, eye cream, sunscreen, face cream, antiaging lip cream, boob cream. (Yes, boob cream.) Lord, if I had back all the time it's taken me to slather all this stuff on every day and night, it'd probably add up to an additional year in my life.

This morning, the body cream I put on costs $175. Line-reducing "elixir": $410. Extra-rich antiaging cream: $365. Eye and lip contour cream: $175. Lip balm: $54. I do the math and realize I'm wearing $1,179 worth of products on my body. And heck no, I can't afford any of it. It's a high-end skin-care line sold at our Canyon Ranch spas across the country, and it's my extremely rough job to try it all out in case journalists have any questions. I decide that no matter what goes wrong today, I'm going to counter it by thinking, *At least I'm coated in $1,179 worth of cream.*

7:01 a.m. Five minutes later, all creams, gels, lotions, and balms are in place, and now I officially no longer look tired. Instead, I look tired and shiny.

7:20 a.m. I am trying to rock the "sexy secretary" look in a pencil skirt, heels, pearls, and crisp white button-down blouse, but it's not working out so well, possibly because my skirt is hanging off me. During the past four months, my weight has dropped from a healthy 128 pounds to a bony 105. As of today, I have also been on my period for twenty-two days. I realize this is not good, and I wonder if we (meaning me, my three cats, my pet hermit crab, and anyone else who happens to be in my galaxy) are about to go through the whole Cervical Cancer Thing again.

Last year my regular Pap smear detected some "abnormalities." Since then I have been sliced, diced, and biopsied (is that a verb?) three times and was later told that my renegade cervical cells are "not normal, but not cancerous." The doctor said, "We Are Keeping an Eye on Them." But since Keeping an Eye on Them was no cakewalk the first few times, I haven't been back lately. I realize this is immature, but I feel like I have been violated by every surgical instrument known to woman, and I'm tired of it.

7:55 a.m. On my way out the door, I step over two weeks' worth of the *New York Times*, all still neatly rolled in their plastic blue bags. Several weeks ago, I had this bright idea that subscribing to the *Times* at home (instead of hurriedly scanning the paper between gulps of coffee at work) would help transform me into a morning person. Instead I have to concentrate on not breaking my neck every morning as I blearily scale the heap by my front door. Time to come up with a Plan B for becoming a morning person.

8:03 a.m. Two months ago, on a whim, I put *Rick Springfield's Greatest Hits* in my car's CD player. It got stuck there. Since then, I have listened to "Jesse's Girl" about 204 times. Argh.

8:08 a.m. I drive by the Immaculate Heart Catholic Church and cross myself. "My Lord, My God, I love you with all my heart, my soul and my strength." My spiritual beliefs have swung from devoutly religious to agnostic, now hovering somewhere in between. Through it all, I have never been able to kick this childhood habit, instilled in me by my never-wavering Catholic mother. Last fall when I visited my family in Tennessee, I was delighted to see my thirty-year-old brother do the same thing when we drove by a Catholic church en route to a bar.

8:11 a.m. At a strictly enforced twenty-five miles per hour, I inch through the pearly gates of Canyon Ranch. (Okay, kidding; they're iron.) Wave at guard. Park on top of a mountain. Wobble all the way down it in high heels to my office. The only thing I truly dislike about this job is the parking situation.

8:30 a.m. Coffee in hand, it's time to start rolling. I direct public relations activities at two Canyon Ranch resorts (here and in Lenox, Massachusetts), as well as at our three SpaClubs in Las Vegas, Kissimmee, Florida, and on the luxury ocean liner *QM2*. I'm also overseeing the rollout of public relations initiatives at our planned living communities, the first one opening this fall in Miami Beach. I supervise a staff of two talented young women who assist me with all of this activity. And frankly, it's an insane amount of activity, but I love it.

8:42 a.m. I get a cryptic e-mail that reads, "Melinda will be calling u for GDV reading." I decipher this message to mean that I finally get to try out our new Gaseous Discharge Visualization machine, which uses electromagnetic finger measurements to track the energy meridians throughout the body. Or something like that. Damn, maybe I just botched that whole description, which is *exactly* why I need to spend some quality time with this machine. I just hope I don't break it with my complete *lack* of energy this morning.

9:00 a.m. Weekly conference call about our soon-to-open Canyon Ranch Living Miami Beach property. It will be the first integrative wellness community in the world, where our condo residents and hotel guests will have access to nutrition-ists, physicians, exercise physiologists, behavioral therapists, and spa services, all without leaving the complex. I flew down in January to look at the property and it's gorgeous. On my end, we're looking for a PR firm in Miami to assist us. Thank God, because I have no idea how my department would handle all the media activity on its own.

9:37 a.m. E-mail from a *More* magazine editor, asking me to call her about a trip to one of our properties for a sleep study. E-mail from a freelance writer, asking me to set up some interviews with our physicians. E-mail from a United Airlines *Hemispheres* magazine writer, asking me to call her. E-mails from a breast cancer expert, an editor at *Allure*, and a writer at *Spa* magazine, all asking me to call them.

9:48 a.m. My assistant comes in my office with a list of all the people I didn't get around to calling yesterday.

10:00 a.m. I am daydreaming about the large bottle of Excedrin I left by my bed, and wishing I would have done the sensible thing and eaten a protein-packed breakfast. Plus, we're having some problems with our thermostat. I think its forty-eight degrees in my office. Outside, there is the sound of a bulldozer in front of my window. Our property is putting a parking lot out there, thank God, but the noise is torture. I just want to put my head down on my desk and scream, "*Stop!*"

But at least I'm coated in $1,179 worth of cream.

10:42 a.m. I am one of twelve people included in an e-mail chain about Ayurvedic medicine. It's one of those chains where some-one hits "reply all," and then everyone starts "replying all," but meanwhile I have had no idea what they've all been talking about since e-mail number one.

11:00 a.m. Conference call with our Lenox property about a bevy of beauty editors who are traveling there to try our new line of

Sisley skin care services. This time two years ago I was working in a grueling PR firm, trying to convince editors that the automotive technician school I represented was worthy of front-page coverage. Today, I'm leading a conference call about spa services and in-room gifts for the editors of *Vogue*, *Marie Claire*, *Town & Country*, and *Elle*. It truly is a Cinderella story, if you don't count the bags under my soon-to-be-thirty-six-year-old eyes.

11:35 a.m. A guy shows up on our property wanting to be a guest lecturer here. Security doesn't know what to do with him so they send him to my office. So glad he doesn't have a gun. I listen to his story and direct him to our functions department. We have so many office buildings here, it's easy to get them confused.

12:09 p.m. Long, draining phone call with the department business coordinator about purchase orders, budget lines, and billing codes. Seventy-five percent of it goes over my head. I want to add, "I don't do math" to my business cards.

12:15 p.m. Lunch. Our staff dining room is modeled somewhat after the gourmet cuisine we serve our guests. Today it's tilapia, chicken, veggie burger, or the entrée of the day, along with two sides, which include spinach salad, fruit, and other healthy choices. The price: a whopping $2.25. And while I'm on the subject of employee perks, we also get to use the workout facilities, attend wellness classes and lectures, and treat ourselves to spa services at outrageously low prices. A "wellness massage," for example, is $20. Nice.

12:30 p.m. I have a ludicrous phone conversation with my boyfriend during lunch, which does not surprise me. We have been dating and breaking up for about a year now, so I don't even know if "boyfriend" is the correct terminology. Sometimes I just call him "my on again/off again whatever-he-is." When he's not running a statewide pest control company, parenting a twelve-year-old, or playing rugby, the man tries to squeeze me into his life. As such, our relationship is slightly strained.

Rugby: "I hope you don't mind, but I made plans for us to go out of town."

Erinn (in slight disbelief): "You did??? Why?"

Rugby: "I thought we should get away and spend some quality time together."

Erinn (heart soaring with joy): "*Get out of here!* Where are we going?"

Rugby: "I booked us a room in Sedona."

Erinn (little cartoon birds tweeting with happiness surround her head): "*Wow*—that was *so sweet* of you—*thank you!*"

Rugby: "All we have to do is sit through this forty-five-minute timeshare presentation . . . "

All over the world, women have boyfriends who whisk them off on romantic vacations. Apparently I don't inspire these types of adoring impulses, but I'm good for a cheap sales gimmick. Sigh.

12:45 p.m. I'm trying to work, but I'm worried about my mother. She's been having bad headaches, and yesterday she finally went in for an X-ray, which showed an "unidentifiable mass" at the base of her skull. What if it's an inoperable brain tumor?

My mother is the lifeline that holds our family together. Without her, my two brothers, my father and I would all crumble to pieces. How did all the women in our family get so potentially cancerous all of a sudden?

12:52 p.m. Call back the editor of *More.* Get voice mail. Sometimes I spend hours a day playing phone tag, trying to nail a story. When I do though, it's sheer joy.

1:00 p.m. Another meeting, this time about our soon-to-be-launched Canyon Ranch skin-care line. We look at box designs and brainstorm sampling plans. It's exciting, but my mind is in a million places at once, and I wonder if my presence at this particular meeting is really necessary. Sometimes I feel like we have meetings to prepare for future meetings, then we have real meetings, then we have meetings to discuss what we just talked about in the previous meeting. I feel like a gerbil running around helplessly, trapped in my Outlook calendar.

Ironically, when I get back to my desk, there's an e-mail from Human Resources: "Please complete this brief survey and tell us what you think about meetings!" I laugh and hit "delete." Sorry, HR, but I literally have 5,353 e-mails in my inbox right now. I need to *work, work, work*.

1:30 p.m. Ground squirrel break. No matter how stressful my days get, the ground squirrels outside my office always seem joyful, digging their little holes and scampering. They make me happy. So, yes, I went to a pet store and bought them squirrel food. And yes, I have tamed them just enough so they'll come up and eat the food out of my hand.

For some reason, this disturbs a few women in my office. One of them approached me the other day. "The ground squirrels are getting aggressive," she said.

I imagined them brandishing tiny baseball bats. "What are they doing?" I asked.

"They're running up to me and looking at me like they want food."

"Damn, that *is* aggressive. You'd better watch out!" I said, smiling.

The ground squirrel controversy makes me sad. I know that feeding them is rightfully frowned upon by some people. (I can just hear my mother wailing, "The germs! The germs!") But what I really want to say to all of them is, "Hey look, my cervical cells are all messed up, my mom is sick, I'm scared, and I'm a little stressed right now. Sometimes the only time the world slows down enough for me to breathe is when a tiny creature trusts me enough to eat food out of my hand. Then my mind stops racing for five minutes, the fear goes away, and I start feeling human again. So get over it."

2:00 p.m. I take two calls, one from National Public Radio and one from a *Today* show producer about possible future coverage. My assistant and I compile a list of our properties' healing retreats to send to various health magazine calendars. Finally, I feel like I have accomplished something today.

2:42 p.m. I get up the nerve to get a referral for another doctor, so we can revisit the whole Cervical Cancer Thing. I can't live in fear like this.

3:00 p.m. I have a meeting with my boss, during which we discuss some PR strategies for our Las Vegas property, our recent meeting with a writer from *Trump* magazine, and a request from Bravo TV producers to film an episode for a reality show at our Tucson property. I can't believe I'm talking about major networks and having conversations with the word "Trump"—as in Donald—in them. I wonder what wonderful thing I've done in a past life to deserve this.

At the end of the meeting, my boss kills my buzz by telling me that a black-and-pink deconstructed hoodie I've been occasionally wearing into frosty conference rooms is unacceptable business attire. I'm impressed that the word "hoodie" has made its way into the corporate lexicon. But damn, it's my favorite one. I'm crushed.

4:00 p.m. I finally get clearance to host a breast cancer survivor for a week at our Lenox property, where she will chronicle her experience for a new magazine. It's this part of my job that fills me with joy, the opportunity to show someone new ways to transition through a difficult period in life.

4:30 p.m. I dash over to our salon to get a couple of broken fingernails fixed, another perk. On the way, I pass our spiritual programming manager. He's holding something like a maraca, and stops me so he can shake it all around me and give me some kind of a Shamanic blessing. That's another reason why I love this job. One minute you're on your way to get a nail fixed, and the next minute you're getting blessed.

5:00 p.m. As I walk back to my office across our desert property, I can feel my breathing slow and my blood pressure lower. The landscape is unlike anything I've ever known growing up in Tennessee. Towering saguaros, small flowering cacti and other natural native landscaping, against the backdrop of the Catalina mountains, create an almost surreal scene. Because animals feel safe here, we have everything from large lizards (some of them the size of cats), to rabbits, to herds of javelina (rodents that look like furry pigs) all wandering around the property. I feel like I work in the Garden of Eden. Except we have cacti instead of apple trees. And we're all wearing clothes (thank God).

5:30 p.m. Before I go home, I get online and pay bills in my office. I'd rather deal with this financial stress here, where the rest of my stress occurs anyway, than take it home. Car payment, utilities, cell phone, credit cards. Yeeks! I'm *so broke*.

6:15 p.m. It's my favorite night of TV. I celebrate by indulging in Stouffer's Fettuccine Alfredo, Ben & Jerry's Half Baked ice cream, and a Corona with a lime (that counts as a fruit serving).

7:00 p.m. I enthusiastically vote for the worst singer on *American Idol*.

8:00 p.m. More mindless TV. I do a bunch of stretches and restorative yoga poses. My mind loosens with my body. I can understand why some people are so religious about their exercise schedules.

I talk briefly on the phone with Rugby, and apologize for being bitchy on our earlier call. He apologizes for trying to trick me into sitting through a timeshare presentation. I can't go to bed mad, but I *can* go to bed irritated, and just talking about all of this makes me want to smack him again. He's a good man, though.

10:00 p.m. I wrap up every day with three cats sleeping around or on top of me. Two of them are fourteen and have been with me through seven jobs, five states, six apartments, and God knows how many boyfriends. I never meant to be a cat lady but I guess it's my destiny. They all take their respective places on my comforter, but not until we turn on my favorite talk show, *Coast to Coast*

AM. With its nightly lineup of alien abductees, Big Foot hunters, time travelers, vampires, people claiming to be the Antichrist, and all kinds of other interesting guests, it's the perfect ending to any day, good or bad.

On March 27, 2007 . . .

57 percent of day diarists said they were working their dream job.

●

Round the Clock

12:10 a.m. Got off the ferry from a long rehearsal and couldn't stop singing, "I am the good Shepherd, I pasture my sheep," I don't know why. It just appeared in my mind and held me captive for three hours!

—*Denyce Graves, 42; opera singer*

2:10 a.m. I fixed a magic prop that broke during my last performance. I'm always so proud of myself when I repair magic tricks!

—*Debbie Leifer, 41; magician*

5:45 a.m. I hate Tuesdays. Every Tuesday for literally the past eight years I have done the same thing—prepare the bulletin for Sunday's service in the church. I am so bored with this job I could actually scream.

—*Mona Howard, 51; church office manager*

5:55 a.m. Should I change his diaper? Should I nurse him? Or should I ignore him? I love his little whimpers. So cute! I wish I knew what to do.

—*Ah-Son Wong, 36; mom of a nineteen-day-old baby*

6:38 a.m. Here comes the bus. Good, no one is sitting in my seat. We always have a place where we like to sit each morning and feel offended if someone else sits there. Don't they know better. Ha-ha.

—*Orietta Brewer, 52; administrative assistant*

7:45 a.m. Head into the school cafeteria for my morning duty post. I love getting called a "fucking bitch" by kids who don't want to stand in line for breakfast.

—*Danielle Mays, 24; teacher*

public relations director, canyon ranch spa and health resort

8:05 a.m. Making first pot of coffee. It will be gone in a few minutes. Everyone waits on me to make it, and brings their oversized cups and fills up.

—Mary Ferguson, 60; administrative assistant

8:15 a.m. The house is a mess and I do not know where to start. I stop at the first bedroom and push open the door. Ugh! I shut it.

—Wanda Garner, 48; "mom" to twenty-seven foster children over the past two years

8:30 a.m. No time to cut fruit to eat on the road. There goes my hemorrhoid prevention plan.

—Melody Lin, 52; hospice social worker

8:40 a.m. Arrive at Revolution, my very groovy eco-retail venture. I check e-mail. Always hoping for a little contact from my "crush." Instead, a message from Greg; the guy who is as "in to me" as I am in to my crush. It's my karmic romantic retribution!

—Kim Souza, 38; store co-owner

8:30 a.m. Driving to work listening to *The 7 Habits of Highly Effective People*. Can't manage to actually make time to read a book, so maybe I'll get something out of it this way.

—Rebecca Lavender, 56; pediatric oncology social worker

8:30 a.m. Look to see if my daughter has updated her blog (no); check my son's Flickr page for new pictures of his art work (no); and work on calculating the amount of an overpayment to an adjunct faculty member.

—Sally Roelle, 57; payroll clerk

8:30 a.m. Another beautiful day at the track. The sun is shining and the grandstands are gleaming, but I have that anxious feeling in my chest about the Indy 500. The adrenaline is coursing through my veins.

—*Cindy Wasson, 38; marketing manager, Indianapolis Motor Speedway*
(two months before race day).

8:45 a.m. We just hired a new guy to replace my co-worker who is off to Iraq to work. The pay is good there, if you survive.

—*Beth Garland, 45; communications analyst,*
U.S. Army master sergeant (served six months in Iraq)

8:49 I didn't even have time to fire up the computer before we got a call that some Security Forces members (cops) drove over a can of 40 mm grenades just a few blocks from where our shop is. This is not the first time this has happened.

—*Sarah Burrill, 22; explosive ordnance disposal technician,*
United States Air Force

8:52 a.m. First autopsy—a traffic accident victim from Idaho. Pills in his pockets. Investigator saw beer in the vehicle. Struck a rail and vehicle airborne.

—*Sally Aiken, 51; chief medical examiner forensic pathologist*

9:00 a.m. Meet with drywall contractor. He stares at my chest and asks what I did last night. I pretend not to hear him.

—*Valerie McVey, 42; real estate investor*

9:00 a.m. Ear is hot, sweaty, beet red from two solid hours on the phone, interviewing professionals on preeclampsia. I'm finally able to call my editor to announce that I can (was there really any doubt?) deliver the story early.

—*Loree Lough, 57; author*

9:30 a.m. I *do not* understand why parents think yelling at a secretary is (1) productive, (2) polite, (3) the way to get assistance for their child, and (4) smart.

—Nina Wallace, 57; school secretary

9:30 a.m. This old, nasty, not nice, matted dog needs pre-clipping and I do not want to use "Mr. Muzzle" on him. I wish the owner would get him groomed more often than every seven to nine months.

—Wendy Booth, 55; pet stylist

9:44 a.m. Was prepared to get up for work but it's nine forty-four. The number four in Chinese often represents death. Obviously, cannot start day by getting up on such an ominous number.

—Sally Huang, 23; video game technical artist

10:08 a.m. Run outside for a smoke. Our CFO's Mini is parked right outside the door. I am so sick of those cars. We did three *Italian Job* roller coasters for Paramount Parks and all the vehicles were little Minis. I know them like the back of my hand.

—Mary Gore, 26; project manager, Premier Rides

10:11 p.m. Tuesday at 10:11 p.m. + 13 hours = 11:11 a.m. Wednesday, Jim's time. I bet he is standing in line to get on a plane to take him back into a war zone. Stay safe, my dear. I love you.

—Becky Clark, 33; army wife

10:30 a.m. A day guest causes a scene, which is nothing new around here, and is banned from the shelter for the day.

—Kandace Carr, 32;, homeless shelter coordinator

10:45 a.m. Contractor is busted. Didn't read my book. I just told a "Moll's Five Must-Nots" joke and he didn't get it. Ha-ha.

—Moll Anderson, 47; chief executive officer and lifestyle expert,
Moll Anderson Home

water cooler diaries

10:46 a.m. Three more surgery/dental cases are completed. Teshla, the tiny Chihuahua with retained baby teeth, turns out to be more difficult a case than I expected. Of course, she came in wearing "clothes" and is a very nervous little dog. •

—Judi Bonner Leake, 50; veterinarian

11:00 a.m. I hear the "ting-shas" sound in the hallway—the death of a patient and our way of marking the moment and letting staff know.

—Susan Vollmer, 47; hospice chaplain

11:00 a.m. Phone call from a worker in the field. We emergently need a hospital bed for a fifteen-year-old child who is eating his feces. There are none available in the state!

—Kathleen Crapanzano, 44; medical director,
Louisiana Department of Health and Hospitals

11:07 a.m. Bad Wendy! No Minesweeper just because the boss is gone!

—Wendy Hardenberg, 24; library assistant

11:10 a.m. Round up last people to get their new ID badge photos. Decide myself to get a new picture. Danged if all the chins don't come through! Oh, well.

—Loretta Mabie, 43; administrative secretary

11:20 That grouchy old fart at the back of the room just kills me! It is *my* lunchtime, even if I choose to sit at my desk. But no, he gets up and walks out of the office to wander around, and expects me to assist customers.

—Suzy Ligon, 41; IT specialist, United States Air Force

11:30 a.m. My stylist, Juls, is finishing up my "do," but we haven't started makeup yet and have only thirty minutes until we start to shoot. We haven't quite figured out how to get my hair to behave; it's trial-and-error, each episode.

—Stephanie McWilliams, 36; host of HGTV's Fun Shui

11:30 p.m. I am sooo frustrated! Medicare denied this little lady is hospice appropriate, and I don't want to discharge her!

—Rayna Bias-Moorer, 37; hospice nurse

12:39 p.m. My husband, Clint, calls and asks the familiar, "What are you doing?" Frustrated at the interruption I yell, *"Writing!"*

—Jennifer Satterwhite, 37; writer/blogger

12:50 p.m. The visiting artist unwraps his work, a piece made from an idea I sent him. This is a moment that I can love or hate—when I see a great piece of art from a crude little sketch I've made.

—Sue Schlabach, 39; art director

1:00 p.m. Back to my office to work on my promotion papers. This is so stressful. I am not one who can brag about myself but to get promoted I must do that. Okay, get busy, start bragging.

—Diane Covington, 54; university librarian

2:21 p.m. I hear over the radio, 10-33 code green, the call for a suspicious/unattended package, and recognize the voice as an officer. I immediately prep BJ, my K9 partner, to go to work.

—Karen Carten, 44; special operations captain and K-9 handler,
Mall of America

2:00 p.m. The dreaded Garage Cleaning Project! I'm in a rhythm now. Trash pile. Goodwill pile. Save pile. Possible eBay pile. Will anyone *really* buy our old crap?

—Stefanie Milligan, 43; stay-at-home mom

2:15 p.m. Back to beading, except the aged feline has just knocked beads all over the floor, ones that I had painstakingly sorted by color and type. Do I kill Kitty now or later? Here Kitty, Kitty . . .

—Veronica Chin, 55, fashion design instructor

2:30 p.m. I take the shark-feeding stick and offer food to the sand tiger sharks. The little one takes a piece of fish readily but the big girl isn't hungry this afternoon.

—*Sarah R. Taylor, 32; aquarist, New England Aquarium*

3:00 p.m. Meeting a potential HR intern for an interview. Yay, free labor. And, of course, I hope she learns something to benefit her.

—*Sharon Ceci, 60; chief operating officer,*
Make-A-Wish Foundation of Michigan

3:10 p.m. A venture capitalist calls. I like that they call now. They turned a deaf ear to me in 2001. Feels good now that I don't need the money.

—*Janine Popick, 39; chief executive officer, Vertical Response*

3:30 p.m. Someone put a half-eaten ice-cream cake on a table near my cube. It's melting. Who is going to clean it up?

—*Renee Wright, 44; executive assistant*

4:00 p.m. Meeting with gem client. She said I was "amazing" because I succeeded in finding the perfect matched pair of incredible, natural blue Burmese sapphires, a truly superb pair, of a quality rarely seen outside of museums.

—*Antoinette Matlins, 61; gemologist*
(the "Ralph Nader" of the gem and jewelry industry)

4:29 p.m. My double-wide cubical looks like a West Texas twister has blown through it.

—*Sherry Maffia, 56; administrative coordinator*

4:45 p.m. I hear one of my team paging me for a call on line three. It's my interview with *USA Today* about the contestants of *American Idol* and their curls.

—*Ouidad; owner of Ouidad Salon ("the Queen of Curl")*

public relations director, canyon ranch spa and health resort

5:20 p.m. Pager went off. Patient just died. Okay, scrap the plans for the tanner. I'm on my way to their house. Note to self—don't put suntan lotion on until you actually get to the tanning salon. Now I'm going to stink like lotion all night.
—*Rachel Malone, 31; registered nurse*

5:25 p.m. Drivers beware—woman driving while listening to iPod and doing Jazzercise routines. I am also sore from teaching last night. Somehow students think instructors don't get sore. I've got news for them. We do!
—*Michele Pelton, 37; UPS flight operations user representative and Jazzercise instructor*

6:00 p.m. Jane, our host at the plantation, knocked down a cocoa pod and split it with her machete. I bite down on the seed to reveal its gorgeous vibrantly purple-colored center. I knew there was a reason I chose purple for my chocolate brand.
—*Katrina Markoff, 34; CEO/chocolatier, Vosges Haut-Chocolat (in Grenada searching for new chocolate flavors)*

6:00 p.m. Come home to a house that looks like a tornado hit it! Clean up and yell at everyone for being so inconsiderate. Calm down and hold my children and hang out with them.
—*Viki Nazarian, 32; executive assistant*

6:37 p.m. At roller derby practice. In attendance: Sister Mary Jane; Rollergazm; Knottie Knoxville; Emme Proper; Chola; Maya Mayhem; Stoli Rocks; Sissy Spankit; Titz McGee; Purr Anna; Hottie Smoochalottie; Lucky Harm (who is leading practice tonight); and myself, Mz. Behavin'.
—*Krissi Montez, 32; teacher and skater, Texas Rollergirls*

6:45 p.m. Headed home from smokejumper rookie training. Feeling good, muscles firing with every step. There really is no comfortable way to carry this seventy-two-pound pack. Left, right, left, right. That's it.
—*Carrie Johnson, 33; rookie smokejumper, National Forest Service*

7:12 p.m. I make myself a watermelon martini and grab a Gatorade for my son. I settle back into the movie just as Morgan Freeman is delivering the bad news to the country that the bombs didn't destroy the comet.

—*Debra Ryan, 50; executive administrative specialist*

7:23 p.m. We've stopped for hot fudge sundaes. Great advertisement for my wellness coaching!

—*Kerri Miller, 28; founder, Holistic Living Resources*

7:45 p.m. Hmm. An e-mail from Jack Nicholson's assistant and a request from Anjelica Huston's. All good. We love those celebrity clients!

—*Jackie Keller, 51; owner/director, NutriFit*

8:00 p.m. I watch *American Idol* and will record *House*. Gwen Stefani is the guest. My husband loves her. They went to the same junior high school in Anaheim, California, but not at the same time. He thinks that links them together. Whatever.

—*Kaye Reshaw, 47; public and media relations, NASCAR (for Bill McAnally Racing)*

9:15 p.m. Soak yet unhealed midlife crisis piercings in sea salt solution. Agonize briefly over dorky bangs. Think of grandmother, realize what's really important in life.

—*Margot Potter, 43; guest jewelry expert, QVC*

9:15 p.m. My hubby is ironing! Great. Made my night. Time to relax for a while.

—*Annette O'Brien, 50; office manager, Merry Maids*

9:27 p.m. Where is my trash can!?! The people who clean the offices at night never put my trash can back in the same spot.

—*Jessica Sexton, 22; software quality assurance engineer*

public relations director, canyon ranch spa and health resort

10:28 p.m. Can't keep my eyes open any longer. I'll post the most recent sermon on the church's Web site tomorrow. I should update quite a few other items but that will be another day, too. It's still Lent and I am trying really hard to give up guilt.

—*Margie Orrick, 53; church webmaster*

Midnight I work a few hours straight, finally finish around midnight. Jump in the shower and get ready for bed. My mind is not even working anymore. I'm numb. Just doing things and not thinking about them. It's only Tuesday.

—*Rajashi Runton, 33; program manager*

Acknowledgments

WE OWE A huge collective thanks to the 515 women who volunteered their day diaries for this book project. Without them, there would be no *Water Cooler Diaries*. We would also like to express our appreciation to Lisa Bankoff, our agent; Katie McHugh, our editor at Da Capo Press; Kim Erlichson of Cohn & Wolfe, who set in motion the National Day Diary Project; and Becky Joffrey, our friend and former partner in the first two This Day books.

Many other friends, relatives, and professional associates (sometimes one and the same) also lent their talents and support to this book project, including Sheron Bates, Kathy Brandt, Klint Briney, Stephen Cole, Jeri Dobrowski, Barbara Dyer, Jennifer Iino-Harvey, Judy Janoo, Kimberly Lawson, Sarah Mac-Coll, Catherine Masters, Cornelia Purcell, Elizabeth Rasberry, Rick Stroud, Maureen Taylor, and Jill Wallis.

In creating this book, our goal was to gather a true diversity of women's working lives by reaching across experiential, socioeconomic, cultural, and geographic boundaries. In this effort we received support from the following organizations:

9to5, National Association of Working Women; American Music Therapy Association; American Society of Indexers; Association of Oncology Social Work; Association of Pediatric Oncology Social Workers; Association for Women in Aviation Maintenance; Association for Women in Technology; Association of Women Veterinarians; Avon; Black Caucus of the American Library Association; Clowns of America International; Doe Run Company; Edmundite Missions; e-Women Network;

Granny Basketball; IMG Artists; International Association of Administrative Professionals; International Association of Bomb Technicians and Investigators; International Game Developer's Association; MGM Grand Hotel and Casino; Make-A-Wish Foundation of Michigan; Merry Maids; Millinery Arts Alliance; Missoula Smokejumper Base; National Asian Pacific Women's Forum; National Association of Executive Secretaries and Administrative Assistants; National Association of Manufacturers; National Association of Medical Examiners; National Association of Professional Organizers; National Aquarium in Baltimore; National Dog Groomers Association of America, Inc.; National Hospice and Palliative Care Organization; National Women's Football Association; New England Aquarium; Oregon Department of Corrections; Outdoor Women of South Dakota; Pennsylvania Amusement Park Association Board; the Professional Doll Makers Art Guild; Seattle Swing Club; South Carolina Farm Bureau Federation; Texas Rollergirls; UPS; Women Anglers; and Women in Mining.

acknowledgments

A Special Thanks . . .

SINCE THE INCEPTION of this book project, we have envisioned a day diary phenomenon in which women could pick a day—any day—and use this simple concept to take stock of their lives and connect. Thanks to the Colgate-Palmolive Company, this vision became a reality. In March 2007, Colgate's Lady Speed Stick 24/7, in partnership with This Day, cosponsored the National Day Diary Project, a Web site inviting women across the country to post a day in their lives at my247life.com. Through Lady Speed Stick's online gallery, thousands of women shared the reality of how they get things done on the job and at home, and how they manage it all in just twenty-four hours.

Among the hundreds of entries created specifically on March 27, 2007, for the Web site, we promised to select one to include in this book. Instead, we have featured three, from contributors Jeannie Hines, Valerie Stadick, and Taylor Collins. We have also included several excerpts from other entries created for the Web site on March 27.

Clearly, when it comes to day diaries, it is impossible to choose just one!

About the Creators of Water Cooler Diaries

Writer and editor **Joni B. Cole** is the founding creator of the This Day book series. She has taught writing workshops for over ten years, and is the author of the critically acclaimed book *Toxic Feedback: Helping Writers Survive and Thrive*. Joni is a frequent speaker at writing conferences and universities and has published numerous feature articles and essays. She lives in Vermont with her husband and two daughters and is currently working on a collection of personal essays.

B. K. Rakhra is co-creator of the This Day series. As a writer, an observer, and an insatiably curious woman, she couldn't say no to a book series that would let her ask anyone—anyone!—what their day is like. Bindi has published articles in a regional magazine, and is currently working on a collection of short stories and a handful of screenplays. She also lives in Vermont, and continues to test her theory that no kids + no husband = eternal youth.

For more information about *Water Cooler Diaries* and other This Day books, please visit www.thisdayinthelife.com, or e-mail joni@thisdayinthelife.com.

Job Index

job index